Sex, Drugs & Magick

OTHER BOOKS BY ROBERT ANTON WILSON

1972   Playboy's Book of Forbidden Words
1973   *Sex, Drugs & Magick: A Journey Beyond Limits
1973   The Sex Magicians
1974   *The Book of the Breast (now 'Ishtar Rising')
1975   ILLUMINATUS! (with Robert Shea)
           The Eye in the Pyramid
           The Golden Apple
           Leviathan
1977   *Cosmic Trigger I: Final Secret of the Illuminati
1978   *Neuropolitics (with T. Leary & G. Koopman)
1980   The Illuminati Papers
1980-1 The Schrodinger's Cat Trilogy
           The Universe Next Door
           The Trick Top Hat
           The Homing Pigeon
1981   Masks of the Illuminati
1983   Right Where You Are Sitting Now
1983   The Earth Will Shake
1983   *Prometheus Rising
1985   The Widow's Son
1986   *The New Inquisition
1987   Natural Law or Don't Put a Rubber on Your Willy
1987   *Wilhelm Reich in Hell
1988   *Coincidance: A Head Test
1988   Nature's God
1990   *Quantum Psychology
1990   *Cosmic Trigger II: Down to Earth
1991   Chaos and Beyond
1993   *Reality Is What You Can Get Away With
1995   *Cosmic Trigger III: My Life After Death
1997   *The Walls Came Tumbling Down
1998   Everything Is Under Control
2000   *The Tale of the Tribe

*Published by New Falcon Publications

Sex, Drugs & Magick

A Journey Beyond Limits

by
Robert Anton Wilson

NEW FALCON PUBLICATIONS
Tempe, Arizona U.S.A.

International Standard Book Number: 0-56184-001-7
Library of Congress Catalog Card Number: 88-83351

First Edition 1973 — Playboy Press
First Falcon Edition 1987
Second Printing 1988
Third Printing 1990
Fourth Printing 1993
Fifth Printing 1997
Second Revised Edition—(Sixth Printing) 2000

Cover by Roy Troepper
Cover Design by Studio 31

The paper used in this publication meets the minimum requirements of the American National Standard for Permanence of Paper for Printed Library Materials Z39.48-1984

Address all inquiries to:
NEW FALCON PUBLICATIONS
1739 East Broadway Road # 1 PMB 277
Tempe, AZ 85282 U.S.A.

(or)

320 East Charleston Blvd. #204 PMB 286
Las Vegas, NV 89104 U.S.A.

website: http://www.newfalcon.com
email: info@newfalcon.com

WHAT CRITICS SAY ABOUT
ROBERT ANTON WILSON

A **SUPER-GENIUS**...He has written everything I was afraid to write
— Dr. John Lilly

One of the funniest, most incisive social critics around, and with a
positive bent, thank Goddess.
— Riane Eisler, author of *The Chalice and the Blade*

A very funny man...readers with open minds will like his books.
— Robin Robertson, *Psychological Perspectives*

Robert Anton Wilson is a dazzling barker hawking tickets to the most
thrilling tilt-a-whirls and daring loop-o-planes on the midway of higher
consciousness.
— Tom Robbins, author of *Even Cowgirls Get the Blues*

OBSCENE, blasphemous, subversive and very, very interesting.
— Alan Watts

Erudite, witty and genuinely scary.
— PUBLISHER'S WEEKLY

STUPID
— Andrea Antonoff

A 21st Century Renaissance Man...funny, wise and optimistic...
— DENVER POST

The world's greatest writer-philosopher.
— IRISH TIMES (Dublin)

Hilarious...multi-dimensional...a laugh a paragraph.
— LOS ANGELES TIMES

Ranting and raving...negativism...
— Neal Wilgus

**One of the most important writers working in English
today**...courageous, compassionate, optimistic and original.
— Elwyn Chamberling, author of *Gates of Fire*

Should win the Nobel Prize for INTELLIGENCE.
— QUICKSILVER MESSENGER (Brighton, England)

to my wife, Arlen
"Blessed Be"

In the province of the mind, what is believed to be true is true or becomes true, within limits to be found experimentally and experientially. These limits are further beliefs to be transcended. In the province of the mind, there are no limits.
— John C. Lilly, M.D., *The Center of the Cyclone*

CONTENTS

PREFACE	To the 2000 Edition	11
PREFACE	To the 1987 Edition	17
INTRODUCTION		26
PRELUDE	Ice Maiden: The Story of Jane	39
CHAPTER 1	Overview: The Brews of Aphrodite	49
INTERLUDE	Slouching Toward Bethlehem: The Story of Leonard	78
CHAPTER 2	Horned Gods & Horny Potions	84
INTERLUDE	Divorce Psychedelic Style: The Story of Tom & Jerri	105
CHAPTER 3	The Smoke of the Assassins	116
INTERLUDE	Drug of Choice: The Story of Bill	145
CHAPTER 4	The Mexican Weed	155
INTERLUDE	Behind Suburban Doors: The Story of George & Martha	173
CHAPTER 5	Powders White & Deadly	180
INTERLUDE	Reject: The Story of Holy Out	200
CHAPTER 6	Tibetan Space-Time-Warp Star-Nova Trips	211
INTERLUDE	Up Against the Wall: The Story of Tyrone	230
CHAPTER 7	2000: An Inner Space Odyssey	238
RISK GLOSSARY	An Alphabetized Reference, With Guidelines & Warnings	253
BIBLIOGRAPHY		271

PREFACE
TO THE 2000 EDITION

And the Beast said:
"By their pee shall ye judge them,
and by thy pee shall ye be judged.
And all will be divided by their pee.
And in the snow shall their names be written."
                              — *The Book of Urinomics*[1]

   This book dates from 1972–73, and the man who wrote it does not exist anymore. Even I, occupying the same body that he did, hardly remember him and quite often do not agree with his opinions at all, at all. I have therefore corrected and updated his ideas in about a hundred places because, frankly, he embarrasses me at times, especially since we share the same name as well as the same body.
   Around the time he wrote this book, Robert Anton Wilson had passed the age of 40, lost the rigid right/wrong ideology he had picked up during the anti-war and anti-segregation move-ments of the 1960s and thought he had outgrown the dogmatic follies of his youth, achieving a middle-aged and mellow agnos-ticism about everything. Ten years later, as Ronald Regan sat in the White House, Wilson reached 50 and, looking back, felt astonished at how much folly had persisted even in his 40s. As he approached 60 a few years ago, he began to realize that he still had his share of human idiocy even in his 50s. Today at 66+

---

[1] Quoted in Revelation X, translated from the original tongues by the Sub-Genius Foundation, Simon and Shuster, New York, 1994.

(beginning to merge with him now), I can only wonder how much of the current Robert Anton Wilson literary output of palaver will embarrass me when I reach 75–80...

Nonetheless, I don't feel particularly disgraced by another printing of this book. Some of it still makes a lot of sense to me, after corrections, and I see that in the semi-fictionalized "case histories" I have accidentally provided a sort of "ideogrammic" history of the 1960s[1]—still the most controversial decade of the century, and well worth looking at again, to learn what we can from both its wisdom and its blunders.

The major blunder I acquired from the 1960s counterculture was the notion that the Enemy (with a capital E), was ignorance and that this could be cured by education. I now feel more inclined to accept R. Buckminster Fuller's description of the four major problems confronting the world as "ignorance, fear, greed, and zoning laws." Being untypically brave (like most fools), I always underestimated the role of fear in human affairs; having simple desires, I underestimated greed; and not being an architect, I never grasped the perfidious nature of zoning laws. Above all, I failed to realize the extent to which the synergy of ignorance-fear-greed-zoning laws in maintaining the tyranny that Fuller calls MMAO (Machiavelli, Mafia, Atoms and Oil)—the banks, the mob, and the energy cartels.)[2]

My current thinking about MMAO derives from Fuller and, in relation to the topics of this book, even more from the Sub-Genius Foundation of Dallas, TX, which refers to MMAO as "the Con."

Many think the Con is just a joke or a parody of other conspiracy theories. To such doubters, the Sub-Genius Foundation says that this is "the *Time of Pee*"—the time foretold, when people would be judged not by works, nor by family, nor even by looks, but by their urine.

---

[1] "Ideogrammic" in this sense means sensory/factual as distinct from abstract/theoretical.

[2] Fuller's ideas on these subjects can be studied in his *Critical Path,* St. Martin's Press, 1981, *Grunch of Giants,* St. Martin's Press, 1983 and at http://www.teleport.com/~px4d.grunch.html on the World Wide Web.

They listen to you through your telephone without its even being off the hook, and record you through satellites that can peer down any street, *anywhere...*

They kick your door in any time they want to. All they have to yell is "DRUGS!" and your spouse is in jail, your kids are farmed out to the state, your car and house are suddenly theirs...

Nobody up there is a friend of yours; nobody up there wants you to have what you would call freedom. The purpose of "government" is to produce consumers and workers who will keep the cost of labor down, and the profits high for the owners...

For this has become so crooked and perverse a nation that your precious bodily fluids are no longer your own, and not even your bladder or bloodstream are private. *There is no place where they may not watch.*[1]

The 1973 author of this book never could have imagined a State so crazily totalitarian, or a population so brainwashed into sheep-like submissiveness, that such absurdities could occur. But then, only Kafka and Orwell in their most eerie satires on bureaucracy-gone-bonkers could imagine an obscenity like our Piss Police. The State in which we live can only accurately be called Urine Nation.

How can this happen in a once-free Republic where searches of the person are forbidden except by court order after probable cause has been shown? Urine Nation, posing as the representatives of you and me, is engaged in an alleged "War on Drugs." That justifies trashing the Constitution.

Now this is, on the face of it, absurd.

1. Wars on drugs or other insensible things (objects, substances) can only be carried on by lunatics. The Con cannot be accused of insanity: of ignorance, yes, and of fear, greed and zoning laws, but not of being batshit crazy. They are not making war on chemicals—or on the laws of physics, or anything of that sort. They are making war on the American people—on all of us, although only a few of us know that yet.

---

[1] http://sunsite.unc.edu/subgenius

For instance, as you may read in *Pissing Away the American Dream*[1], on January 1989 the Minneapolis police smashed down the door of the home of an elderly Black couple, using "flash bang" grenades which accidentally set the house on fire and killed both old people.

The cops were looking for "drugs," but never found any. The chief of police justified the murders of two innocent citizens (and the total violation of the Fourth Amendment) by saying, "This is war."

The war is being waged against people, not chemicals, and it is people who get killed.

2. Even within the off-kilter logic of its own rhetoric, the "War on Drugs" is nonsense.

If you go out your door and drive a few blocks, they say, you will find at least one store boldly declaring that they sell DRUGS, although some say PHARMACY, which can only be deciphered by those who know Greek roots; and in these stores, hundreds of drugs are available. Nearby is a supermarket where you can buy cigarettes, containing nicotine, a drug more addictive than heroin according to former Surgeon General Koop. Next door is a BAR where you can buy dozens of varieties of C_2H_3OH, a heavily addictive substance, statistically linked to wife and child battering, divorce and violent crime.

Urine Nation, thus, is not making war on *all* drugs, or drug-users, but only on some. The government asserts that the drugs on their taboo list are the worst ones; skeptics like me say they are merely the ones that are either (a) cheap and effective, like herbal medicines, and/or (b) not easy to monopolize, like marijuana or (c) better than the higher priced drugs manufactured by the large pharmaceutical corporations that financially support both political parties.

The only people literally "at war" with drugs—*all* drugs—are the Christian Scientists. Eight of them are currently appealing their convictions for refusing to give their children the drugs ordained from on high by the Con/MMAO.

---

[1] *Pissing Away the American Dream,* edited by David Ross, Digit Press, PO Box 91066, Norcross, GA.

As Count Bismarck once said, "Laws are like sausages: you have much more respect for them if you haven't actually seen how they're made."

Many of the chemicals and herbs forbidden by the Con are not only harmless, but are widely believed to be beneficial. The war against the users of these substances is just as vicious as the wars against all other substances on the taboo list.

Over the past 10 years, the Food and Drug Administration has engaged in raids on alternative health companies—companies operating openly and, they thought, legally—that more and more tend toward the violence of DEA raids on suspected crack dealers. In every case, the companies were selling vitamins and herbs that a growing minority of the medical profession approves but which MMAO and the FDA do not approve.

For instance, in 1990, the FDA raided the offices of Dr. Jonathan Wright, a fully qualified physician with an M.D. from the University of Michigan Medical School, terrorized the staff with drawn guns, and seized all the vitamins and herbs they could find. They never did file criminal charges against Dr. Wright for the heresy of giving his patients cheap medicines instead of expensive ones[1], but this raid was only one of hundreds of similar Gestapo-style operations, creating what libertarians call "a chilling effect" on scientific freedom.

As the Life Extension Foundation wrote:

> … The FDA's strong-arm tactics are used to intimidate and terrorize Americans into toeing their police state party line on healthcare and medicine. The FDA's purpose is not just to destroy the business and lives of their targets, but also to spread fear and terror throughout the land so that others who may be tempted to rebel against the agency will remain meek and submissive.[2]

In the 1980s, a Fundamentalist couple named Randy and Vicki Weaver fled to a mountain top in Idaho, to get as far as possible from the U.S. government, which they considered a Zionist conspiracy. However goofy that idea was, it was the only "offense" of which the Weavers were guilty. They didn't annoy

---

[1] See *Trajectories,* Vol 1 No. 12, Spring 1993.
[2] http://www.livelinks.com/sumeria/health/raids.htm

their neighbors and they didn't plot an insurrection against the government: they just tried to avoid and evade it. This alone was too much for the Feds. They sent in an informant to make friends with Randy and eventually entrap him into selling a shotgun. With that excuse, the FBI and ATF made war on the Weaver family, killing Vicki while she stood holding her baby in her arms, killing the older son, and even killing the family dog.[1]

The Weavers sure had a lot of nutty ideas; nobody but another Fundamentalist would deny that. But maybe their idea of the nature of the current U.S. government, and its attitude toward its serfs and subjects, was a hell of a lot more accurate than the ideas you read in liberal journals.

Robert Anton Wilson
http://www.rawilson.com

---

[1] *Every Knee Shall Bow,* Jess Walter, HarperCollins, New York, 1995.

PREFACE
TO THE 1987 EDITION

This book was originally written under the title *Sex, Drugs and the Occult* in 1972. It was published by Playboy Press in 1973 under the title *Sex and Drugs: A Journey Beyond Limits.* The change was ordained by an editor who explained, "Hef says only women and fags buy books on the occult."

I have no idea whether Hef actually uttered that paleolithic sentiment or not. After five years working for *Playboy* magazine as Associate Editor (1966–1971) and having three books published by Playboy Press (1972–1974), I have learned that Hugh Hefner is at least as mythical as the Playboy Bunny, the Easter Bunny or Harvey the six-foot-tall white rabbit in the famous film. On many occasions, editors have attributed to Hef ideas and attitudes which later turned out to be based entirely on myth, rumor, delusion and the madness of middle-rank executives.

I saw *Playboy* magazine take a marked turn to the right, politically, between early 1966 and late 1967, entirely because Hef said something vaguely favorable about Ayn Rand, which got exaggerated to the report, "Hef has become an Objectivist," and then I saw it turn markedly left-of-center again because Hef said, on another occasion, that he liked Rand's ornery heroes but was personally a New Deal liberal on social issues.

Nervous editors are always trying to guess the publisher's prejudices from minimal clues and they often guess wrong, which, of course, makes them more nervous in the future. That's probably why Gene Fowler uttered the immortal aphorism, "Every editor should have a pimp as an older brother, so he'd have somebody to look up to." The Big Bunny Empire has always been a warren of extremely lapine editors.

Playboy Press seems not to have published this book in the ordinary sense but to have released it on a need-to-know basis, or something of that sort. There were marvelous advance-of-publication blurbs from heavyweight figures like Alan Watts, William S. Burroughs and Timothy Leary; there were enthusiastic reviews in a dozen counterculture newspapers and magazines; and then there was a stifled and prolonged silence, as if I had killed a cat in the sacristy. Every place I went to lecture or give seminars, people had heard of *Sex and Drugs* by word of mouth but complained that they were unable to find it in any bookstores. Very quickly, it went out of print. I have never earned a penny in royalties on it, which event I fully expect to reverse from the Falcon Press edition. [And which, indeed, has happened. Ed.]

Even more curiously, as years passed and other books by me sold well and were reprinted regularly, no publisher was, for 13 years, willing to reprint *Sex and Drugs*. This has often puzzled me.

In retrospect, I can't help recalling that in the early 1970s—when this book was first published and immediately disappeared like a brick thrown in mud—many other weird things were happening to advocates of unpopular ideas in America. Paul Krassner's *Realist* (the magazine that first published me, in 1959) was driven into bankruptcy by what Paul has always claimed was an FBI conspiracy. Dr. Leary, for poor usage of the first amendment, was in solitary confinement in the basement of Folsom Prison, in the cell next to mass murderer Charlie Manson. John Lennon was shot by another of the "deranged lone assassins" who were as common in America at that time as empty beer cans on a beach. Stop-and-frisk laws, curfew laws, no-knock laws and other Sovietic measures were selectively enforced on certain segments of the population, at least at first. Now it seems they can crash into anybody's house and steal the family jewels, if they claim they suspected drugs were on the premises. Most "underground" newspapers and magazines followed *The Realist* into bankruptcy in a period of only a few months after the large record companies abruptly and very mysteriously stopped advertising in the only publications read regularly by the young people who buy most records. Psychiatrists and psychologists who once told me they agreed with Dr. Leary's ideas became as pale and silent as moonlight on a gravestone.

I draw no definite conclusion from this. I merely report the facts. The 1970s were a period in American history when a President accused by Congressional investigators of more high crimes and felonies than any five Mafia Godfathers, was allowed to resign and appoint a successor who immediately granted him a full pardon for all crimes known or later to be discovered.

The most important comment I wish to add to this new edition is that, since cocaine has become a great deal more popular than it was when I wrote this book, I wish I had been even more unfavorable in my references to that nefarious compound. Having seen a lot of coke-heads in recent years, I am convinced that you can get exactly the same results over a period of a few months by repeatedly shoving talcum powder up your nose, rubbing it in with sandpaper and then burning everything you own in a backyard bonfire.

Or, as Richard Pryor once said, cocaine is just nature's way of telling you that you have too much money.

I also regard cocaine as pernicious because most of the profits from the coke industry go to enrich the Mafia, the Vatican and the worst dictators in South America. You can find the documentation to support this charge in David Yallop's *In Gods Name,* in Penny Lernoux's *In Banks We Trust* and in my own *Everything Is Under Control.*

A few additional comments might be helpful in clarifying the thesis of this book, since many of the ideas herein are totally unfamiliar to most people in the Western world.

This book was originally called *Sex, Drugs **and the Occult*** because it deals with the interface of those *three* intensities of experience and not just with two of them. It thus violates all the taboos of middle-class, middle-brow readers.

Sex has many facets—biological sociological, esthetic, psychological, compulsive, ecstatic, tragic, playful, loving, perplexing and (I am told), even on occasion boring—but in this text is considered chiefly in its "transcendental" aspect. By this, I mean simply that in orgasm everybody experiences, to some degree, an explosion/implosion of the normal ego and a melting, merging, "oceanic" sensation of at-one-ment.

There are many types of drugs in the world—antibiotics;
anesthetics; analgesics; narcotics; hypnotics; psychedelics;
uppers and downers; dreamers and screamers—but here I am
concerned with drugs that act centrally upon the higher nervous
system and alter ego-definitions and perceived reality-tunnels.
That is, drugs that produce "transcendental" or transpersonal
states.

It is obvious that sex and drugs together can lead to more
extraordinary and paranormal trans-ego experiences than either
sex or drugs alone. This is an ancient Tantric "secret" and the
present book was, as far as I know, the first ever published in
America to discuss it explicitly, without using alchemical or
other codes to obscure what was actually being said (a technique
of disguise that had been used by writers as diverse as Thomas
Vaughin, Titus Burkhardt, Arthur Waite, Aleister Crowley and
Israel Regardie). In retrospect, I am not disappointed or astound-
ed that the distributor of the original edition appears to have
buried the books in the cellar instead of placing them in book
stores. I think I am lucky not to have landed in the cell next to
Dr. Leary and Charlie Manson.

H.L. Mencken once defined puritanism as "the haunting fear
that somebody, somewhere, might be having a good time." (See
the recent career of Kenneth Starr.) One deeply entrenched reflex
of Western culture is that post-puritan hangover which Dr.
Wilhelm Reich called *pleasure anxiety.* This can be defined non-
technically as the suspicion that maybe the puritan god exists
after all and, if we do manage to have a good time, he will rear
up and give us bloody hell for it. The intensity of sex-phobia and
drug-phobia in a large and loud part of the U.S. population was
known to me when I wrote this book, but I thought it would lead
to "controversy." I was too naive to realize that by touching on
both sex-and-drug phobias simultaneously I would produce, not
controversy, but repression and scotoma.

The third theme of this work, "occultism," has even more
contradictory aspects and conflicting meanings than sex or drugs.
It includes superstitions, silly pseudo-sciences, authoritarian
cults as nutty as a kangaroo in a Mozart quartet, and, in some
places, a true science of psycho-neurology or *rapid brain change*
as valid as, and often more valid than, most of what passes for

"scientific psychology" these days. The last is best represented by Crowleyan "Magick," so I have used that word in this new edition.

I am interested only in the latter kind of occultism, and even there I am leery of the high nonsense quotient that infests most writings in this field. My aim has always been to learn what occult practices produce concrete results and to reformulate what I have reamed from occultists into scientific and experimental language, as far as that is possible at this date.

Time magazine, with their usual *dummheit,* once did a cover story entitled, "The Occult: A Substitute Faith." If this was all that could be found in occultism, I would not touch the subject with the proverbial ten-foot pole. The world already has enough "faith" to guarantee that the Idiots are always, as Ambrose Bierce said, the largest and most influential political party in any society. Occultism interests me, not as a substitute faith, but as a *substitute for faith.*

Organized religion, which is based on faith, has been, as Mencken once wrote, the greatest fomenter of hatred in the history of the world. The only political parties to rival religion as causes of human suffering and horror are Nazism and Communism, which are also based on blind faith and rigid dogmatism. My basic attitude has always been that the greatest drug any chemist could possibly invent would be an anti-gullibility pill, to cure humanity of its addiction to faith and dogma.

The kind of occultism that interests me is based, not on faith, but on the same experimental method as the more objective and less controversial physical sciences. This is the occultism that you will find, for instance, in the appendices (the practical part) of Aleister Crowley's *Magick in Theory and Practise.* As Crowley writes:

> In this book it is spoken of the Sephiroth and the Path, of spirits and conjurations, of gods, spheres, planes and many other things which may or may not exist. It is immaterial whether they exist or not. By doing certain things, certain results follow; students are most earnestly warned against attributing objective reality or philosophical validity to any of them.

In other words, traditional occultism has come down to us with the vocabulary and metaphors of past ages attached. This

vocabulary and these metaphors have proven useful for centuries, and may still prove useful to those not entirely alienated
by their archaic flavor, but the essence of a practical occult
system has nothing to do with vocabulary or metaphors. The
essence is "doing certain things" as Crowley says. These things
one does, or *operations,* are sometimes called "rituals" and
sometimes "exercises," but it is not at all extravagant to call
them "experiments" or "explorations."

The reason Crowley warns against attributing "objective reality" to the *operations* (rituals, exercises, experiments, explorations) of practical occultism is that these operations deal only
and always with non-objective realities (plural).

A popular fallacy holds that there are no non-objective realities: that objective reality is the "only" reality. The error of this
view can clearly be seen when one contemplates the range of
non-objective realities encountered and endured by different
people on ordinary days, without any occult operations being
performed at all:

Mr. A has a headache and is irritable. Ms. B just passed her
mathematics test and is happy. Mr. C is worried, irrationally, that
the Communists are putting poison in his food. Ms. D is worried,
rationally, that she can't pay the rent. Mr. E is so involved in a
medical research project showing good results that he elatedly
thinks all disease is about to be abolished next Tuesday after
lunch. Ms. F is so depressed by a year of losing battles for the
rights of farm workers that she thinks the human condition is
hopeless and the bad guys always win.

Any one-level theory of objective reality that ignores the separate reality-tunnels in which these people are living existentially
has no validity in psychology, and, with a little analysis, it is
obvious that no such one-level theory has any general validity in
sociology either. To understand *human behavior,* we have to
understand *human evaluations* (neuro-linguistic programs) and
modern social scientists of all schools increasingly recognize that
human evaluations (internal reality-tunnels) depend on both the
external environment (setting) and the internal environment
(neuro-linguistic programs).

You can easily kill yourself with negative mind-sets, by
developing ulcers, heart problems, high blood pressure, etc., or

by drunken driving, or simply by getting so depressed you jump in front of a train. Conversely, you can survive "objective realities" that would mentally or physically destroy others, if you are maintaining a positive mind-set.

The operations and experiments and training exercises of practical occultism are concerned with "causing change in consciousness by act of will" as the psychoanalyst Violet Wirth wrote under the pen-name she used on her occult books, Dion Fortune. Such rapid brain-change is an art well worth mastering in a world that is full of nasty shocks and discouraging social problems. I have tried here to tell as much about this art as I can, in plain English, without hiding anything, and without using supernatural or mystic metaphors for events that can be described more economically in the languages of neurolinguistics and neurosomatic medicine.

The major lesson to be learned from practical occultism has already been stated several times in this brief Preface and will be stated again, in other metaphors, throughout this book. It needs to be stated in many ways, redundantly, because most people cannot understand it without experience of the operations, experiments and exercises of rapid brain change. Here is one more attempt to state it simply and directly:

NO "EXTERNAL" SITUATION MAKES
A MENTAL STATE "INEVITABLE"

Whatever is going on around you, your experienced reality-tunnel is still a synergetic product of both internal and external environments (set and setting). You do not "create your own reality," as Pop Mysticism says, but you create the larger part of it by how you evaluate, respond and give "meaning" to what happens. Your freedom is much, much greater than you realize until you start experimenting with alternative reality-tunnels and rapid brain change.

This book, then, is basically an informal history of how certain long-hidden practical secrets of Tantric Buddhism crept into the Western world in the middle ages, were crushed and/or driven underground by the Holy Inquisition, have gradually been rediscovered since around 1900, suddenly emerged as a major social-revolutionary force in the 1960s, and were once again crushed and driven underground.

Fifteen years after the first edition, I think I understand better why these secrets of mind-programming have been so carefully hidden and why they are so ferociously persecuted whenever they are leaked to a large section of any population. Tantra survived in the East precisely because it *did* hide its secrets and never attempted to become a revolutionary force for social change. Tantrists, like other Buddhists, believe that breaking free of mechanical consciousness—learning to change consciousness by acts of will—can only be accomplished by one person at a time, and that trying to liberate the whole world is impossible and counter-productive. "When eating an elephant, take one bite at a time" is their motto.

My own preferred reality-tunnel is precisely the reverse of this Buddhist conservatism. Despite the tone of fashionable cynicism in a few pages of this book—the one form of disguise I used to get the text past the original editors' prejudices—I have been convinced for some time that the present worldwide technological society is much like a *dissipative structure* in the mathematical quantum chemistry of Illya Prigogine. Such a complex structure, once achieved, immediately becomes mathematically unstable and must quickly transform itself radically, either into a more chaotic state or into a more coherent state. If this mathematical model really fits our planetary village today (and Dr. Prigogine himself thinks it does), then we are certainly moving, very rapidly, either into chaos or into higher order.

In human terms, that means that either your favorite Doomsday scenario is about to happen or else some form of totally new world society will emerge from our current instability. The accelerated changes we are experiencing are symptoms either of radical *breakdown* or of radical *breakthrough* to a new level of human evolution. As Buckminster Fuller said repeatedly in his last ten years, the only choices left for us are Utopia or Oblivion.

Since it is fashionable, *chic* and "the in thing" to bet on Oblivion, I think it is worthwhile to consider the case for Utopia. The arguments for this unfashionable and unpopular alternative are presented in my *Prometheus Rising* (Falcon Press, 1983). Briefly, here, I will say only:

(1) until the future arrives, the outcome is uncertain, so Doomsday scenarios, however popular, are not definitive and,

for intellectual honesty and clarity, deserve to be criticized and challenged;

(2) for the reasons sketched above, and developed more fully in the text to follow, I do not think pessimism is the *only* possible outlook on the universe, but merely the one that is currently ubiquitous;

(3) many sociological behaviors are the result of self-fulfilling prophecies, so it is worth the gamble of experimentally breaking the group hypnosis of defeatism, and experimentally testing to see what the results of more hopeful scenarios might be, and;

(4) Prigogine's math indicates that the odds actually favor the optimists, since dissipative structures are more likely to evolve into more information-rich (intelligent?) forms than into more primitive or chaotic forms.

In this context of skepticism toward the modern Idol of Existential Despair, I think the programs of rapid brain change suggested in this book are worthy of experimental testing by anybody who isn't yet ready for suicide.

Perhaps there are resources of courage, creativity and higher intelligence latent in each of us. Perhaps a sociological chain reaction can still be set in action if enough people learn how to transcend fashionable self-pity and make an effort to become happier and more efficient. Perhaps we are not dead yet, but only hypnotized by morbid and moribund philosophies. Perhaps the powers of the human brain have never fully been released in the paleolithic, neolithic, feudal, capitalist or socialist games. Perhaps the limits that seem to restrict us are only bad habits and we can transcend all of them.

And—this is the major theme of the pages to follow—perhaps the human brain can be used for fun and profit; perhaps the brain is not designed for failure, as current intellectual dogma holds, but for "total success in Universe" as Bucky Fuller claimed.

Those who are willing to consider these heretical and blasphemous notions might find profit in the upcoming chapters.

One final 1987 postscript to this 1972 book. No cure has been found for AIDS yet. Far be it from me to criticize anybody's lifestyle, but—if you must be promiscuous, remember that in the age of AIDS casual sex *without a condom* is like Russian roulette.

INTRODUCTION

We're all Bozos on this bus.

— The Firesign Theater

In Berkeley, a young man is chanting a Hindu mantra while exuberantly balling a female member of his commune. Incense is burning, there is a chalked pentagram on the floor around the bed, and they have been copulating—unbelievably, without reaching orgasm—for nearly two hours, with occasional stops for additional sniffs of cocaine. If you tell this fellow that all this magick is unscientific and silly and that, with continued use, the coke will ruin his nasal septum, he will dismiss you as a hopeless square. He has found the real meaning of religious ecstasy in the newly faddish works of magician Aleister Crowley (who died in obscurity in 1947). This program of drugs plus artificially pro-longed Tantric (sexual) yoga has raised him to a plane of beauty and joy where the warnings of the rationalist are meaningless.

Meanwhile, in Chicago, a hip young lawyer with a more hard-boiled attitude is smoking a joint of Panama Red marijuana with his lady of the evening before they climb into bed. He does not consider himself a magician and he knows nothing about Tantric yoga. But he, too, is part of the new cult of drug-drenched sexual mysticism, even if he says "vibes" without real-izing that this is a shortening of "astral vibrations." He is just looking for a bigger and better orgasm, and expects weed to produce it.

In Darien, Connecticut, where the Mad Avenue crowd retreats at sunset to become suburbanites, a high-school student and his teeny-bopper sweetie pie are also combining drugs, sex and a little mysticism. They are nude but not yet engaged in intercourse; he is reading the "Sex Chakra" chapter from Timothy Leary's Psychedelic Prayers *aloud to her, while 500 mikes of "windowpane" acid are circulating in their bloodstreams. "Lie quietly in the slippery union of male and female," he intones, and they move together toward a mounting posture, utterly free of the furtive guilts of their parents. They are quite convinced that what is transpiring is more religiously meaningful than anything that ever happens in the local church on Sunday.*

The preceding paragraphs are not fiction; they are composites based on people I have actually known. We are living in a time in which—together with thousands of other social changes—the Drug Revolution has combined with the Sexual Revolution to bring forth amazing progeny. Chiefly, what has happened, and is continuing to happen as more and more converts climb on the eroto-psychedelic bandwagon, can be described—paradoxically—as an upsurge of interest in the *nonphysical* side of sex.

Even though the concept sounds like an oxymoron at first, we all know about the nonphysical or metaphysical aspects of our own eroticism. It is the emotional—or energetic—force that gives sex a flavor or a color quite independent of its physical spasms, albeit capable of enriching and even prolonging the physical aspect.

According to Masters and Johnson, a woman can achieve a higher intensity of physical pleasure through masturbation than she can ever experience in coitus with a man. This fact has been seized upon as proof that men are unnecessary to female sexual gratification by a certain vehement fringe of the Feminist movement. To nobody's great surprise, however, most women continue to prefer copulation to masturbation.

Similarly, many propagandists for Gay Liberation insist that fellatio gives a man a more explosive orgasm than coitus. Although they have no authority equal to Masters and Johnson to support them in this claim, they may well be right. Our President seems to agree with them; and Judge Murtagh of New York, in his book on prostitution called *Cast the First Stone,* points out that a high percentage of the men who go to whores are married and are seeking fellatio, which either they are too timid to ask from their wives or their wives are too prudish to provide. This would seem to indicate that fellatio, at least occasionally, provides a certain something extra (as Mad Avenue would say) that pene-vage just doesn't have. Nevertheless, again to nobody's surprise, most men are quite devoted to the old "missionary position" most of the time.

Obviously, there is more to sex than the twitching of a few muscles and the excretion of a few glands. Every adolescent boy who has ever held a pin-up in his left hand while masturbating knows this. Every woman who has ever been irresistibly drawn to a man who looks like Adonis but acts like a son-of-a-bitch knows this. And so does every husband or wife who has fantasized a different partner while in the arms of his or her actual spouse.

The mysterious nonphysical part of sexuality is variously known as "mind," "spirit," or "emotion." Sigmund Freud called it "libido" and then cautiously backed away from defining what he meant. Wilhelm Reich, M.D., the *enfant terrible* of modern psychology, called it "orgone" and insisted it was a real energy that physical scientists hadn't noticed because they had never thought to turn their instruments on men and women in a state of erotic passion. Russian scientists have been trying to measure it lately, and several have claimed success; they cheerfully inform us that it extends several feet beyond the physical body.

Whether Reich and the Russians are right or not, there is a clear sensation, which most of us know very well, that some sort of field of emotional energy is aroused by sexual excitement. This subjective streaming sensation generally rises and falls in proportion to the more specific bioelectric charge in the primary and secondary sexual organs; but not always. The difference between this psycho-energetic "thrill" and the more localized genital sensation explains why a woman prefers a man to her own middle finger, even though masturbation can produce more of the localized charge and discharge; why an adolescent enjoys masturbating more when a photo is building up a mental charge to aid and abet the physical charge produced by his onanistic hand; why a man will want copulation on one occasion and fellatio on another.

The local sensations are entirely the product of the celebrated "technique" taught in sex manuals; the general emotional field effect is partly (though certainly not totally) independent of this, and depends mostly on psychological variables—the conscious and unconscious feelings, needs, whims, fantasies and yens of the individual.

Timothy Leary, Ph.D., the prophet and martyr of the drug kulch, likes to refer to Konrad Lorentz' ethological research which is oddly *apropos* here. Dr. Lorentz discovered that geese—in order to be attracted sexually to other geese—must be immediately "imprinted" after birth (i.e., they must acquire the image of a goose as a source of emotional gratification). They acquire this "imprinting," in the ordinary course of nature, by nesting with their mothers. Due to Dr. Lorentz's careful attention to his experimental birds, a few of them were "imprinted" with his image as the protective, maternal object, and pursued him sexually when they grew to adulthood. Another gosling, more strikingly, was accidentally "imprinted" by a ping-pong ball. Consequently, he spent his adult life in frustrating attempts to make love to these plastic spheres.

As Dr. Leary says, this anecdote

> is both amusing and frightening. It reminds us that each of us sees the world through perceptual structures (biochemical-neurological) which were laid down accidentally in our earliest moments. It raises the uneasy suspicion that…we may be simply chasing the particular Ping-Pong balls which, at those sensitive shutter moments, had been imprinted on our cortical film.

My own experience illustrates this. My wife has red hair. Looking back, it occurs to me that I have been involved sexually with more red-headed women than mere chance and accident can explain. Seeking some light on this, I asked my mother about the early female influences on my infancy. She remembered that, at that time, I was especially fond of one baby-sitter—*a girl with red hair.* It doesn't take much imagination to assume that, if the baby-sitter who was so kind to me had been male, I might be homosexual today; or that if she had been cruel, I might be a masochist; and so on.

This analysis is not intended merely to trigger the trite reflections about "nothing human is alien to me" or "there, but for the grace of God, go I." More significant is the realization that, however and whatever imprinted us in youth, we bring this sub-merged history with us to each sexual encounter. It is one—only one out of many—of the factors that determine whether our emotional field becomes highly charged when our genitals are being stimulated mechanically.

I sometimes think that the most profound lyric ever uttered by bard or poet is the old Rocky Mountain folk tune:

> From here on up, the hills don't get any higher;
> From here on up, the hills don't get any higher;
> From here on up, the hills can't get any higher;
> But the valleys get deeper and deeper.

Ultimately, what we find in any experience, sexual or other-wise, depends upon our own emotional energy field. We can see a small mountain above a deep valley, or a shallow valley with a tall mountain towering over it.

Way back in the innocent pre-LSD days of the 1950s, Carl Rogers, a distinguished psychologist who invented what is called "client-centered therapy," wrote a paper on the changes in per-ception that occur during psychotherapy. He pointed out that patients entering treatment usually see rather subdued colors and hear a great deal of chaotic noise in their environment; moreover, they are also generally surrounded by negative and unpleasant stimuli in such areas as odor and temperature. On the other hand, patients who have completed a successful psychotherapy tend to see brighter colors, hear more attractive and rhythmic sounds, and generally perceive a more pleasing world. It seems evident that the changes occur in the patients, and not in the environ-ment.

Even earlier, poet Carl Sandburg told a yarn about a farmer sitting on a fence when a stranger passed on the road and asked him how folks were up in the town ahead. "How were folks where you came from?" asked the farmer. "They were a pretty mean, selfish and unfriendly lot," the stranger said bitterly, "and that's why I left." The farmer shook his head sadly. "I'm afraid you're in for a disappointment. Folks in the next town are just the same."

A while later, a second stranger came along the road and asked the same question. "How were the folks where you came from?" the farmer asked again. "They were great," this fellow replied. "A kinder, more helpful lot of people I never saw. I really hated to leave." "Well," the farmer said, "don't be sad. You'll find the same kind of folks up ahead."

We all find it hard to believe that reality is as much our own creation as Professor Rogers' research and poet Sandburg's parable suggest. Conservatives, who pride themselves on having a "hard-nosed" and "realistic" attitude to the "brute facts" of life, are suspicious of anything that introduces the subjective element or implies that the "brute facts" may exist only in their own heads. Liberals, dogmatically committed to what they believe is scientific skepticism (mostly, in fact, popularizations of obsolete pre-Einstein physics), are wary of any idea that seems to open a door to "mysticism" or (Got forbid) traditional otherworldly religion. And radicals, of course, react like a bull toward a colored cloth when confronted with notions that imply (in Shakespeare's words) that "nothing is but thinking makes it so," since that could easily lead to telling the poor that the proper mental attitude, and not more government spending, is the cure for their miseries.

In spite of all these powerful prejudices, most of us acknowledge that *other people* are fairly subjective in their perceptions and are frequently inclined to what Freud called "projection"— seeing what they expect, or hope, or sometimes what they fear. Under philosophical cross-examination we will even admit that the same self-deception occasionally does manifest itself in ourselves—although very seldom, of course. A cult called CSICOP believes this "projection" or "self-deception" happens to everybody else except themselves.

The drug revolution of the 1990s has brought this issue home to all of us, where it had previously occupied a murky area of philosophy and occasionally intruded on the technical proceedings of those psychologists and neurologists who were specialists in perception theory. Somewhere between 10 and 70 million Americans have experimented on themselves with marijuana or other drugs that are loosely classed as *psychotomimetics*, or *hallucinogens* or *psychedelics*. The conflicting names for these chemicals indicate the disagreement in the scientific community about what actually happens when these drugs enter the human biocomputer. *Psychotomimetic* means that which imitates psychosis, or puts us temporarily in the world of the insane; *hallucinogenic* implies that which distorts or warps our perception; *psychedelic* means merely that which alters or enlarges consciousness. Obviously, the first two terms suggest that the drug voyager is seeing nothing but illusion and delusion, while the third leaves open the possibility that *some* of the newly acquired perceptions might be as accurate as normal awareness, or even more accurate.

The latter, needless to say, is the claim of those who see the psychedelic movement as a political or cultural force; it is the dogma of such new religions, based on these drugs, as Dr. Leary's League for Spiritual Discovery, the Neo-American Church, the Church of the Awakening, the Church of Psychedelic Venus, and so on. To a large degree, social policy toward this whole movement will depend upon how open we can be on this issue of the validity of the perceptions of others. Do we think that the world we perceive *is* the real world, as Ayn Rand (for example) insists? Or do we admit that everybody lives in his own world and that each person's universe is partly valid and partly an artistic creation?

I was an early participant in the Drug Revolution. I took peyote, the sacred psychedelic cactus of the American Indians since about 1000 BC, with a Sioux Indian friend in 1961. I experienced the explosion (or implosion) of my previous universe and the creation of a new universe. I know what Dr. Leary and the other ideologues of the "new consciousness" are talking about. At the same time, I have a wife and four children to support and a Brooklyn boyhood's training in the arts of survival, which means that I am a constitutional non-joiner and non-crusader. I have known the psychedelic activists and liked many of them, but my own temperament has always been skeptical. I do not have the glands of a True Believer.

My friend, novelist William S. Burroughs, liked to say that "anything which can be accomplished by chemical means can also be accomplished by non-chemical means." I have personally found this to be true. There is no area of new perception and expanded awareness discoverable through peyote (or LSD or similar drugs) that cannot also be reached by techniques well-known to Oriental yogis and Western occultists. The sensory withdrawal techniques pioneered by Dr. Lilly and the new biofeedback machines also duplicate most of this expanded awareness. Other scientists are investigating even easier techniques. As this new knowledge becomes increasingly available to the layman, I am convinced that it will have the effect that the Washington solons *aim at but are unable to achieve through prohibitive laws*: the drug revolution will lose its momentum and shrink a bit. (I doubt that it will ever vanish totally. It has been around, as we shall see, since at least 15,000 BC.)

Meanwhile, the chemical revolution is doing "quite nicely, thank you." There were, for instance, probably no more than a few hundred thousand pot smokers in this country when Congress outlawed the weed in 1937; the figure now hovers around 50–70 million—and the number seems to be increasing. Many of them have gone through perception changes similar to those of Dr. Rogers' patients and are living in a reality unknown to, say, Reverend Billy Graham or the chairman of the board of your local bank. Those who take drugs laugh at different things, love in a different fashion, get angry for different reasons and generally seem to many of their elders like invaders from another planet.

The first "drug joke" that I ever heard, back in the mid-1950s, seemed mysterious to me in my youth and innocence. It concerned two pot-smoking bop musicians who are walking on the street when a fire engine races by at full throttle. "Man," one says to the other, "I thought they'd *never* leave." Today, even the straightest citizen knows, at least by hearsay, the point of that yarn: marijuana expands time as if it were silly putty. It also confronts us with Einstein's paradoxes: Is my time real or is yours more real? Is our train moving or is it the train on the next track? Are the hills getting higher or the valleys deeper? For the first time in the history of the development of Anglo-Saxon law we are confronted with that most accursed of all metaphysical questions—*What is Reality?*—and our tolerance, or intolerance, toward around 40 percent of our citizens depends on our answer.

Perception does not exist in a vacuum; what we see determines how we feel and relate to the world. Our answer to "What is Reality?" is never an abstract or academic matter, however abstruse the question itself may seem. Those who share what anthropologist Carlos Castaneda has called "a separate reality" also develop a separate lifestyle and ethos—which is widely called "the counterculture." As Richard R. Lingeman writes in *Drugs from A to Z:*

> As long as the mystique surrounds the drug, the curious will want to try it, and the adept will orient their lives around it. There will probably continue to be agitation for the drug's legalization by its advocates... Dedicated LSD users are characteristically, almost compulsively, proselytizers for the drug, but it remains to be seen whether their efforts will have any widespread effect in our society, *for the meditative, non-aggressive, inward orientation of self associated with the drug runs counter to the values of an extroverted, aggressive, acquisitive society.* [Italics added]

This book can hardly hope to resolve such complex epistemo-logical and sociological conflicts, but it is my hope that I will be able, at least, to clarify some of the issues somewhat. My subject is the effect of drugs on sexuality, but I cannot separate this from their effect on life and feeling generally, and upon philosophy, law and politics. It is my hope that, at minimum, the ordinary reader will gain some increased understanding of the real conflicts involved in the subject, as well as in such deceptively simple words as "reality," "hallucination," "consciousness," "consciousness-expansion," and so on.

It is not at all true, for example, that the average pot smoker or acidhead has lost the ability to distinguish an obvious hallucination from an inescapable reality. However, the line, for such enthusiasts, has certainly grown more problematical and puzzling than it has for most people; they are less dogmatic in saying "this is real" or "this is hallucination." But please note that (a) this is also true for the greatest minds in science, who recognize much more ambiguity in this area than the man-in-the-street does, and (b) except under very rare circumstances and for very brief moments (i.e., under a solanaceae drug or a very high dose of LSD), the average drug user will have no more trouble than Jesse Helms in distinguishing a real speeding car from a vision of the one-eyed, one-horned, flying purple people-eater.

This is worth emphasizing because a popular misunderstanding has it that the "drug cultists" have lost all critical judgment and believe in all sorts of illusions and hallucinations that they experience on their weed or their acid. This is hardly true of men as sophisticated as Aldous Huxley, William S. Burroughs, Alan W. Watts and many other distinguished persons who have said that drugs enabled them to know more of reality, and it is not even true of the *lumpen* users in our colleges or hippie ghettos.

For instance, under a drug like hashish, a man might, in a few hours, pass through a program or scenario in which (a) all colors become brighter and lovelier, (b) he suddenly discovers abnormally succulent flavor in a product like corn flakes, (c) he sees a werewolf in the window, (d) he spends a half hour in hopeless giggles over a subject that never does become clear, (e) he suddenly realizes that his last quarrel with his girlfriend was sparked by unconscious resentments against his mother left over from infancy, (f) he thinks he understands what Hindus mean when they say that everything is God, (g) looking at himself in a mirror, he sees an old man (or a corpse), (h) he sees something in a Van Gogh painting that he never noticed before, and (i) he goes to bed with his girl and has the best orgasm in months.

Afterwards, mulling over this experience, the voyager will *not* assume that (c) the werewolf was really at the window. He will also probably decide that (b) the corn flakes really are a fairly bland food and that the hashish was just programming him with memories of better food in the past. He might even be skeptical enough to wonder if his great Freudian insight (e) into infantile traumas was a real memory or just a reflection of what he has heard or read of Freud's works. He might, however, decide that colors (a) really are brighter than he usually "sees" them as being, and that his normal perception of drab or dull hues is, like that of Carl Rogers' patients mentioned above, a result of his own partial crippling by our repressive society; that giggling (d) is probably better for you than worrying, whether or not you understand the cause of your laughter; that the old man or corpse (g) in the mirror, although hallucinatory, is a spiritual reality—one's ultimate fate—which should be faced instead of being avoided as it usually is; that all the preoccupation with God (f) might be worth more thought; and that the super-orgasm (i), however you describe it, was certainly worth experiencing.

Let us examine the matter of better orgasm in more detail, since sex is the major topic of this book. Asked what actually happened, our hypothetical hashhead might say—we will see actual quotes to this effect later—that his consciousness centered entirely in his penis; that he felt as if he were nothing but a penis, and one of gigantic dimensions. He might add that his girlfriend seemed to be nothing other than a gigantic, very warm, delightfully moist vagina. At the same time, the emotional field mentioned earlier seemed to be peculiarly aglow or illuminated. (This sensation, oddly or not so oddly, has been reported also by all the great mystics of East and West for at least the last 2000 years. A synonym for "illumination" appears in all the mystical writings of every language I have investigated.) At the moment of orgasm, ordinary consciousness was totally suspended, at least for a few seconds—quite in the manner described by D.H. Lawrence and Ernest Hemingway (and by Dr. Wilhelm Reich), even though "realistic" sex manuals tell people not to expect such an apocalyptic cosmic storm at the sexual climax.

Did something unique happen physically, or was it "only" psychological? As long as the experience was truly overwhelming for the participants, what purpose can such a question serve? (After all, happiness, bravery, zest and all the other desirable qualities can also be explained away as "only" psychological.)

But we go too fast, perhaps. The general reader, and, even more, the skeptical psychiatrist, will be quite convinced that the reduction of consciousness down to the dimensions of the penis *must* have been a hallucination, and this will taint the entire experience. Here is where the gap between "straight" society and the drug world appears insurmountable. Our hashish smoker, if he is an articulate exponent of the psychedelic philosophy, will deny that his perceptions constituted a hallucination.

He will point out that our notion that consciousness is in the head has been created socially for us and is not at all innate. The Chinese, for example, think of the consciousness as being in the solar plexus; the ideogram that we translate as "mind" actually shows the heart and kidneys. The Hindu yogis believe that consciousness can be moved anywhere, and perform daily exercises of moving it around from foot to calf to knee, up and down the torso, into the head and out again, and so on. And he will add that any notion that these two vast nations, whose populations comprise close to a third of the human race, are hallucinating constantly is rather provincial.

And he might even comment further that all our skepticism can be answered by a little first-hand experience. Our fear of such experience, he will even suggest, is a measure of the lingering influence of Puritanism on us. Western society, at least since St. Paul, has tended to regard the sex act as more or less deplorable, and it is this tradition that causes so many of us to regard Oriental lingering on the details as effete, frankness in erotic art as pornographic, and drugs that enhance sex as degenerate—or hallucinatory. This last is, after all, a way of removing a temptation—one simply declares it to be nonexistent.

The hash smoker has become more "open," but not necessarily more gullible.

Then again, the most fruitful drug experiences are probably those that fit the classic pattern described in the Zen Buddhist proverb about the course of the mind during yogic contemplation: "First the mountains are mountains and the valleys are valleys, then the mountains are no longer mountains and the valleys are no longer valleys, and at the end the mountains are mountains and the valleys are valleys again." That is, the process of breaking down conventional perception is profoundly educational on one level, even if the very same perceptions are restored at the end of the process. In the course of taking these perceptions apart and putting them back together, one will have learned something of great value about one's own mind. John Lilly, M.D., calls this "metaprogramming the human biocomputer" and points out that it gives one much greater freedom in choosing between later programs. The difference resembles that between a man who doesn't know how to turn the dial on his television set and must look at the same channel every night, and the man who is able to turn the dial and try an alternative.

It must be added that some of the alternate programs are, as Dr. Lilly nicely puts it, "potentially lethal." It is this, of course, that lies behind our usual commitment to conventional programs—ordinary perceptions, ordinary feelings, ordinary levels of awareness. *Once one steps outside those limits, which have been selected by both evolution and social history as fairly safe, one is living dangerously.* Some acidheads have killed themselves rather than face new programs to which they have inadvertently "tuned in."

Establishment harping on that fact has not discouraged the drug revolution one whit, because the quest for adventure and for risk is innate in our species, especially in the young. Besides, all drug experimenters know what the Establishment never cares to admit: many of the alternate programs are benign, thoroughly charming, even glorious.

This book cannot hope to end this perennial quarrel between the conservative Establishment and the adventurous young. All I reasonably can try to accomplish here, in treating mostly the sexual aspect of the drug revolution, is to shed some light on these "benign, thoroughly charming, even glorious" aspects of the alternate programs and alternate perceptions that certain drugs create. This should at least give the ordinary reader some insight into the motives of those who subscribe to the drug revolution, which is hardly the insane scramble for self-destruction portrayed by its most hostile critics.

And, to those readers who—after reading this Introduction—still feel that they know exactly the dimensions of all male mountains and female valleys and that no drug can possibly alter their sexual sensations, I can only add, in Shakespeare's words:

There are more things in heaven and earth, Horatio,
   Than are dreamt of in your philosophy.

Ice Maiden:
The Story of Jane

To worship me take wine and strange drugs whereof
I shall tell my prophet and be drunk thereof.
They shall not harm thee at all.
                                    — *The Book of the Law*

"Does LSD cure frigidity?" Jane asked me.

Her question was posed after hearing me deliver a lecture for the New York Society for General Semantics. My topic had been "The Game of Semantics and the Game of Psychedelics," and I had argued (this was back in the optimistic early 1960s) that the psychedelic drugs tended to confirm the non-Aristotelian/non-Euclidean/non-Newtonian picture of the universe urged by Count Alfred Korzybski, the founder of General Semantics. That is, the world of the LSD voyager is precisely one in which opposing ideas are true simultaneously (non-Aristotelian), space is geodesic rather than linear (non-Euclidean) and cause and effect are unreal (non-Newtonian).

Jane came up to me afterward and asked her question about frigidity in a tense and serious tone.

I am no psychologist, emphatically not a psychiatrist, and I was not about to commit myself on such a controversial subject. I told her that I had read a paper by an English psychiatrist who was using LSD plus Ritalin (a stimulant drug) in the treatment of frigidity and had been obtaining some remarkable cures. I added that "remarkable cures" are always reported when a new therapy is first tried, and that their numbers always fall off somewhat, after a while; they are partly a result of the hope and enthusiasm of the experimenter (and, of course, of the patients also).

She asked me if I knew where she could obtain some LSD. Now, as stated above, this was only the early 1960s and there were no anti-LSD laws yet. Nevertheless, the controversy was already raging, Leary and Alpert had been asked to leave Harvard and never darken its door again, and a few magazines had published frightening and apocalyptical exposés of "bad trips" and suicides resulting from unwise and unguided experimentation. I knew about five good sources for pure Sandoz Laboratories acid, but I was also wary. Jane seemed too desperate, too fragile.

I gave her the name of a psychoanalyst who was experimentally using LSD (dispensing it in psycholytic doses[1]) on some of his patients. Whatever happens, I thought, will be on his professional conscience, and not on my amateur shoulders.

A week or so later, my wife Arlen *(not* Arlene) and I encountered Jane on the street and discovered that we were neighbors. We invited her up for cocktails one night soon thereafter, and as it happened she and my wife got into a deep and private conversation while I was (as usual) playing the fool for the other guests.

I was given a partial report on the conversation later.

"Poor Jane," Arlen said. "She's got an absolutely horrible problem and after seven years in psychoanalysis it's as bad as

---

[1] The distinction between *psycholytic* and *psychedelic* doses of LSD is used in many scientific publications but seems to be ignored by popularizers who either preach the "LSD utopia" or warn of the "decline of the west." A *psycholytic* dose, generally 75 or 100—or at most 200—micrograms, causes a rush of thoughts, a lot of free association, some visualization (hallucination) and abreaction (memories so vivid that one seems to relive the experience). A *psychedelic* dose, around 500 micrograms, produces total but temporary breakdown of usual ways of perceiving self and world and (usually) some form of "peak experience" or mystic transcendence of ego. "Bad trips" usually occur only on psychedelic doses.

ever. Four times a week! And the shrink hasn't helped her yet. After seven years!"

"*Four* times a week?" I said. "What the hell does she do for a living? Is she chairman of the board of some bank?" At that time, I had not met anybody whose economic level made such fees conceivable. The few people I knew "in analysis" were going once a week and bitching about the $25 cost in those days.

"She's something very big at X," my wife said, naming a prominent ad agency on the Avenue of the Mad. I was impressed. A woman who had risen to a top position in that gladitorial arena must have had the sweet lusts of a headhunter.

"And she's frigid," I said thoughtfully.

"How did *you* know?" Arlen asked.

I repeated my previous conversation with Jane. "It doesn't take Sherlock Holmes to add that two and two together," I concluded.

The next time I saw Jane she again asked how she might obtain LSD. I countered by asking her if she had seen the doctor I had recommended. She replied, with some bitterness, that the newspaper scare stories had frightened him off and that he wasn't using LSD therapy anymore. "He gave me the name of another shrink in Los Angeles," she said. "But I'm not going to quit my job and move out there. There's lots of underground acid around New York. I'll find some and do it up in my own apartment, without a therapist."

Jane was a striking woman, but very frail—the first strong gust of wind would carry her away, you might think. The thought of her experimenting with LSD all alone bothered me. "I know where you can get some hashish," I said, breaking the New York State narcotics law, which at that time made it a crime not only to sell cannabis drugs but to conspire to help others sell them. I gave her the name of a man in a cigar store on 42nd Street.

In the days to come I worried considerably about what I had done, because I had known people to have the blue terrors on hashish if they approached it the wrong way. Nevertheless, it did seem wiser than letting her experiment with LSD without professional guidance.

My worries were premature. The next time I saw Jane, she was more bitter and frantic than ever. Arlen and I got her slightly drunk, in fact, and encouraged her to talk out her desperation.

Jane, it appeared, had a new boyfriend, a pilot, who was the Romeo of her dreams and all that jazz. Although they had made love several times, he didn't know yet that she was frigid—which made me decide privately that Romeo was a little bit dense. To make matters worse, her shrink was talking more and more in terms of "acceptance" and "reconciliation"—"the way they talk to faggots," she said bitterly. "You know—'the mature acceptance of things as they are.' All it means is 'I can't change you, so you had better just grin and bear it.' That may be okay for faggots—they've got some kind of sex life, after all—but it's not why I've been paying the bastard $160 a week for seven years! If he can't help his patients, he should give back his license and take up plumbing." And so forth. I had heard the same general rap from patients undergoing Freudian analysis many times before.

I suggested a behavioral therapist. "They concentrate just on relieving symptoms," I pointed out, "and what you want is relief from one specific symptom." Jane didn't care for the approach. "It's an offense against human dignity," she said, somewhat slurring her words due to the bourbon we'd been feeding her. "They think we're just machines."

"Does that matter, if they can help?" I asked.

It was no use. Jane regarded B.F. Skinner as the reincarnation of the mad scientist Karloff used to play in the 1930s and she wanted nothing to do with "conditioning or brainwashing or that kind of thing." She wanted acid. An actress she knew had boasted of being cured of frigidity by one single acid trip, and Jane was sure the same miracle would happen to her.

"Did you try the hashish?" I asked.

She had. She had contacted my friend at the cigar store and she had even gone to a "head shop" (they were new and glamorous then) to purchase a small metallic "hash pipe." Because she knew the dose I had recommended was minimal (enough thin powder to cover the nail of the little finger) she had deliberately tripled it before her last date with the pilot.

And nothing happened. All through dinner, she kept waiting to "turn on" and feel those "vibrations" and see those colors, but she felt the same as ever. When they returned to her apartment, before going to bed she surreptitiously smoked another, stronger dose in the bathroom. "I was determined I was going to feel *something,*" she said furiously.

Nothing. It was the same as all her other sexual experiences. A slight tension, a few twinges of something that might be very muted pleasure, and then a sudden numbness when his excitement escalated toward climax. "And I did my usual Academy Award performance, to keep him from guessing," she added. The flying Adonis was a flying fathead, I decided again.

A short while later, Jane and the pilot broke up. I had never met him—which was strange, considering that I already had an opinion (unfavorable) about his sexual prowess.

Then, one day, I was invited to a peyote party. It sounded interesting: The peyote was not to be eaten (which always causes vomiting—an unpleasantness that the Plains Indians claim is God's way of ensuring that nobody but the spiritually prepared will enter the domain of this sacred hallucinogen), but was to be sipped in a kind of tea. This was the practice of the Indians of Wisconsin, and was reputed to provide a gentler, more gradual and totally non-nauseous trip. Best of all, the host was an anthropologist, which in my opinion made him just as qualified—if not more so—than most of the shrinks or clinical psychologists I knew. An anthropologist seemed the next best thing to my Sioux Indian friend.

I asked if my wife and I could bring another couple, and we were told "the more the merrier."

We invited Jane, and she accepted eagerly. Her new boyfriend, it appeared, was about ten years younger than she, a graduate student in physics at Brooklyn Polytechnic, very serious, but intrigued by certain aspects of the psychedelic revolution. When I met him, before going to the peyote feast, I learned that his interest derived from a report he had read about another physicist who had said while on LSD, "Now I not only understand that matter is energy—I can *feel* it!"

I explained to Jane, privately, that on the basis of the underground lore I had acquired, she should not look for any sexual effect from the peyote during the first four hours. "Wait until you're sure you've 'peaked'—you'll know what that means when you get there—and then take him home and try your sexual experiments."

Our host was very scientific, but very genial and relaxed. He warned us that he was taping the proceedings, and would later include it in a book, but assured us that none of us would be identified. Our responses, without ritual and tradition, would be compared with those of Indians who approached the sacred plant guided by awe-inspiring rites and age-old legends.

Very light and melodious classics were playing on the stereo—Vivaldi, Mozart, nothing heavy or "religious." I wondered about this, but decided that our host's main purpose, at the beginning, was to create a sense of party and relaxation. The tea was poured, and he added one minor touch of ceremony, saying very soberly, "May we all find what we are looking for in this journey." As was my pattern in those days, I very quickly entered a Laughing Buddha state (+12 on the Gurdjieff scale of altered consciousness) and began pondering various Zen riddles and mathematical theorems that were obsessing me. All of this led into hilarious revelations. People soon began to ignore me, because they couldn't make any sense out of my few remarks— e.g., "Hey, do you know what? All things really are the same size!" (This odd thought also appears in the writings of the Taoist philosopher, Chuang Chou, and in certain modern theories of the infinite derived from Cantor's transfinite numbers. Peyote-consciousness brings me to paradoxes but not to absurdities.)

The physicist was on an energy trip, as he had hoped, and was discovering "auras" around things. He would have a lot of thinking to do the next morning, deciding whether the auras were something real or a hallucinatory visual expression of something that was there in less visual form or just plain delusion.

A woman who had seemed rather distant and nervous at first spent the next hours beaming at everybody and repeating "my God" and "you're all so beautiful" over and over.

Jane looked increasingly unhappy and kept saying "I don't feel anything yet."

After a few hours, Arlen and I had a yen to walk. We wandered around a while, digging the street lights and the neon signs

(Edison's gifts to the psychedelic era) and discussing things that don't belong in this chapter. When we found an automat we both had the same profound esthetic experience contemplating *a bowl of cherry jello*—which some readers will understand immediately and others will regard as an idiocy.

When we returned to the party, Jane and her physicist had left. Our host was now playing Beethoven's *Ninth Symphony* and everybody had drifted out of their chairs onto the floor, where they were lying, with their eyes closed, following Ludwig in his pursuit of one of the grandest fantasies humanity has ever conceived. I closed my eyes, too, and followed the music into a strange vision of Beethoven himself turning into what appeared to be a gigantic *female* bull. If that sounds ridiculous, find your own metaphor for what the last movement of the *Ninth* seems to invoke.

The next day, a Saturday, Jane came to our apartment almost in tears. Her hashish adventure had repeated itself. Nothing had happened. Nothing. I was faintly incredulous. I had read of some catatonic patients who had been given LSD and hadn't shown any reaction, but I had never heard of such a thing outside the schizophrenic wards. Peyote is almost as strong as acid, and everybody I had ever heard of had reacted in *some* way.

Jane was vehement, however. She had seen no new colors, felt no new sensations, experienced no new emotions. Above all, she had had no orgasm.

"It was terrible," she wailed. "And the damned peyote must have made him extra sensitive, because he knew I was faking. He felt very sorry for me, and went down on me and tried to suck me off. Oh, God, and I usually feel *some*thing with that, even if not a climax, but this time I was so nervous I didn't feel *any*thing. He was very upset and guilty and kept blaming himself. It was *awful.*"

We calmed and consoled her as much as we could. Meanwhile, I made a private resolution to never again help her toward psychedelic adventures. She was obviously not the type.

The next few times we saw her, she was more interested in LSD than ever. It was quite clear in her mind that her failures with hashish and peyote had been due to the comparative "weakness" (!) of those drugs and that she needed the "mama of them all, Dr. Leary's panacea," nothing but pure Sandoz Laboratories lysergic acid diethylamide (which we call LSD because Sandoz's name for it, in the original German, was *l*yserg *s*aure *d*iethylamid). It was equally clear, in my mind, that she would have to obtain it without my help.

The climax—in every sense of the word—came a few weeks later. I was at home one evening, writing, and Arlen was at the second typewriter doing the same, when the phone rang. Arlen answered. In a moment, she signaled me to pick up the extension.

Jane was calling us, and she was in a state of ecstasy. "It's happening," she kept telling us. "The colors, the music—everything. I haven't felt so at home in the world since I was a little child. It's wonderful, wonderful." She insisted that we come to her apartment immediately and witness the miracle for ourselves.

Her excitement was so infectious that, in spite of our involvement in our writing, we allowed ourselves to be persuaded. What we saw when we got there was a sight to make Dr. Leary burst with pride. Jane, always an attractive woman, was radiantly beautiful: every harsh and angry muscle in her face and body had relaxed. She was laughing constantly, weeping occasionally, and generally out of her head with sensations of pleasure that she literally had not experienced since childhood. Her physicist friend was equally high, if in a more subdued and introspective way, grooving on my own sort of mathematical and structural mysticism about the shapes and forces of things. They had obtained some black market acid from a Greenwich Village painter.

"This is the way I was born," Jane said once, giggling. "This is the way we were all born, the way puppies and kittens are born—absolutely at home in this world and delighted with it. I haven't felt like this since I was about three years old. God, how our society destroys us..." There was more of that sort of talk, the usual reaction to the first trip, but it was touching coming from somebody who had been as miserable as Jane.

I soon began to suspect something that made me uncomfortable. Jane hadn't called us merely to witness her new acquaintance with joy; she and her physicist hadn't made love yet and she was looking for a distraction to avoid that very peculiar acid test. I needn't have worried. After about an hour of hilarious and incoherent conversation, Jane got her nerve back. She dropped a few hints, and we took our leave.

The next morning I was curious and nervous. It had all been so beautiful to see the night before; I hated to think that the bubble might have gone smash as soon as they got to the bedroom.

Again, I needn't have worried. She called at around ten and spoke to Arlen, privately. I watched and saw wisps of shared happiness on my wife's face: the news was good. When she finally got off the phone, she said, "What do you know? A perfect cure in one night. She says she reached climax eight times, and she still sounds dizzy." She added, "It's nice to hear somebody sound happy in this city."

I had been unafraid of the psychedelics before that experience, and intellectually intrigued with the mental trips they had set me on the few times I had experimented with them. Now, I became more positive and was inclined to join the Holy War that was beginning to appear in our mass media, taking the side of the Huxleys and Learys and other prophets who saw a new path to salvation in these strange, unpredictable chemicals.

We moved to Chicago shortly after that. The last time we saw Jane, she looked about ten years younger. She didn't have to tell us that her new orgasmic capacity was still with her. It was obvious in her new radiance and sparkle.

A few months passed, and one day an old friend from New York was in Chicago and we had lunch together. We began chatting about people we'd known and Jane's name came up.

"Poor Jane," he said.

"Poor Jane?" I exclaimed. "What happened?"

"She's in a private mental hospital. Committed herself. She was having depressive fits and made a few half-hearted attempts at suicide."

As the 1960s wore on, the national mood shifted toward the Kafkaesque: Some Americans burned their draft cards and others burned the ghettos in which they lived and some, in total repudiation, even burned themselves in public; and I was to become familiar with the pattern, which also appeared in encounter and yoga groups (where it was less publicized) as well as in the drug kulch: an uptight person would find liberation, the energies would flow, the neurotic armor would fall off, a new and naked

soul would be born—and then the old patterns would reassert
themselves and the person would sink into depression, if not
psychosis or suicide. The pattern became more than familiar, it
even became commonplace, as did the quest for a drug cure for
sexual problems. However, it was all new to me in the early
days. As the results of these experiments began coming in, I felt
a wave of almost supernatural dread: *There, but for the grace of
God, go I...*

"In a mental hospital?" I repeated stupidly. It was all so new,
back then.

Years later, Dr. John Lilly was to write of certain types of
transformations produced by LSD:

> For a time, the self then feels free, cleaned out. The strength
> gained can be immense; the energy freed is double... Adult
> love and sharing consonant with aspirations and reality (out-
> side) gain strength... Humor appears in abundance, good
> humor... Beauty is enhanced, the bodily appearance becomes
> youthful... These positive effects cam last as long as two to
> four weeks before reassertion of the old program takes place.

This would be a good parable for an anti-drug book (from the
U.S. Government Printing Office) if I were to stop here. In reality, however, there are no ends; things flow on. I met Jane again,
about five years later. She was living on welfare, being unable or
unwilling to write advertising copy any longer. Her lover was a
boy in his teens, who obviously thought of himself as a genius
and struck me as a fool. She was practicing yoga daily and
looked young and trim. Although she didn't give me details, it
looked from the outside as if her sex life was much more satisfactory than it had been before the LSD.

She was writing articles (for no money) that appeared in little
publications of a new movement that called itself Women's
Liberation.

I suppose most people would have a strong opinion about
whether her new life is better or worse than her old life. I am not
at all sure. All *I do* know is that, just as you read in the anti-drug
propaganda, she went from acid to a mental hospital; and, just as
you read in pro-drug propaganda, she ultimately appeared to
have been reborn as a new person.

1

Overview:
The Brews of Aphrodite

Hearasay in paradox lust.

— James Joyce, *Finnegans Wake*

It is a psychoanalytical truism that many people turn to the desensitizing drugs, such as morphine or heroin, in order to flee from their sexual problems, that is, to turn themselves off erotically. This, you might say, is the modern form of the religion of Attis, whose devotees literally castrated themselves.

The drugs that we will be most concerned with in this book are sensitizers rather than desensitizers, *turn-ons* rather than *turn-offs*. In all probability—we will see the evidence later—many who have turned to those drugs are also seeking relief from sexual problems, like Jane in our Prelude. It is not to be assumed, however, that they can be lumped together with the first group. They are not so much fleeing from their sexual problems as attempting—rightly or wrongly—to grapple with them. They are exercising what the heretic of modern psychiatry, Thomas Szasz, M.D., calls "the right to prescribe for yourself." They think (and may be right in thinking) that their drugs of choice—marijuana, the psychedelics, cocaine, the amphetamines—are actually sexually beneficial.

49

And some of them, I am sure, could not be considered sexual cripples by anybody's standards. Their erotic life was quite satisfactory when they began experimenting with these charismatic chemicals—they merely discovered that the *good* can be even *better.*

The drug-sex underground had no definite time of birth. One can hazard a guess that it all began when Leary said flatly in 1966 that LSD was "the greatest aphrodisiac in the world." Or maybe it began in 1968 when the Beatles placed sex-magician Aleister Crowley on the cover of *Sgt. Pepper* among the "people we like." But it may be possible to date the new religion of ecstasy to an even earlier date: sex-and-cocaine scandals rocked Hollywood in the 1920s; jazz was born out of the marijuana-wreathed whorehouses of New Orleans in the 1890s.

Tallulah Bankhead once said that "Americans have a bad case of sex in the head, and that's a hell of a place to have it." Actually, all sex is in the head, always—for, as modern scientists know, everything we see, hear, smell, taste or feel is inside our brains. It follows, then, that spicing up the chemistry of the cortex and frontal lobes will alter the entire nature of human experience. Our ancestors discovered this salient fact several thousand years ago. Primitive man, wherever anthropologists find him, has a considerable lore concerning those local weeds, fruits, berries or vines that are good to eat or smoke in order to pep up the brain and experience a "different" reality. (In one shut-away plateau of Central Asia, according to biochemist Robert DeRopp, Ph.D., explorers found that the local gentry had devised a way of fermenting *horse* milk and getting high from *that.*)

What is unique about contemporary America is not its putative "drug problem," but the Establishment attitude that this age-old and universal human habit is criminal, sinful and altogether reprehensible. That joyless WASP philosophy, alas, not only inspires increasingly absurd legislation but distracts everybody's attention from the questions that are really worthy of investigation such as: Which drugs are most dangerous? Which are least harmful? How can the risky ones be handled with the least possible danger? Under what circumstances do the normally safe ones become unexpectedly troublesome?

The Establishment attitude is based on the self-justifying argument, "Everything we've made illegal in the past is terribly, terribly harmful, and everything we've left legal is perfectly safe." The underground attitude tends to turn this argument on its head with the assumption that only the illegal drugs are safe and that everything else, from aspirin to the meat at the supermarket, is, as W.C. Fields used to say "fraught with peril." Finding where the truth lies between these extremes is not easy.

Meanwhile, we might all remember the verdict of Count Bismarck: "Laws are like sausages: you respect them more if you haven't actually seen how they're made."

Drugs in Perspective

Alcohol is the most widely used and abused drug in America. Dr. Joel Fort, director of the Center for Special Problems in San Francisco, estimates that 100 million Americans drink booze occasionally, which means that about one out of every two of us at least sips. One out of five of these, or 20 million Americans, are classified as "problem drinkers," and there are at least six million hard-core alcoholics.

Without doubt, a great deal of this compulsive guzzling has a sexual motivation. Booze helps people to relax, to shed their inhibitions, and to feel happy and self-confident. It is, in fact, the classic "make-out" drug. (In a Peter Arno cartoon, a man is sitting next to an attractive girl at a bar and leeringly tells the bartender, "Fill 'er up!" His motivation is obvious.) And this is a tragic irony, because Shakespeare was right about alcohol and sex: booze all too often "increases the appetite but diminishes the performance."

Masters and Johnson, in fact, consider booze one of the primary causes of "secondary impotence"—that is, sexual dysfunction in men who are normally virile, as distinguished from "primary impotence" or lifelong inability to function. Typical of this pattern, a man drinks too much, attempts to make love, finds himself impotent and begins worrying. The worry (sometimes assisted by more alcohol) provokes future failures. In time the man comes to regard himself as impotent and may stay that way, sometimes for several years, before he is able to bring himself to seek therapy.

Better knowledge of the drug called alcohol could prevent this psycho-physical torment. A little liquor is a fairly good sex stimulant—hence, the traditional split of champagne on the first night of the honeymoon—but a lot is a different matter entirely. In large quantities, alcohol is an anaphrodisiac, an anti-aphrodisiac. The Romans used plenty of it at their orgies, and this has given it a sexy reputation, but the satires of Juvenal and Petronius leave no doubt that the Romans were also chronically afflicted with impotence, just as heavy drinkers are today. For the erotic drug users, then, the rule on alcohol should be: Use only a little. Bring the grapes to your orgy, if you want to be classical, but leave the vats of wine in the cellar.

The second most common drug in America is tobacco, used by 75 million—but this is almost neutral sexually, except that it will eventually produce illnesses that will probably include impotence.

Well below booze hounds and compulsive smokers is the third largest drug culture around: the pill poppers. About 35 million of us are swallowing sedatives, stimulants or tranquilizers. None of these drugs have any sex-enhancing qualities at all, and some of them—such as Tofranil, prescribed by doctors more often than psycho-pharmacologists think wise—actually produce temporary impotence in some cases.

The next largest group of drug takers around are the potheads. While it may not be true that every marijuana user is employing this drug as an aphrodisiac—which was once charged by the archenemy of grass, former Narcotics Commissioner Harry Anslinger—most users are aware that the weed has charming and delightful effects on their boudoir experiences. Probably the majority of regular users regard sex without grass (or grass without sex) as distinctly inferior to sex with grass.

Then there are the acidheads which, for our purposes, means users of any of the strong, LSD-type psychedelics. A breakdown of specific drugs is impossible here, since most people who like acid also like mescaline or DMT (dimethyltriptamine) and *vice versa.* Besides, independent studies of black market supplies have been made by scientists who were able to purchase various pills from these sources, and subsequently analyzed them in a laboratory. Each of these studies has shown that a large portion of what is sold is labeled incorrectly; much street acid is really mescaline. Sometimes the mescaline is really acid, and almost all the THC (tetrahydrocannabinol, or "synthetic" pot) on the underground circuit has actually turned out to be a dog tranquilizer used by veterinarians. Approximately one million Americans have tried an LSD-type drug, and something like 200,000 take regular trips. Although none of these drugs are, contrary to Dr. Leary, real aphrodisiacs, many users find quite stimulating sexual effects in them.

Heroin—the most sensationalized drug—is a problem only because it is illegal. The drug's illegality has driven the cost of a fix upward from a few cents (the free market price) to $100–$200 a day or more (black market), forcing most users into thievery or prostitution. The stereotype of the "junk-crazy rapist" is entirely inaccurate; heroin is more of an anaphrodisiac than even alcohol and barbiturates, and the first sign of true addiction is permanent impotence and a total lack of interest in sex.

Finally, we come to the category that ends every list—"miscellaneous." Nobody knows how many Americans are users of hashish, jimson weed (also called "moon flowers"), morning glory seeds, airplane glue, and other minority preferences. No generalizations are safe here, since these drugs are very different from one another. Jimson weed (*datura noxia*), like belladonna, mandragora, and other members of the solanaceae family, is very dangerous and potentially fatal if one takes an accidental overdose. While erotic responses are occasionally reported (sometimes bordering on erotomania), this is unpredictable and the trip is always delirious and basically schizoid. Morning glory seeds produce the same effects as LSD or mescaline, plus nausea and vomiting (because they are coated with insecticide). Airplane glue definitely damages the liver and probably also damages the brain; the high is brief and doesn't relate to sex at all.

And then there's hanging your head over a tub full of ammonia—"the washwoman's kick"—or nutmeg, or drinking wood alcohol. These, again, are last-ditch expedients and frequently fatal. The real sex drugs, then, are marijuana, hashish, the psychedelics in small doses and cocaine.

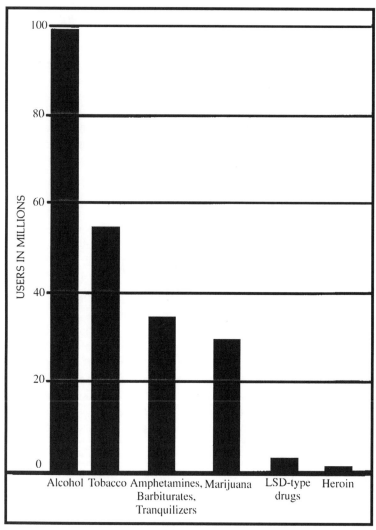

Figure 1
Drugs in Perspective

Marijuana & the Mystics

Pot lends itself to every form of sensory enrichment and has been associated with both sex and religion for a long time. In

India, Hindus of the Shivite sect are often seen stumbling out of their temples, stoned into the middle of the next week, muttering the marijuana mantra, *Bom-Bom-Mahadev,* which translates as "Boom! Boom! Great Big God!"—a sensation that even irreligious pot smokers will vaguely recognize. There are also several religions based on the weed in Brazil and the Caribbean area.

In the Middle East, a stronger cousin of marijuana (also derived from the Indian hemp plant and called hashish) played a leading role in perhaps the most remarkable eroto-religious movement in history, the Ishmaelian sect of Islam, also known as the Assassins. This order was founded by one Hasan i Sabbah, circa 1092, and wrought havoc with the orthodox Moslems and the Christian crusaders for some centuries thereafter. Hasan's followers were utterly unafraid of death because they *knew* they were going to paradise, whereas most people can only hope for postmortem glorification; they knew, because they had already been to paradise once, through the magic of the noble Lord Hasan, and he had promised to return them there if they remained perfectly obedient to him throughout their lives.

The secret of Hasan's power—the trip to paradise given to all his followers—rested upon the powerful combination of hashish and some talented young ladies, as we shall see in Chapter Four. Filled with hashish-stuffed food, the candidate for initiation was ushered into a certain Garden of Delights in Hasan's fortress temple of Alamout, high in the mountains of Afghanistan. There, the ladies, pretending to be the supernatural houris described by Mohammed in his vision of heaven, performed in such a manner that the men came out of their hashish trance with very clear memories of "divine" sexual experiences and other unearthly delights. None ever doubted that they had been in heaven.

The last indicates strongly that Hasan was more than just a good drug dealer; that he was, in fact, an expert programmer of other people's trips long before Timothy Leary conceived of such an occupation. Undoubtedly, the explanations or exhortation given by Hasan before the candidate went on his astral trip to the Garden of Delights, and the words and behavior of the houris therein, were all well-calculated to produce what psychologists now call a "peak experience"—an ecstasy far beyond that of the normal sexual spasm of civilized man.

Figure 2 illustrates a pot-plus-sex "peak experience." One begins with quite ordinary sensations, but as the sexual activity continues and the drug takes greater hold on you, the sensations intensify. The penis feels bigger, stiffer, and strangely "rubbery." Sensations of pleasure expand to more areas of the body than usual. One is "floating" or "high." If one is self-programming the trip, via one of Dr. Leary's manuals or the rituals of some older occult tradition, the "astral" or hallucinatory stage soon begins: the lady may give forth a divine effulgence, a light that seems cosmic and eternal—this is the meaning of Aleister Crowley's mantra "Every man and every woman is a star"—or, perhaps, she may appear covered with jewels or flowers. With real luck and some skill at self-hypnosis (or real magical ability, as true believers would say), a "peak experience" will occur shortly before orgasm. This is the terminology that Dr. Abraham Maslow uses and, like similar terms from other sources (Freud's "oceanic experience," the *satori* of Zen Buddhism, the Hindu "samadhi," Gurdjieff's "waking up," etc.), it is difficult to define. It is simply the experience of total ecstasy, usually involving a paradoxical sensation that the whole universe is actually your own body.

This concept represents the general idea; it is more commonly experienced, probably, as a kind of jagged up-and-down as concentration wobbles (see Figure 3).

An important minority of so-called occultists, from Hasan i Sabbah on, has made an effort to devise "rituals" (which Leary and the moderns would call "programs") to direct the trip ever upward and thereby avoid the "wobbling" sensation.

After contact with the Assassins, the Christian order known as the Knights Templar developed some very peculiar doctrines. In 1307, the grand master of that order and 122 members were burned at the stake for heresy, blasphemy, sodomy and various other charges that seem to have been tacked on just to disgrace them utterly. The Templars had been trying to introduce sex into the Christian sacraments and ambiguous references to a sacred plant or herb appear in their surviving manuscripts.

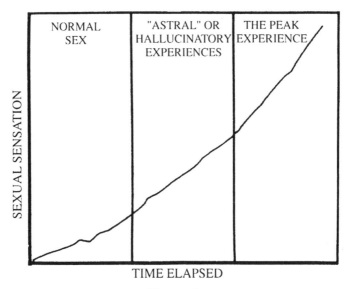

Figure 2
Sexual Sensation With Peak Experience

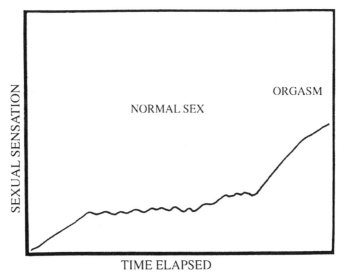

Figure 3
Sexual Sensation

Late in the 19th Century, the Ordo Templi Orientis appeared, claiming direct descent from the Knights Templar. They used Tantric sex yoga in association with the traditional astral projection of the European occult tradition and, when Aleister Crowley became their Outer Head—what an appropriate name! Outer Head!—drugs became a secret part of their teachings, at least in some of the higher grades in certain of their lodges.

Crowley's interest in drugs centered on hashish, cocaine and peyote. He used the first two in conjunction with sexual matters, both homosexual and heterosexual; peyote he used only for non-sexual visions and trances. Presumably, he was the first white man to fully appreciate the religious uses of the latter drug, which is the central—and legal—sacrament of the Native American Church, having 150,000 American Indian members in the United States and Canada.

Like booze, marijuana can double-cross you; if you overdose just a little bit, you might find yourself impotent. However, many heads who have reported this experience point out that they had ejaculative impotence, not erectile impotence; that is, they didn't lose their erections, which were firmer and more long-lived than usual, but they simply could not reach orgasm. Some say that the non-orgasmic vibes were so good that they didn't even regret the absence of a climax.

Acid: Instant Zen?

LSD, in contrast with marijuana's romantic history, began in the laboratories and had only a shadowy existence in obscure experimental work until Dr. Timothy Leary discovered what was going on, plunged into the research with zest and quickly informed the world that God was alive and well; it has been impossible to separate LSD from mysticism ever since.

Leary, moreover, was not just rationalizing his own liking for this particular trip. Novelist Aldous Huxley, theologian Alan Watts, and numerous others have reported that religious experiences took place while they were under the influence of LSD. Whether the government likes to admit it or not, many white acidheads are just as sincerely pious as the peyote-eating Indians on the reservations, and are having precisely similar astral or hallucinatory experiences.

Nobody connected LSD with sex, however, until Leary claimed it was an aphrodisiac. Responsible voices immediately announced that this was false. Irresponsible and underground voices just as quickly began claiming the reverse. In fact, this question seems to hinge on the exact meaning of the word "aphrodisiac." If one means a drug that will *create sexual desire in somebody one wishes to seduce,* or that will *create potency in the previously impotent*—the two miracles usually attributed, inaccurately, to the spurious aphrodisiacs of the past—then LSD is bound to disappoint. No known drug can perform those feats.

On the other hand, many seasoned trippers now agree that acid can enhance a sexual experience, just as grass or hashish can, if desire and potency are already present in both partners. The ecstasy, when this is successful, is far more intense than it is with the hemp drugs; but sometimes this goes awry, because too much is happening at once for the mind to concentrate on sex exclusively. The experience can resemble trying to copulate while a rock band is playing full blast, or while a good movie appears to be playing on the ceiling and God Himself is trying to shout something important in your ear.

Sex-and-acid cults sprang up in the early 1960s, and one of the first was the charming Kerista, founded by a former Air Force pilot named John Presmont after a "voice" spoke to him (while he was reading the Koran and smoking hashish) and told him to found the world's next great religion.

"Why me?" asked Presmont, awed.

"Because you're so gullible," said the voice.

Presmont followed the call, and there were soon Kerista chapters in most major cities. The teachings were summed up by Presmont—who changed his name to Jud the Prophet—in a statement called *The 69 Positions.* Each "position" began with the word "legalize" and the first ten were: "Legalize prostitution. Legalize adultery. Legalize fornication. Legalize bigamy. Legalize sodomy. Legalize cunnilingus. Legalize group sex. Legalize pornography. Legalize homosexuality. Legalize lesbianism." And so on, for 59 additional "positions."

Kerista quickly acquired a reputation for being a group sex cult, which irked Jud when I interviewed him for *Fact* magazine in 1964. "We don't force any trip on our members," he said to me. "If some of them want to be monogamous, that's their own business. Why, we've even got one member who's a *virgin!*"

The Keristans all took religious names, just like Pope John Paul II or Mohammed Ali, except that their names were peculiar to the Keristan philosophy. I remember interviewing a Tree, a Pied Piper, a Tao, and a Mordecai the Foul. There was also a youngish girl of unknown name, who never said anything but "fuck." Literally, it seemed to be the only word she could—or would—speak. Some might have considered her mentally unbalanced but the Keristans regarded her as possessed by a wise spirit.

Jud claimed that he himself was in constant communication, in those days, with the ghost of the late Russian mystic, G.I. Gurdjieff, via Ouija board. (Once, he reported, he picked up John Fitzgerald Kennedy, or some low-plane spirit who pretended to be Kennedy. The Message, curiously, was: *We shall win Jackie is an ego bitch Farewell.*)

Despite Jud's liberalism about monogamy and even virginity, most Keristans were heavily involved in group sex. This presented the usual problems. One week, the entire New York commune got the clap within a few days. Jud was especially vexed because it was traced to a man who had picked up a non-Keristan girl in Washington Square. "If I believed in commandments," Jud told me morosely, "I'd pass an ordinance against balling outside chicks." He paid for everybody's medical treatment out of his government pension—which he received, much to his amusement, for being mentally unbalanced. The proof of his mental instability was his compulsion to form a new religion, and the pension paradoxically allowed him to avoid working for a living and to devote his full time to that compulsion.

Perhaps significantly, Jud was the very first person I ever heard use the now popular word "vibes," meaning astral vibrations.

Eventually, Jud and his most loyal disciples moved to Central America to get away from drug busts and other hassles that orthodox United States society was inflicting on them. Little has been heard of Kerista since then.

In the absence of Kerista, more sinister alternatives appeared such as the Manson family, in which each new female member was initiated by an LSD trip (or any other drug, including some weird ones, if acid wasn't available) during which Charlie cunnilinged her to orgasm several times. After that experience, these girls—like Hasan i Sabbah's followers before them—were ready to follow any orders, including murder.

There are quite a few other sex-and-acid cults flourishing, but I won't mention their names as they wouldn't appreciate the publicity. Most derive either directly or indirectly from the Crowley/Ordo Templi Orientis influence and Pop Zen and are inclined to quoting from Robert A. Heinlein's sci-fi classic, *Stranger in a Strange Land,* a great deal. Their influence has made Heinleinese—such as "deep grokking," "share water with me," "may you never thirst," and "Thou art God"—familiar jargon in every freaky or hippie hangout from coast to coast. Most of them are harmless and just as horrified by Manson's bloodletting as you or I. Whenever one of these groups is busted for possession of a drug, though, the newspapers generally headline the event, "Manson-style cult raided," and ma and pa in the suburbs shiver with images of knives glittering in their heads.

Too old and too respectable to be considered sinister, Louis T. Culling has headed a sex-occult group called the G.B.G. (Great Body of God) since the 1930s. In *A Manual of Sex Magic,* published in 1971, Culling frankly admits his debt to Crowley's teachings. Only in an appendix does he grant that some find that this magic works even better with marijuana, and then he adds that the G.B.G. does not recommend this since it involves breaking the law.

Contemporary witches are tight-lipped about their historical connection with strange brews. Gerald Gardner, the English eccentric largely responsible for the contemporary revival of witchcraft, never mentioned sex or drugs in his books, although it is charged by Francis King, the most sober and scholarly historian of occultism, that all Gardnerian rites end with the priest and priestess copulating, in traditional fashion right out of the Middle Ages, before their congregations. Many of the covens one finds in big cities these days believe that the Witches Sabaat was traditionally an orgy. They therefore practice it that way, with the help of pot, acid or some other trippy and flippy substances, sometimes including cocaine.

Cocaine: Heaven & Hell

William S. Burroughs has described this last substance, derived from coca leaves, as "the most exhilarating drug in the
world." The Peruvian Indians have used it for centuries to keep
up energy on long trips across the mountains. They chew a few
leaves every time they get exhausted, and are then able to continue. There is a brief hit, like a sun exploding inside, and then a
long afterglow of a few hours. Cocaine was fashionable with the
jet-set in the 1970s (a fact which was a pivot in *Easy Rider*), not
only for its intrinsic properties but because it was harder to
obtain than pot, more exotic, faintly sinister because it looks like
heroin and, above all, expensive.

Sex on cocaine is much like sex on high-grade pot or hashish—very intensified, but without the hallucinatory muddle often
characteristic of acid and the stronger psychedelics. What is
especially attractive to experienced heads is that, with cocaine,
you have greater control than is usual—sniffing a few grains
more when you seem about to come down, waiting a while if you
think that you are too high.

What is not so attractive is the aftermath, especially if use is
chronic. Depression is inevitable, it seems, and irritability usually
follows. If one continues sniffing coke, day after day (and why
not?—the user reflects—it's *so much fun*) the depressions and
grouchiness subtly escalate until you have a full-blown paranoid
condition, cops hiding under the bed, your best friend planning
to poison you, the landlady doing something sinister with the
duster when you pass her on the stairs, people skulking about the
streets in a most furtive and conspiratorial manner.

The old myth that cocaine is addictive for all users (it isn't)
seems to have been based on the fact that most cocaine users
who come to the attention of the authorities are addicts—of
something else—Seconal, or Demerol or heroin—usually a
sedative drug that undoes the galloping anxiety that results from
too much cocaine stimulation. Aleister Crowley made himself
unpopular in 1920 by insisting that this pattern of cocaine *abuse*
is not typical of intelligent cocaine use.

The same issue still haunts us. The problems of pot, hashish
and the psychedelics—all of which are not physically addicting—are constantly befuddled by the Establishment's refusal to

recognize a difference between *use* and *abuse.* Any user, however moderate and harmless, is treated as a menace to society and himself; any melodramatic story of horrible and reckless *abuse* is widely published as an example of what these "dangerous drugs" lead to. Users grow more and more contemptuous of accepted public opinion and the credibility gap widens and widens.

Bad Trips

The end result of this credibility gap was illustrated in a story from *Playboy,* October 1972: When students at San Mateo High School in California were asked what famous person they would trust as a narrator of an anti-LSD film, they answered bluntly, "Nobody."

While on the staff of a large magazine a few years ago, I wanted to print the fact that four grams of niacinamide (Vitamin B-3) will abort most bad LSD trips. The editors rejected this because "it might encourage kids to think they can take acid without risks." Now, that argument may be valid, but it reminds me of the old assertion that automobiles should not have safety belts because such protection would just encourage drivers to be more careless. People who are going to be damn fools probably can't be stopped no matter what restrictions are placed on them, but those who want to minimize risks should have safety information available to them.

Similarly, scare stories about bad marijuana trips occasionally break into the press, and then get repeated endlessly in "drug education" material distributed by the government or schools. (The classic, about an adolescent who committed murder with an ax while on pot, actually happened in 1928 but is still reprinted as if it happened yesterday and is typical of pot smokers. It isn't.) The important information is that these panic reactions usually occur to inexperienced smokers, seldom last more than a few minutes if treated sympathetically and intelligently by the novice's friends, and always come to an end within hours.

This happens even without proper supportive treatment, if the victim doesn't fall into the hands of the authorities (who will treat him like a lunatic and convince him that he has, indeed, lost his mind). This fact has long been documented by Dr. Alfred

Lindsmith of Indiana University, but has yet to be included in most so-called educational pamphlets. Novices are left to think that if they experience any frightful or unexpected sensation, they are going to land in Ward Eight and stay there for months or years.

So, too, bad acid trips are publicized endlessly, although almost all the evidence suggests that they are increasingly rare. George Peters, who founded Naturism, Inc., to treat LSD panics in the Chicago area some years ago, recently said to me that he seldom sees a bad trip these days and spends most of his time treating speed freaks (people strung out on too much methamphetamine). Dr. David Smith, of the Haight Ashbury Clinic, has also commented on the scarcity of acid panics and is now giving most of his attention to the heroin problem.

The drug culture, as Dr. Lindsmith predicted back in 1967, has learned how to treat its own acid terrors, just as it earlier learned how to treat adverse reactions to pot. Quiet, sympathetic friends with consoling and reassuring voices, aided perhaps by a tranquilizer or vitamin B-3, will almost always abort such flipouts.

These bad trips, curiously, may have had much to do with the creation of our sex-and-drugs or sex-drugs-and-magick movements. That is, quite aside from wandering missionaries who learned something from Kerista or Ordo Templi Orientis and went forth to teach others, many may have stumbled onto these pleasant linkages while just trying to cope with a drug panic. It is common underground lore that repeating a consoling mantra (such as the famous *Om Munnee Pudmeh Hom!* or even a prayer from one's childhood in Sunday school) often quiets such an anxiety attack. It is also known that holding, cuddling or petting with a loved person also has this sedative effect. Many trippers, therefore, might have found themselves praying and balling, without any knowledge that this is an old tradition, but just to stave off paranoid and frightful feelings.

It is difficult to determine how many people are combining sex and drugs regularly. Travels and conversations around the country suggest that more than half the drug users in the nation think that a good high is being wasted if it doesn't climax in the bedroom. If we assume that half of the people who have tried pot smoke it regularly, and that half of *them* are also psychedelic users, this gives us approximately five million sex-drug freaks. As increasing numbers of them become involved in the occult aspect, due to the proselytizing of the zealous missionaries that seem to pervade every freak neighborhood, Leary's old argument—that drugs which are part of religious celebration are protected under the First Amendment—may become the most bitterly fought civil liberties issue of our age.

The present Supreme Court attitude—which allows peyote to Indians for their ceremonies, but denies similar drugs to whites and blacks of similar sincerity—is transparently racist and discriminatory, but that is no reason to assume that it will change in the near future. This battle has already continued into the third millennium, and may linger on forever. "Thou shalt not suffer a witch to live," says the Bible; and the witches—those who prefer their religion of ecstasy to the Christian religion of austerity—are always going to have a rough time in Bible-thumping nations. After all, Genesis says that an angel was set at the front door of Eden to keep us out, and those who find chemical gimmicks to sneak around through the back door are always going to seem heretical.

Holy War

It is probably worth examining this religious tradition in somewhat more detail. After all, in virtually every tribe there is some version of the Garden of Eden story. Our earliest ancestors or our first parents, we are told, lived in a virtual paradise. Private property did not exist, and neither did envy, jealousy, robbery, murder, war or government. "It was the Golden Age," says Cervantes' Don Quixote, summing up what is common in the Greek, Jewish and Christian versions of the myth. "In those days amorous ideas found simple, natural expression in the very form and manner in which they were conceived. Neither fraud, nor deceit, nor malice had yet interfered with truth and plain dealing." And then came the first sin, the first error, the first transgression. We have been wandering in the wilderness ever since and (as said above), an angel is stationed at the front gate of Eden "with flaming swords turning in every direction," to make sure that we never again find our way back to that earthly paradise.

Psychiatrists and other social scientists have some interesting theories about the origins of this universal myth pattern. Freudians believe that its basis is in our memories of early infancy, when we were given everything that we wanted (as soon as we cried for it) and no conflict had yet risen to frighten or frustrate us. Otto Rank, another psychoanalyst, suggested more imaginatively that Eden is our distorted memory of the womb, and the "fall of Man" is our traumatic recall of the shock of birth. Some Marxists and women's liberationists believe that there was a Golden Age of brotherhood, sisterhood and socialism between the agricultural revolution of 12,000 BC and the urbanization of 4000 BC.

Some ethologists believe that the myth is a memory of the hunting stage of much earlier prehistory (circa 4,000,000 BC to 1,000,000 BC), when we were living in accordance with our "instincts," and hadn't become fully socialized and invented unnatural taboos to make ourselves miserable. There is even a charming theory, put forth by Theodore Lasar of New York, that the alleged Great Comet of 8000 BC, hypothesized by Dr. Immanuel Velikovsky, made mankind mad with fear, and that the golden age legend is our insane recollection of the time when we were sane.

But whatever the source of this worldwide legend, the psychological fact to which it attests is obvious: people can imagine an ideal condition of happiness, but are usually *not* capable of imagining that they, personally, are able to achieve that ideal. There is everywhere a consciousness of some gate, or door, or barrier, between desire and reality. Men and women everywhere tend to feel partially impotent and incapable of achieving what they want to achieve.

This psycho-spiritual barrier corresponds fairly well to Saint Augustine's concept of "original sin," which "clouds the intellect" and gives the soul "a permanent inclination toward Evil." It also corresponds to Freud's notion that *everybody* is neurotic and—even more—to Dr. Wilhelm Reich's startling diagnosis that humanity suffers from "pleasure-anxiety," an internal fear that causes us to repress our "primary drives" and always substitute "secondary" and "substitute" goals, like the archer who dares not aim for the bull's-eye but must always force himself to miss it by at least a few millimeters, or more often by miles.

There is a minority viewpoint. It was stated eloquently in a movie called *They Might Be Giants,* starring George C. Scott, who plays a famous lawyer who once dedicated himself to fighting for the poor and weak, but has now become insane and believes he is Sherlock Holmes. As his psychoanalyst (named Dr. Watson, of course) tails him around New York City, this genial maniac finds clues everywhere, leading him ever onward in his search for "Professor Moriarty," the Satan in his myth. "You see," Scott explains to the audience at the end, "we were never put out of the Garden of Eden. It's still all around us. You only have to learn to look..." And, as the therapist, now a pupil of the former patient, looks into the distance, the screen turns white and the movie ends.

It was the Gnostics, during Christianity's early centuries, who first proposed that man could live in paradise "while still in the flesh." Condemned as a heresy in every church council from then until now, the Gnostic viewpoint has never quite died out. Even *Time* magazine stated, a few years ago, that it was the most important idea in the modern world, underlying such tendencies as socialism, communism, anarchism and even liberalism. Even more, it permeates all the utopian heresies that have separated out from orthodox modern psychiatry—Reich and his Orgone, Brown and Marcuse with their prophecy of future societies that will exist without the repression of Eros, R.D. Laing's theory of a mental state as far superior to normalcy as normalcy is to paranoia, the joyous hopes of the Gestaltists and sensitivity trainers, and the whole Human Potential Movement.

The acme, or seed center, of all these messianic visions, in our time, is the Psychedelic Revolution foisted upon us by those very naughty and mischievous shamans Timothy Leary, Doctor of Philosophy; Alan W. Watts, Doctor of Divinity; and Aldous Huxley, Secretary of Nature. Others, of course, aided and abetted, in one way or another—poet Allen Ginsberg, novelist William S. Burroughs, Dr. John Lilly, Dr. Humphrey Osmund, Dr. Houston Smith, novelist Ken Kesey—the list actually is endless. Whoever deserves the lion's share of the credit (or blame), the event is upon us. Millions of our citizens, especially among the young, are chemical Gnostics and are searching busily for a molecular back door to the Garden of Eden.

These "green revolutionaries" do not believe that we must forever impotently fall short of the bull's-eye. They refuse to admit original sin, or inborn neuroses, or even the theosophists' "Lurker at the Threshold" (one who supposedly eats the heads of those people rash enough to invade the higher planes without an invitation). They will not accept the perpetual barrier between desire and reality lamented by T.S. Eliot in his poem "The Hollow Men." According to Eliot's quite orthodox Christian view, there is a "Shadow" that always falls between "the idea and the reality," "the desire and the spasm," "the motion and the Act." This Shadow is, of course, Original Sin and by definition no man or woman can remove it.

The Drug Revolution says, like Buddha, "But it's *only a Shadow*—only an appearance, an illusion." At most, the ideologues of this cause would grant that Shadow the status of an old tape playing in the mental stereo, imprinted with the social fears and prejudices of our parents; and any program of that sort can be erased and replaced by a better program if one knows the proper neurological or yogic techniques. And, they would add with a missionary gleam in their eyes, these techniques are known by many, can be taught to others, and are exquisitely accelerated by the use of the proper chemicals.

Think of your desires as realities, the slogan of the French student revolution of 1968, is the seed-mantra of the whole dope mystique and even appears, in different words, in so sober a scientific student of psychedelics as the gifted polymath Dr. John C. Lilly, who says in a passage worth quoting twice:

> In the province of the mind, what is believed to be true is true or becomes true, within limits to be found experientially and experimentally. These limits are further beliefs to be transcended. In the province of the mind, there are no limits...

This is what scientists call a *pragmatic* statement. That is, it is not truth as known to the theoretician or the pure scientist in the ivory tower; it is a generalization useful to the troubleshooter dealing with actual events in the laboratory. (In this case, of course, the laboratory is the human head.) What Dr. Lilly is saying is that the distinction between desire and reality can safely (even profitably) be ignored by the psychedelic experimenter. Whatever you truly believe you can do, you actually can do. Any limits to this statement are themselves axioms of impotence, to be transcended by reprogramming your belief system. New limits, discovered after this reprogramming has taken place, are further errors to be removed by further reprogramming. If this process does not continue to infinity, it continues far longer than one is willing to believe before attempting such mind expansion.

But that was heresy to the church fathers, and it is still heresy. Our society is firmly committed to the dogmas that we are "conceived in sin and born in corruption," that "there is no health in us," and that this world is necessarily and forever "a vale of tears." These expressions came from three of the best-known and most reiterated of all Christian prayers; they represent the essential pessimism that is the bedrock of Christian theology. He who denies this view is not Christian.

This is the most marked difficulty in communication between a psychedelic shaman and a man who was educated as a Christian. Anthropologist Carlos Castaneda states it very eloquently in describing (in *A Separate Reality*) one of his problems with the Yacqui Indian sorcerer don Juan:

> What impressed me about don Juan was that he did not make a point of being weak and helpless, and just being around him insured an unfavorable comparison between his way of behaving and mine...
>
> "You're plagued with problems," he said. "Why?"
>
> "I'm only a man, don Juan," I said peevishly.
>
> I made the statement in the same vein my father used to make it. Whenever he said he was only a man he implicitly meant he was weak and helpless and his statement, like mine, was filled with an ultimate sense of despair.
>
> Don Juan peered at me as he had done the first day we met.
>
> "You think about yourself too much," he said and smiled...
> "Therefore, all you have is problems. I'm only a man too, but I don't mean that the way you do... I've vanquished my problems. Too bad my life is so short that I can't grab onto all things I would like to. But that's not an issue; it's only a pity."
>
> I liked the tone of his statement. There was no despair or self-pity in it.

But don Juan, whose separate reality is created by the same magic mushroom that originally turned on Dr. Timothy Leary, would be pronounced guilty of the "sin of pride" by orthodox Christian theologians. As Thomas Szasz, M.D., points out in *The Myth of Mental Illness,* many people in our society develop neurotic symptoms or psychosomatic illnesses because the only way to become important in Christian culture is to be conspicuously more pitiful than others.

Of course, the United States was not originally intended to be a Christian nation. Jefferson, Washington, Franklin and most of the founding fathers were skeptics or Deists; they specifically intended a secular government with an "unbreachable wall" between church and state; they even wrote into the treaty with the Moslem nation of Tripoli a clear statement that, unlike European countries, the "United States is not, in any sense, a Christian nation." (So clearly understood was the principle of separation of church and state in those days that this treaty passed Congress without any debate on that clause, and President John Adams signed it at once, without any fear that it might jeopardize his political future.)

But the simple ideas of the men who wrote the Constitution are no longer acceptable in modern America, as everybody knows. Our rulers—and, perhaps, a large number of our fellow citizens—have decided that the open-ended government of the founders is too radical, and an official Christian code of morals and beliefs has been written into our statute books. You cannot hold office in some states without believing in an anthropomorphic form of god; you cannot make love to your own wife, in *many* states, except by methods found acceptable to tinhorn Baptist legislators. And, of course, you cannot practice a psychedelic religion—or, at present, pursue psychedelic scientific research—in any state.

So this is a book, not about ordinary criminals, but about heretics. It is not about a "conflict of generations" as the popular oversimplification would have it; it is about a religious civil war—the worst that Christendom has experienced since Protestantism split off from the Church of Rome in the late Middle Ages. It is about two opposing views of mankind and the *odium theologicum* that their conflict has generated. It is, in short, a postscript to Andrew Dickson White's famous thousand-page tome, *The History of the Warfare Between Science and Theology,* except that, in this case, orthodox science and orthodox theology are on the same side. These old enemies have united against a handful of radicals who have infiltrated both camps.

Nobody—not even Newt Gingrich—should be so naive as to believe that this conflict will be settled easily once all the heretics are imprisoned and silenced. Our ancestors learned— after they had toasted one million to nine million "witches" according to various estimates, and perhaps an equal number of fellow Christians since the Inquisition was founded in the Eighth Century—that ideas cannot be burned at the stake. Nor can prisons be built fast enough to hold all those who, every day, become converted to the psychedelic faith in "better living through chemistry." This is especially true because the real heart of the Drug Revolution—hardly ever mentioned in public, but nevertheless widely suspected—is, and always has been, sex.

The Witch Hunt Metaphor

The first overt admission of the central role of sex in the Psychedelic Revolution appeared in the September 1966 issue of *Playboy,* in which Dr. Timothy Leary said bluntly in an interview:

> The sexual impact is, of course, the open but private secret about LSD, which none of us has talked about in the last few years. It's socially dangerous enough to say that LSD helps you find divinity and helps you discover yourself. You're already in trouble when you say that. But then if you announce that the psychedelic experience is basically a sexual experience, you're asking to bring the whole middle-aged, middle-class monolith down on your head...
>
> The sexual ecstasy is the basic reason for the current LSD boom. When Dr. Goddard, the head of the Food and Drug Administration, announced in a Senate hearing that ten percent of our college students are taking LSD, did you ever wonder why? Sure, they're discovering God and meaning, sure, they're discovering themselves; but did you really think that sex wasn't the fundamental reason for this surging youthful social boom? You can no more do research on LSD and leave

out sexual ecstasy than you can do microscopic research on tissue and leave out cells…

The LSD session, you see, is an overwhelming awakening of experience; it releases potent, primal energies, and one of these is the sexual impulse, which is the strongest impulse at any level of organic life.

Once this is admitted, we have obviously come full circle back to the days of the Holy Inquisition, for it is precisely this double diabolism—drugs plus sex—which was the "crime" of the majority of accused "witches" burned at the stake by that august body. If one looks through Margaret Murray's *The Witch-Cult in Western Europe* or G. Rattray Taylor's *Sex in History,* one will find that the same general charges appeared again and again in the witch trials. The same charges, virtually without a shred of difference, occur in contemporary newspaper stories, whenever a youngsters' "commune" is raided by the police. One can even put this into a table, as follows:

Table 1

Typical European witch trial circa 1490	*Typical American drug bust circa 1990*
The accused are arrested in a woodland meeting place	The accused are arrested in a rural "commune"
The accused are said to worship a Horned God, perhaps Satan Himself	The accused are said to worship Hindu or American Indian or other non-Christian divinities
The accused are alleged to have engaged in "obscene" or "bestial" orgies	The accused are alleged to have engaged in "obscene" or "bestial" orgies or, at least, to be sexually casual
The accused are said to seek religious visions with drugs, most commonly belladonna, thorn apple or mandrake	The accused are said to seek religious visions with drugs, most commonly LSD, hashish, peyote or marijuana
The accused are typically defiant, in the manner of heretics, not guilty in the manner of ordinary criminals	The accused are typically defiant in the manner of heretics, not guilty in the manner of ordinary criminals
The accused usually come from either the lower class (peasants, serfs) or from the young scholars	The accused usually come from either the lower class (Negroes, Mexican-Americans) or from the young intelligentsia (students)

The offense is a "crime without victims" or a crime by definition, not a real crime against persons or property	The offense is a "crime without victims" or a crime by definition, not a real crime against persons or property
But society paradoxically demands harsher penalties than are given for crimes against persons or property	But society paradoxically demands harsher penalties than are given for most crimes against persons or property
General charges of Satanism, anarchism, black magic, murder, etc., are often directed against the class of offenders (the "witches")	General charges of treason, communism, black magic, "un-Americanism," etc., are often leveled against the class of offenders (the "dope fiends")

According to a popular school of rationalistic historians of the last century, there never were any "witches" and the Holy Inquisition was just an outbreak of paranoia among the celibate priests of Roman Catholicism. According to Dr. Margaret Murray's revisionist theory, there were "witches"—worshippers of the pre-Christian horned god of fertility, best known as Pan or Dionysus—and the "paranoia" of the churchmen consisted only of ingrained religious bigotry that compelled them to believe that any pro-sexual religion must be Satanic in inspiration. According to Rev. Montague Sumners and other pro-Catholic revisers of Dr. Murray's revisionism, the witches were *so* Satanists after all and delighted in all manner of murder and atrocity. Whatever the truth concerning those tragic trials of 400 and 500 years ago, it is obvious that the same psychological pattern is at work in our psychedelic struggle today.[1]

That pattern can be defined in a number of ways, but most fundamentally it is a conflict between those forces that Freud called the superego and the id. The superego—the self's "harsh master," Freud called it—is the angel guarding the door to Eden with a flaming sword; its archetypal religious expression is Christianity, that most social of all religions, which asks each individual to consider all others before himself. The id—the

---

[1] Perhaps, in the year 2598, some historians will claim that there never were "hippies," while others will claim that hippies existed but didn't actually smoke marijuana, and a third group will insist that the hippies, always stoned out of their skulls on belladonna, ran through the streets attacking innocent bystanders.

primordial raw power of instinct itself—is the force that sends us around to the back of Eden, looking for another entrance; its archetypal religious expression is Dionysianism, the cult of deliriant drugs that burst into Athens from somewhere in the East during Greece's prehistoric period, approximately between 1000–900 BC. The German philosopher Nietzsche said that history is coming, in our time, to take the form of a final conflict between Christ and Dionysus, and that certainly seems to be the case in America today. The Reverend Billy Graham, the classic "pale Christian," sits as an adviser to Presidents, while Dr. Timothy Leary, the Dionysian spirit of dope and ecstasy is sentenced to 40 years and flees into exile, only to be recaptured.

The distinguished literary critic Leslie Fielder was not exaggerating when he said:

> In fact, I would say this particular generation gap might almost be called chemical warfare—the pot-heads versus the booze-heads. Actually, though, it would be more accurate to call it religious warfare—but only the pot-heads realize that there is a religious issue at stake...
>
> Drugs have always been considered either sacred or diabolical. The background of drug use in history involves charms, magic potions, holy sacraments and Devil's orgies. In more advanced societies, the same cluster of ideas carries over into our modern distinctions between legal intoxicants, which are good, and illegal dope, which is bad. But that is purely a matter of social definition.

In the *Playboy Panel* on drugs during which Professor Fielder made these remarks, Baba Ram Dass (formerly Dr. Richard Alpert) commented:

> Precisely. Every religion is a way of arriving at a certain state of consciousness and every society is based on a particular religion. Naturally, since any state of consciousness can be induced by a specific drug or group of drugs, you are going to find each society accepting certain drugs and bitterly condemning others.

In this holy war, I write as a war correspondent, awash in a deluge of propaganda from both sides. I have tried to gather the most accurate information available on the actual effects of various drugs on sexual drive and sexual performance. Since we are concerned here with a theological and legal conflict as well as a scientific field for investigation, there is little consensus. Trying to find out what a drug really does to the human mind and body, in America today, is like trying to find out who shot first at Waco or Ruby Ridge. "Only God knows for sure, and He isn't telling." All that the objective reporter can do, then, is to print the claims of both sides and let the reader decide for himself who can be trusted.

What I have tried to show is that the current "psychedelic genocide" (as Michael Aldrich, Ph.D., has called it) is not unique in history. We have been through all this many times in the past (the witch hunts were only the last large-scale example) and, with so much emotion involved, the real facts (even when they can be discovered) will scarcely change anybody's mind.

Do you deny that? Just imagine what would happen if LSD were proven to be as dangerous as the automobile—i.e., if it killed 50,000 of us per year. Would acidheads then give up this drug? No more than drivers will give up their cars despite the mathematical risk; the acidheads will decide, just like automobile drivers, that the statistical risk is worth the rewards. Similarly, if it were demonstrated that marijuana cures cancer, would Washington then legalize it? If you think the answer is "yes," you are wrong. There is already evidence—which we will quote later— that marijuana is useful in treating AIDS, cancer, headache, neuralgia, melancholy and depressive psychosis, insomnia, loss of appetite and that, moreover, it may be more effective than any tranquilizer currently on the market. None of this has lessened the *odium theologicum* against the weed in governmental circles.

In 1996, for instance, the voters of California approved the legalization of marijuana for some medical uses (AIDS and cancer, chiefly) if prescribed by a qualified physician. President Bill Clinton—whose middle name, ironically, is Jefferson—immediately proclaimed that the people of California had no right to meddle in their own affairs. Further rumbles from Washington, chiefly from the Justice Department, threatened doctors who wrote prescriptions for the taboo herb. Two years later, a few brave and humane physicians continue to prescribe the "devil weed" for patients who seem to really need it, but the majority of M.D.s are afraid to take the risk no matter how many patients suffer painful deaths. It reminds one of H.L. Mencken's verdict that cowardice is the strongest force in human behavior. Doctors seem to have more of it than most professions.

So: We have here a religious war; and theological bias, rather than scientific objectivity, determines what most writers will say on the subject. *The writings themselves are all war propaganda.* Nonetheless, an objective investigator can hope to disentangle some of the truth from the worst of the lies, and that is attempted here. I will endeavor to state what each drug discussed here will probably do to your sex drive, and what side effects (if any) will probably come in its wake. What you do with this information is your own business, and you do it at your own risk.

Of course, the whole religious dimension of this problem is often denied these days. Huston Smith, Ph.D., Professor of Religion at Massachusetts Institute of Technology, has his own brief way of answering those who insist that drug experiences and religious experiences are totally different and unrelated. He merely asks such skeptics to read the following two autobio-graphical passages, and decide which is an account of a "tran-scendental" experience *with* drugs and which is a "transcenden-tal" experience *without* drugs. Both are entirely typical of the "mystic" writings of the past, and of current psychedelic confes-sions. Which is which?

Passage A

Suddenly I burst into a vast, new, indescribably wonderful uni-verse. Although I am writing this over a year later, the thrill of the surprise and amazement, the awesomeness of the revela-tion, the engulfment in an overwhelming feeling-wave of grati-tude and blessed wonderment, are as fresh, and the memory of the experience is as vivid, as if it had happened five minutes ago. And yet to concoct anything by way of description that would even hint at the magnitude, the sense of ultimate real-ity ... seems an impossible task. The knowledge which has infused and affected every aspect of my life came instanta-neously and with such complete force of certainty that it was impossible, then or since, to doubt its validity.

Passage B

All at once, without warning of any kind, I found myself
wrapped in a flame-colored cloud. For an instant I thought of
fire ... the next, I knew that the fire was within myself. Directly afterward there came upon me a sense of exultation, of
immense joyousness accompanied or immediately followed by
an intellectual illumination impossible to describe. Among
other things, I did not merely come to believe, but I saw that
the universe is not composed of dead matter, but is, on the
contrary, a living Presence; I became conscious in myself of
eternal life... I saw that all men are immortal; that the cosmic
order is such that without any peradventure all things work
together for the good of each and all; that the foundation principle of the world ... is what we call love, and that the happiness of each and all is in the long run absolutely certain.

Dr. Smith points out that when this problem was first submit-
ted to his students, twice as many guessed wrong as guessed
right. To give the skeptical reader ample opportunity to work on
this fairly without cheating, I have buried the answer in a later
chapter.

And for those who cannot see any link between sex and religion, I offer the words of 11th-Century French poet, Pierre
Vidal: "I think I see God when I look upon my lady's body
nude." Vidal, according to the biographies I have seen, was not
even on drugs when he wrote that pious sentiment.

Slouching Toward Bethlehem: The Story of Leonard

Marijuana addicts are gregarious and prefer to smoke in the company of others rather than alone... There is a loss of time and depth perception... There is a general loss of inhibitions and the user indulges in behavior he or she would not normally even consider... Crimes of violence such as robbery, burglary, assault, rape, and homicide are common to persons under the influence and it usually is in this condition that the user tries his first injection of heroin...

— *Drug Abuse is an Escape to Nowhere*
Green County Sheriff's Department (Ohio)
Revised 1972 edition

"Would you mind if I jack off? Leonard asked. His wife, in the chair next to him, smiled—she was accustomed to his whimsical ways.

I was just learning Leonard's habits, however. "Right here in my living room?" I asked stupidly.

"Why not?" he asked suspiciously. "Do you still have some of those lingering Puritan hangups?"

I was stumped. The ordinary American would tell Leonard he was a nut and throw him out the front door, but I have long been a spokesman for an extreme right-wing libertarianism that prides itself on being more radical than left-wing anarchism. I would not want it to be known that I had inflicted any subjective prejudices on somebody else's sexual freedom. "Well," I said gropingly, knowing I had a reason but not quite remembering it, "my kids, you know. They're all under six, and they talk about everything they see. By the time they tell the neighborhood kids about you beating your meat with the rest of us sitting around watching, it'll be a pretty weird story. I don't mind being chased out of town for my own eccentricities, but I don't want to be in trouble for yours."

It sounded weak to me, but Leonard was an ultra-libertarian also. He nodded thoughtfully. "Yeah," he said, "I shouldn't make *you* pay for *my* trip." He got up. "I'll be in the john for a few minutes," he said.

For Leonard—as he was in those days—this was a fairly typical experience. Unlike Jane, whose story was told in the Prelude, Leonard was not an adult with a fully-formed and fairly well-set personality structure when the Drug Revolution of the 1960s began. He was, in fact, 12 years old when Dr. Timothy Leary ate four magic mushrooms in Cuernavaca, Mexico, in 1959 and had an experience in which "the space game came to an end, the time game came to an end, and the Timothy Leary game came to an end." Leonard was only 16 when Harvard asked Dr. Leary to go elsewhere in 1963, and he was 18 when most of the anti-LSD laws were passed in 1965, which was when I met him and his wife, a 22-year-old psychology major named Sandra.

Leonard was a kid whose adolescence was shaped and molded, in numerous ways, by the Drug Revolution, by the Sex Revolution, and by the Political Revolution, all of which were at their peaks in those years.

Leonard was an anarchist, a communist, a mystic, a bit of a fascist, a social creditite, a technocrat, a back-to-nature agrarian, and, above all, a sexual revolutionary, all more or less at the same time; or so it seemed since these enthusiasms came and went so quickly that they seemed to occupy his passions simultaneously. He claimed, also simultaneously, that everybody should reside on farms and have all their work done for them by machines, that we should live in harmony with nature and build bigger and better computers, and that the government should distribute purchasing power (social credit) to everybody, whether they were in need or not (to *discourage* them from unnecessary labor), and that there should be no government because the tribal form of society was most in keeping with our primate biology.

Naturally, he had a very high IQ. Dimwits do not acquire such remarkable notions.

Above all, however, Leonard believed that our "bullshit society" had alienated us from our true drives. Unlike Freud, Reich, Marcuse and others who have taken a similar position, Leonard did not assume that he knew what our true drives are. Quite the contrary, he was dogmatic in opposing all dogmatism about this delicate issue; he insisted that our true drives had to be *discovered*. He was trying to discover these primal instincts by doing everything forbidden by society; if he enjoyed an experiment, then it was one of our primal drives; if he didn't enjoy it, then it was a perversion.

Hemingway seems to have had the same empirical approach when he wrote that "the Good" is that which makes you feel good.

Leonard liked me because I was almost as confused as he, having left a good job in the city to work at slave wages on a small-town newspaper, just to provide my children with a rural environment. I also believed in technocracy while I was fleeing from it personally, and from my own right-wing perspective, I believed that many of his "fantastic" dictums might be more plausible social programs than the panaceas usually prescribed by liberals.

Nevertheless, I did look with some skepticism on his changing sexual and dope enthusiasms.

One day he and his wife Sandra drove over from the college they were attending and he immediately told me his latest discovery in the field of primal instincts. He had tried on some of Sandra's underwear and liked it. "I'm wearing her panties and girdle right now," he said gleefully.

Nobody would have guessed it. On the surface, he appeared to be the very picture of a 1965 college student—that is, he looked like a very poor cowboy. His ragged levis and sweatshirt certainly didn't suggest transvestism.

"How does it feel?" I asked in my best non-judgmental tone—the one I used when interviewing John Birchers for my newspaper.

"It's groovy," he said. "Every time I remember what I'm wearing, I start to get a hard-on."

This phase lasted a few months. Every time I saw Leonard and Sandra, he had some new items of women's underwear to brag about. By this time they had worked out a routine: they would walk into a ladies' wear store together, the ideal young marrieds—and nobody guessed that the frilly silks that they bought were actually for him.

Then there was Leonard's anal phase. Even before *Myra Breckenridge,* he decided that there was a primordial instinct which demanded that men be buggered by women. (Are you reading this, Andrea Dworkin?)

"Er, how do you manage that?" I asked when he bragged about this latest discovery.

"With a Coca-Cola bottle," he said.

"Oh," I said thoughtfully. "I'm not sure, but you ought to look up *prolapsed anus* in some medical books. I think you can turn your asshole inside out and really hurt yourself with a bottle that way. It creates a vacuum, I think."

"Oho!" he cried. "Maybe that's why I was bleeding the last time we tried it."

Sandra was always very quiet and repressed, like most psychology majors. Aside from helping Leonard in his various sexual manias, she didn't seem to have any personality traits to distinguish her from a million other white, Protestant, Midwestern girls her age. Maybe that was *why* she helped him.

"You were right about that prolapsed anus," Leonard told me the next time I saw him. "We gave up that Coke bottle and bought one of those fancy vibrators. Wow, man—wow!"

Naturally, Leonard and Sandra had to make the orgy scene eventually.

"It was groovy," he told me later. "They had cocaine and I was sniffing and coming, sniffing and coming, all night long. Out of fucking *sight!*"

Before the reader rushes out to lay in a year's supply of cocaine, let me remind you that Leonard was 18 at that time.

Many young males around that age are (for a few years) as multi-orgasmic as mature females may be without cocaine.

Leonard's dope manias were as frankly experimental as his sex adventures.

For a while, when I first met him, it was grass. Grass was the millennium. It not only expanded consciousness, enriched sex and proved the existence of God, but it absolutely turned all users into pacifists. "All we gotta do is turn everybody on and there'll be no fucking Third World War," Leonard proclaimed on one occasion.

"The Hell's Angels smoke a *lot* of grass and they're not exactly pacifists," I pointed out, gently. "And then there was Hasan i Sabbah..."

"Well, there's something in that," Leonard admitted. "Some people need a hell of a lot more grass than others before it begins to loosen them up. Besides, the Angels louse it up by mixing it with booze and that's always a *down* trip."

That's what I liked about Leonard. He always listened to your arguments and even thought about them, at least briefly. He was never really insane.

Later, of course, Leonard's panacea became LSD.

"I was fucking Sandra," he'd tell anybody who would listen, "and the acid made all my consciousness go into the very top eighth inch of the head of my penis. That's all I was—just that fragment of flesh entirely surrounded by cunt and pulsating with joy. Then—boom!—I wasn't even that. I was nowhere, and yet I was everywhere. Now, that's exactly what the Hindus call Samadhi—union with the All."

It was, of course, his dream to put acid in the Washington water supply. "Even LBJ will fall in love with the world and stop killing people," he would enthuse.

Leonard suffered a terrible depression when it was widely published in the underground press that LSD breaks down into inactive components when placed in running water under sunlight and therefore would be wasted if put in the water supply. "Christ," he said, "things are never as easy as they seem. We'll have to find another way to get to LBJ."

The blood of the rebels runs thin, as Bernard Wolfe once remarked; after a few years, small-town life palled on me and I began hunting for a big-city job again. I moved back to New York and lost touch with Leonard and Sandra.

We did meet again—East Village in a coffeehouse. His then current passions were cocaine and homosexuality.

"I think the coke fucks up your brain," he told me worriedly, "but I'll stop before it does any *serious* harm. You'd be surprised what it does for your orgasm, baby. Oh, Lord, Lord!"

I asked if he was still married to Sandra.

"Oh, yes, man, she's still my mother angel," he said rhapsodically. "We're balling the same guy. All three of us sniffing and coming, sniffing and coming, all night long."

Of such is the Kingdom of Heaven, I thought whimsically.

Years passed; I got older; it was 1972 and the optimism of the 1960s revolutionaries was just an ironic memory. One day I was in a post office in Chicago and a voice at my right shoulder said, "Bob Wilson?"

I turned and looked at a face I didn't quite recognize. There was a new beard, conservative clothing and some of the veneer of adulthood—but one feature remained. There was that unmistakable glint in the eyes—the glow that revealed one who was still in hot pursuit of "truth" and had finally caught "it" by "its" shirttails and was about to possess it whole. "Leonard?" I asked.

"Yes," he said, "and I've often worried about the bad influence I must have been on you in the old days. The terrible things I used to do, and how hard I tried to get others to do them, too!" (Uh-oh, I thought.) "But I have found peace now, I have been reborn through our Savior Jesus Christ, and I..."

"It's always good to see an old friend," I said quickly, "but I have to rush to catch a train." I was already in flight.

"Wait, wait," he said, "take this pamphlet..." I could still see his mouth moving as I hurried out the door.

2

Horned Gods & Horny Potions

One must sell it to someone, the sacred name of love ... all thinking all of it, the It with an itch in it, the All every inch of it, the pleasure each will preen her for, the business each was bred to breed by... The law of the jungerl.
— James Joyce, *Finnegans Wake*

The human brain consists of about two and one-half pounds of an oatmeal-like goo. (The stiffer, starchy-looking brains seen in laboratories or movies are dead; the rest of the body looks equally plastic after death.) In this goo—"this enchanted loom," neurologist Sir Charles Sherrington called it; "this hive of anarchy," novelist Bernard Wolfe said more poetically—there are several billion separate cells, each one of which might be in an electric hook-up with any one, any dozen or any thousand of the others at one time. Each such circuit is a registration or response to something that has been impinging on the nervous system, either from deep inside itself in muscles, glands or cells, or from as far outside as the stars at night.

Architect-poet Buckminster Fuller sums it all up in one, fine, unforgettable paradox: *"Everything we see,"* he says, *"is inside our own heads."* That is, we do not see with our eyes, but with our brain-plus-eyes working as a unit.

Thus, if a person has been blind and has his sight restored by an operation, he will not see what we see. He will see a whirling chaos, and it will probably frighten him; it is only gradually, over a period of months, that he will learn, through coaching by his doctors and nurses, to see what we see. We will not regale the reader with the neurological theories that attempt to explain why an LSD trip sets the experimenter into this same whirling chaos.

Needless to say, we also hear with brain-plus-ears, taste with brain-plus-tongue and, in general, know everything only through its registration inside our heads on what William S. Burroughs calls "the soft machinery" of our brain tissue.

Thus, under hypnosis, a person who has been given salt and told that it is sugar will taste it as sweet—thereby illustrating the brain-plus-tongue phenomenon. Similarly, a hypnotized subject shown a green circle and told that it is red will see it as red. That is because we see with brain-plus-eye.[1]

Now, obviously, anything that affects the brain will affect our perceptions of the whole universe. Frontal-lobe epilepsy—a disease of the brain that has afflicted such illustrious persons as Julius Caesar and the Russian novelist Feodor Dostoevsky—illustrates this process clearly. In his attempts to describe this condition, Dostoevsky sounds exactly like a modern acidhead, saying that, despite the pain associated with the fit, "I feel entirely in harmony with myself and the whole world ... for a few seconds of such bliss one would gladly give up ten years of one's life, if not one's whole life." It is nonverbal, like acid and other trips we will be discussing, because our language was invented to describe other, more statistically normal perceptions. Dostoevsky (and other frontal-lobe epileptics) even describes a great "white light" that also has been seen by LSD trippers and Oriental yogis. (A rock group called The Clear Light is evidently named after this experience, which philosopher Alan W. Watts—who experimented on himself with LSD while it was still legal—

---

[1] In other experiments, the subjects have not seen the green circle as red but as a color close to red (orange or yellow). This is not understood, but the reader can have some fun trying to dream up his own explanation.

suggests might be the brain's perception of itself when all the electrical circuits are turned on at once. Maybe.)

But (and the reader must know we have been leading up to this), a more common way of transforming the brain is via drugs, which can be self-administered, unlike epilepsy, which has to be inherited. It is also true (despite the hysteria in Washington) that quite a few drugs are, if taken in small doses, considerably less unpleasant than epilepsy. (They are also less unpleasant than cancer. If such moderate statements sound like pro-drug propaganda, I am truly sorry; as Dr. Humphrey Osmund has said, it has been difficult, since about 1965, to make any true statement about drugs without sounding like a part of the dreaded "drug cult.")

The discovery of mind-expanding, mind-blowing, mind-bending and mind-transcending properties of drugs seems to go back to the Neolithic ("New Stone") Age, if not earlier. Our Neolithic ancestors in the Near East buried their dead facing east (suggesting some form of sun worship) and placed marijuana in the grave (suggesting some psychedelic or religious use of that plant). In Mexico, statues dated at 1000 BC or earlier show the "magic mushroom" *psilocybae mexicana* with god-figures emerging from it, strongly suggesting that the religious use of this hallucinogenic (which was observed by the invading Spaniards in the early part of the 16th Century and still exists today), dates back at least that far. The first brewery was built in Egypt in the third millennium BC.

It is not to be assumed that our ancestors had any theoretical scientific knowledge of how these brews and herbs were affecting their brains. Rather, their knowledge must have been crudely empirical—like that of American teenagers today: "Hey, man, just chew this berry and see what happens!" (Yes, there is a hallucinogenic berry—the Pakistani—and it is known throughout the Middle East, and, according to William S. Burroughs, is quite like the South American hallucinogenic vine, *yage.*)

Needless to say, if drugs can change the way in which the brain sees, hears, smells and assembles meaningful form out of the chaos of sensation, they can also radically transform the nature of sexual feeling.

This undoubtedly is the point at which our ancestors (who were just as horny as we are) became acutely interested in the subject of drugs. The search was soon on for potions of Aphrodite—chemicals with uniquely sensuous kicks. And, since this was before the invention of Christianity, these erotic eucharists were more often identified with religion than with sin.

The Solanaceae

Back in college, most of us encountered John Donne's poem "Song" that begins:

> Go and catch a falling star,
> Get with child by mandrake root,
> Tell me where all past years are,
> Or who cleft the Devil's foot.

Some readers may even remember the footnote to the second line, which explains that the Elizabethans believed a woman could become pregnant via the mandragora or, as it was then called, mandrake. Actually, that was one of the later superstitions to be connected with this plant. Earlier, it was believed that the mandragora was a powerful aphrodisiac, and this belief was preceded by the notion that the plant was connected with religious visions and the peculiar frenzies of the death-and-resurrection cults that came into Greece from the Near East shortly before the time of Plato (Fourth Century, BC).

These cults, which are treated at length in Sir James Frazer's classic of anthropology, *The Golden Bough,* worshipped a series of gods said to have died and then risen. These include Dionysus, Attis and Tammuz from the East, and Osiris from Egypt. Like Christianity, which appeared several centuries later, these cults held out the promise that every worshipper could repeat the gods' miraculous feat. Unlike Christianity, however, they offered a kind of "proof" of this assertion—that is, an experience that apparently convinced the worshipper that he had been dead and returned to life, or had been to a place where life and death were not opposites but parts of the same continuum. This experience involved the use of mandragora and, also, on occasion, henbane and thorn apple.

These three drugs have two things in common: They are all of the solanaceae family, and they are all reputed aphrodisiacs.

Solanaceae drugs, like psychedelics but unlike true narcotics, produce excitation rather than torpor and lethargy; they also produce hallucinations which, for a time, completely overwhelm reality—which is often *rumored* to happen, but virtually never *does* happen with a true psychedelic. For example, on LSD, confusing misperceptions shift rapidly and, therefore, are never taken seriously. The situation rather resembles Lewis Carroll's poem:

> He thought he saw a banker's clerk descending from a bus
> He looked again and saw it was a hippopotamus

With mandrake, what is seen tends to remain constant and to be believed, even if it is something as implausible as a polar bear in a black turtleneck sweater lounging in the corner of the room. (This was actually seen by Ronald Weston, an advertising executive who experimented with belladonna, another drug in this family, and wrote about his experience for *Fact* magazine, Vol. I, No. I, 1963.) These drugs, unlike psychedelics, are also quite toxic and it is easy to overdose and kill yourself. Hence, our information about them is less copious than about psychedelics; there have been fewer experimenters, or, at least, fewer who lived to tell the tale.

This explains our cautious remark that such drugs are "reputed aphrodisiacs." Responsible medical opinion now holds that there are no true aphrodisiacs. (Sorry about that.) These chemicals do appear, however, to function *part of the time* as if their properties *were* very much like those of a true aphrodisiac.

Witches & Orgies

The Dionysian revels in Greece at which these deliriants were used had a very ripe and ribald reputation. At the witches' Sabbaths of the Middle Ages, where a similar Horned God was worshipped and the same drugs (plus belladonna) were copiously imbibed, an orgy usually occurred—at least, according to the confessions that the inquisitors obtained under torture. R.E.L. Masters, in *Eros and Evil,* tells of a Goettingen professor who experimentally tried one of these witches' brews from a formula found in a medieval manuscript, and experienced hallucinations of flying to a witches' orgy. Masters also tells of a woman who

used these drugs for asthma relief. Due to an accidental overdose, she made lesbian advances to her landlady and tried to
seduce a male visitor as well.

The conventional explanation of such seemingly aphrodisiac
effects is autosuggestion. That is, the people in question knew
what the drugs were supposed to do to them and, therefore,
unconsciously programmed themselves for such effects. Unfortunately for this theory, R.E.L. Masters claims that the woman in
the second anecdote did *not* know the reputation of the drugs in
question. Skeptical psycho-pharmacologists would not accept
such an anecdotal "testimony" and would demand a statistical
survey of several subjects under controlled laboratory conditions.
In such an experiment, one would be able to test the distinct
possibility that the woman, as is often the case, knew more than
the doctor realized.

Like psychedelics, these drugs seem to lend themselves exceptionally well to outer- or auto-suggestion. For instance, Akron
Daraul, in his *History of Secret Societies,* tells of an interview
with a Tibetan lama who virtually projected Daraul's "soul" out
of his body. Daraul, who had kept a specimen of the dinner
served to him before this interview, later had it analyzed at a
chemical laboratory and found elements of mandrake/mandrag-
ora as well as scopolamine, a derivative of henbane, which is
often referred to as "truth serum." (Actually, what the subject
"reveals" is not the precise truth, but what the questioner seems
to want to hear. Scopolamine was used originally by some police
departments in Europe to obtain confessions from suspected
criminals. If the suspect were actually guilty, the confession
would be detailed and accurate. If he were innocent, the confession would be equally detailed, but inaccurate.)

Under good conditions, then, a subject who *believes* that such
drugs will produce a wild sexual experience is quite likely to
have a wild sexual experience. In *Drugs and the Mind,* Robert
DeRopp, M.D., gives a classic example from the old witchcraft
days:

> In this particular trial the proceedings were made all the more
> piquant by the fact that Lise, from whose confessions the trial
> resulted, was the sixteen-year-old daughter of the local pastor.
> This Lise was decoyed into evil ways by her lover, who per-

suaded her to take part in the secret ceremonies to be held at midnight in the depths of the Harz Mountains. The participants, having assembled in their secret meeting place, prepared with suitable incantations a drink of which all partook freely.

(Dr. DeRopp concludes from other details that the drink and the salve mentioned later probably consisted of mandrake, henbane and/or belladonna.)

Soon after partaking of the drink, a frenzy seized them all, including young Lise, who, abandoning all restraints of feminine modesty, stripped herself naked, as did the others present, and was anointed with the "witches' salve." Next she engaged in a frenzied sexual orgy accompanied by the most vivid hallucinations, in the course of which she became convinced that every devil in hell had enjoyed her body, that she had mounted a broomstick and soared over the mountains, that she had seen the ovens of hell and even smelled the aroma of roasting sinners. So vivid were these hallucinations that she firmly believed them to be real and, in a subsequent fit of remorse, related them to her father. That worthy pillar of the church had no hesitation in handing over his daughter to the authorities, who forthwith instituted a hunt for the other members of the midnight party and, in an orgy of torture, wrung from all of them confessions of their misdeeds. Thereupon the entire group was ceremoniously burned alive in the public square, the whole town turning out to watch the event.

Evidently, if Lise had expected to meet Jesus and his 12 apostles and copulate with all of *them* in turn, that is what she would have remembered afterward.

The inquisitors—aided, it must never be forgotten, by instruments of persuasion that might have turned Carl Sagan into a spiritualist—obtained many confessions of orgies that would make Lise's experience seem like a girl scout hike by comparison. Many alleged "witches" confessed that incest was common at these celebrations, not only between brother and sister or father and daughter but between son and mother as well. (Kinsey found that the first two mentioned varieties of incest are more common than is generally believed, but that the last—despite its popularity as a theme in folklore, Greek tragedy and psychoanalysis—is as rare as the abhorrence for it would lead one to expect. He never found a single real case, although he investigated the matter for several years.) Others confessed to varieties of sex murder (killing the person one was copulating with) or necrophilia, and to various kinds of sadism and masochism. Cannibalism was also prominent in these confessions.

Most of this testimony can be explained as the result of the thumbscrews and other devices used in interrogation. Others, very likely, are real memories of hallucinations experienced under the influence of mandrake, belladonna or thorn apple. And, of course—witness the Manson Family—a few are probably genuine.

The inside view of the use of sexuality in witchcraft is given in *The Book of Shadows,* which, it is claimed, is a manuscript passed on for several centuries through various covens of the British Isles. Here, for instance, is the Second Degree Rite, which involves a good deal of kissing, some oralism, and mild sadomasochism but is not quite so frantic as Lise's confession.

High Priestess:
   Hear ye, Ye Mighty Ones. (Initiate's witch name), a duly consecrated Priestess/Priest and Witch is now properly prepared to be elevated to the Second Degree.
   To attain this degree it is necessary to be purified. Art thou willing to suffer to learn?

Initiate
   I am

High Priestess/High Priest says:
   I purify thee to take this oath rightly

High Priestess strikes three on the bell. Scourge 3, 7, 9, 21[1] then says:
   Repeat after me. I (initiate's witch name), swear on my Mother's womb, and by my honor amongst men, and by my Brothers and Sisters of the Art, that I will never reveal any secrets of the Art, except it be to a worthy person properly prepared in the center of a Magic Circle, such as I am now in. This I swear by my past lives and by my hopes of future ones to come and I devote myself to utter destruction if I break this my solemn oath...

---

[1] That is, the lucky candidate is whipped three times, then seven times, then nine times and, for a grand climax, 21 times. Great fun, if you happen to be a masochist.

High Priestess/High Priest makes the Pentagram on the genitals, right foot, left knee, left foot, genitals and says:
I consecrate Thee with Oil. [kiss]
I consecrate Thee with Wine. [kiss]
I consecrate Thee with Water. [kiss]
I consecrate Thee with Fire. [kiss]
I consecrate Thee with my lips. [kiss]

High Priestess:
Seventh, the Cords—bind the High Priestess/High Priest.

Initiate does this and High Priestess/High Priest gives a kiss.

High Priestess says:
Learn that in Witchcraft thou must ever return triple. As I scourge thee, thou must scourge me, but triple. Where I gave thee three strokes, return nine, seven strokes, return twenty-one, nine strokes, return twenty-seven, twenty-one strokes, return sixty-three. That is 120 strokes in all. Take up the Scourge.

Initiate does so and purifies the High Priestess with 120 strokes, then unbinds High Priestess/High Priest who gives a kiss. High Priestess/High Priest then says:
Thou hast obeyed the Law but mark well, when thou receiveth good, so equally art thou bound to return good threefold.

The actual use of coitus in witchcraft, according to *The Book of Shadows,* is decidedly decorous:

In ancient times the Great Rite was practiced but I do not know of any Witches in America or England who still practice the Great Rite. You may reject it, or if you feel closer to the Gods by returning as much as possible to the worship of the Ancients, then by all means do it.

THE GREAT RITE—at the end of each Sabbat Rite, the ancient ones had to "Earth" the power that had been raised within the Circle so that the power raised would not remain in the atmosphere afterwards. They earthed the power by committing the "Sex Act," which brought them down from the mystical to the material level. Each Sabbat Rite ended with this act and it was called "The Great Rite."

The Great Rite is performed as an act of worship to the God and Goddess. Obviously, if everybody indulged in lovemaking at the end of the rite, within the Magic Circle, it would look as if an orgy were taking place. Mostly the coveners did this in private after leaving the Magic Circle. Sex Magic is one of the most powerful of all acts of Magic and not to be taken lightly and certainly I believe should be performed in private before the Gods.

It is only fair to add, lest the reader accept this too easily, that no copy of *The Book of Shadows* has been produced that is more than a few decades old. Gerald Gardner (the English bureaucrat who after his retirement from public service became the chief spokesman for modern witchcraft) seems to have produced the first known copy of this text, and the very scrupulous occult historian Francis King says bluntly in his *Rites of Modern Occult Magic* that Gardner "either forged, or procured to be forged, the so-called *Book of Shadows.*" Nevertheless, modern witches accept this book as authentic, and its rites are, therefore, practiced widely today, and something very like them is, indeed, charged in the historical records of witch trials of the past.

If all this sounds rather perverse, the reader should remember that the whipping is also practiced by many Christians even today (such as the *penitentes* of Mexico) and has long been a tradition of the Jesuits. The sex rite (and the solanaceae drugs associated with it) is a part of a far older tradition.

Hierogamy, or Sex Magick

Behind this whole mystique is "sympathetic magic," the primitive notion that imitating a desired result will cause it to happen. Thus, to make rain, tribal shamans in many parts of the world will pour water through a vessel that has holes in the bottom. Or, to kill an enemy, a wizard will make a doll in his image and stick pins in it. That which is most desired by the tribe, of course, is fertility in the broadest sense of that word—more food, more crops, more animals and more children so the tribe will be strong in fighting men if they are attacked. To obtain fertility by sympathetic magic, the act of generation must be imitated. Hence, as Frazer demonstrates at exhausting length in *The Golden Bough,* some form of sexual magic or hierogamy appears in almost every culture. In certain cultures it takes the form of the orgy, in which every man and woman copulates in the fields on nights that are astrologically important—May Eve, Midsummer Day, Halloween, and so on; in others, it becomes the pure hierogamy in which the ritual copulation of exalted figures, the

king and his sister usually, is assumed to serve this function of
keeping nature green and abundant.

Figure 4
Phallic Leaden Tokens from the Seine

Thomas Wright, in his famous *History of the Worship of the
Generative Organs,* actually tried to prove that such sex worship
was the origin from which all later religious ideas developed.
Anthropologist Ashley Montague, a spokesman for the more
conservative and cautious approach, indicates that, in his opinion, Wright's theory may not be far from the truth. He writes:

> [Wright] is not quite so sound when he goes on to say that
> such beliefs and practices prevailed universally. The fact is
> that such practices and beliefs were very scarce among the
> American Indians... But Wright was near enough to the truth;
> such practices and the sexual symbolism associated with them,
> if not universal, were in one form or another well nigh to being
> so.

In other words, if you leave out the American Indians, Wright was right.

I insert here a few of Wright's famous illustrations (figures 4 to 7). Please bear in mind, while looking at them, that these are *religious* emblems—a concept that might be difficult for Christians or Jews to understand. And note that these idols do not come from India, like the erotic sculptures of the famous Tantric temples. These are European, and they indicate the alliance (or identity) of sexuality and religion in ancient times.

Figure 5
Monument Found At Nimes in 1825

According to philologist John Allegro in his speculative *The Sacred Mushroom and the Cross,* these links between eros and religion also link back to mind drugs—specifically, to the phallic-looking *amanita muscaria* mushroom, whose effects are similar to belladonna's, and which is still used for magic purposes by Siberian shamans. Moreover, according to Allegro's hypothesis, it was worshipped as a god throughout Europe and Asia in the late Stone Age.

The 20th Century has added little to the tradition. Charlie Manson, called the "LSD madman" by the press, was able to convert his followers to believe that he was both Jesus and Satan *only after he had supplemented that acid diet with heavy doses of these deliriant drugs,* especially belladonna and jimson weed (the American botanical cousin of mandrake). According to Ed Sanders' account of the Manson cult, *The Family,* one of the disciples suffered a 40-point IQ drop after a few belladonna trips with Charlie, and is now in a California mental hospital.

Jimson weed owes its name to the original Jamestown Colony in Virginia, of which "jimson" is a corruption. A group of soldiers stationed there found it by accident, with typically unsettling results. According to Robert Beverley's *History and Present State of Virginia* (1705):

> ... the effect ... was a very pleasant Comedy; for they turned natural Fools upon it for several Days. One would blow a Feather in the Air; another would dart straws at it with much Fury; and another, stark naked was sitting up in a Corner, like a Monkey grinning and making Mews at them; a fourth would fondly kiss and paw his Companions, and sneer in their Faces, with a Countenance more antik than any in a Dutch Droll. In this frantik Condition they were confined, lest they in their Folly should destroy themselves; though it was observed that all their Actions were full of Innocense and Good Nature. Indeed, they were not very cleanly; for they would have wallow'd in their own Excrements, if they had not been prevented. A Thousand such simple Tricks they play'd and after Eleven Days, return'd themselves again, not remembering anything that had pass'd.

The nudity, combined with the kissing and pawing, again suggests that this family of drugs does seem to have a sexually uninhibiting effect, *some* of the time, on *some* of its users. (The most recent report of jimson weed that I have seen, however, suggests that it is distinctly non-sexual. The report was a newspaper story about some kids in California who got hold of some and tried it for kicks. They were apprehended by the police while running down the street screaming that red, white and blue alligators were pursuing them.)

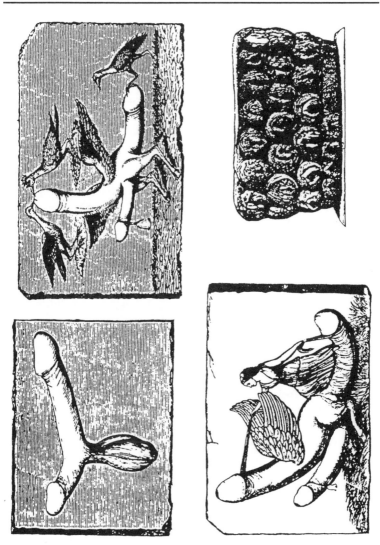

Figure 6
Roman Sculptures From Nimes

Figure 7
Ex Voti of Wax, From Isernia

Some of the reports on these drugs from ancient Greece are
even more hair-raising than the medieval accounts of girls flying
over mountains on broomsticks. The Greek *bacchantes,* or worshippers of Dionysus, were not only reputed to engage in frenzied and spasmodic sexual orgies but also, according to sober
contemporary authors, often ran amok and tore up sheep and

other small mammals—sometimes certain authorities say, even human children. In Euripedes' tragedy, *The Bacchae,* King Pentheus attempts to stamp out these rites, but Dionysus lures Pentheus' mother Agave into the cult and, stoned out of her gourd on these potent potions, she dismembers Pentheus without knowing what she is doing. That, every reader must admit, is considerably worse than anything claimed against currently popular drugs.

The aphrodisiac reputation of the mandrake, incidentally, is broadly hinted at in one of the more confusing of the tales in the Old Testament, which reads as follows:

> And Reuben went in the days of wheat harvest, and found mandrakes in the field, and brought them unto his mother Leah. Then Rachel said to Leah, Give me, I pray thee of thy son's mandrakes.
>
> And she said unto her, Is it a small matter that thou hast taken my husband? And wouldest thou take away my son's mandrakes also? And Rachel said, Therefore he shall lie with thee tonight for thy son's mandrakes.[1]

If the language of King James' translators is a bit obscure here, what is being told is that Rachel is allowing Jacob to return to sexual relations with Leah for one night in exchange for the wonderful mandrakes. The story concludes:

> And Jacob came out of the field in the evening and Leah went out to meet him, and said, Thou must come in unto me; for surely I have hired thee with my son's mandrakes. And he lay with her that night.
>
> And God hearkened unto Leah, and she conceived and bore Jacob the fifth son.[2]

Anyone with a knowledge of sexual magic will recognize that the mandrakes (which, physically, happen to look like erect penises) are being used as sympathetic magic to cause pregnancy in this yarn. On the other hand, it is also a bawdy tale in the classic tradition of sex humor, and you could retell it today (with one young chick stealing another's old man and then lending him back for a night in exchange for the currently fashionable mari-

---

[1] Gen. 30:14–15.

[2] Gen. 30:16–17.

juana) and still get some laughs. Except from Bible readers, who wouldn't recognize the source, and would be shocked at your levity and disrespect for marriage.

Gerard, in his *Herbal,* recounts many legends about the mandrake. One is of special note: "They added further that it is never...to be found growing naturally but under a gallowse, where the matter that hath fallen from the dead body hath given it the shape of a man." That is, according to an old superstition, every hanged man has an ejaculation as he dies, and it is from this seed, our ancestors believed, that the phallic mandrake grew.

Moses Maimonides, most learned of the medieval Jewish theologians, regarded the mandrake as useful in virtually all forms of sorcery; and, as late as the 18th Century, it still had a reputation as an aphrodisiac, and was mentioned by de Sade.

Its latest appearance in literature—a last, dying whimper perhaps—is in Terry Southern's screenplay of *Dr. Strangelove,* where one of the characters is simply named Captain Mandrake. (Others in the cast had such similarly coded names as President Merkin Muffley, General Buck Turgidson, Dr. Strangelove himself, Bat Guano, General Jack D. Ripper and Captain "King" Kong.)

Nightshade

In present-day America the easiest of these solanaceae drugs to obtain is belladonna, also called "deadly nightshade." (In New York City, this became so popular in the 1960s that asthma sufferers can no longer buy the popular remedy asthmador without a prescription. It contains belladonna, and the drug-kulch kids were having some wild trips on it for a while.)

A college student I know told me of trying belladonna in a frat house in Boston. He immediately went into a coma and woke up in the hospital to which his friends had rushed him, and where his stomach had been pumped. Belladonna, however, leaves the belly and enters the bloodstream fairly quickly, and he was still tripping, although not aware of the fact. As he watched, partly embarrassed and partly entranced, a nurse took off her uniform, stripped with bumps and grinds out of her underwear, and climbed into the next bed, where she made loud, passionate and prolonged love to the delighted patient there. It was not until the next day that my friend realized that this whole Mitchell Brothers sequence had been a hallucination.

And that is all he remembers of his belladonna trip. Probably, he had many other interesting hallucinations, but it is characteristic of solanaceae drugs to create micro-amnesia, which seems to remove all memories for from one to several hours. It is also interesting, considering the erotic reputation of this drug, that my friend's one retained hallucination was of a voyeuristic nature. Presumably, with a different set of mind he might have imagined—see the adventures of Lise a few pages back—that the nurse, or a dozen other nurses, had balled him in his delirium.

I have interviewed two other people who went into coma after trying belladonna. They remember nothing, not even the stomach pump.

William S. Burroughs, author of *Naked Lunch,* told me that in his days as a heroin addict he once inadvertently bought some alleged morphine that was actually severely cut with belladonna. A short while after taking his fix, he noticed that he was out of cigarettes and went to the window, sticking one leg out before a visiting friend asked him what the hell he was doing. "Going down for cigarettes," was the reply—and the friend grabbed him before he completed the trip out the window, which was on the third floor. The next day, typical of belladonna, Burroughs did not remember this experience and had to be told about it.

Another friend, who also tried belladonna while at college— these stories say something about the kind of drug education available in America, don't they?—had a more colorful experience. A friend came into his room after he had swallowed a cup of belladonna tea, and they had a long talk. Then the friend came into the room again, and our tripper realized that he had hallucinated the whole first visit and its associated conversation. As soon as he began to wonder whether this second visit was yet another hallucination, the visitor vanished. Our hero then went outside, got into his car and took a long drive. (He didn't own a car at the time.) The next morning, he woke up in a ditch several miles from the college. His right shoe and right sock were missing, but the rest of his clothing was intact. He never found his motorcycle—apparently that was what he was riding while he thought he was driving a car.

I once asked Dr. Timothy Leary if he had ever met anyone who had had *a good* belladonna trip. He replied flatly, "No, never."

A Separate Reality

Jimson weed, the only other solanaceae drug easily available in America, has been mentioned previously in connection with the Jamestown freakout and the kids chased by red, white and blue alligators. Further information about it can be found in *The Teachings of Don Juan* and its sequels, by anthropologist Carlos Castaneda. Don Juan Mateus, a Yacqui Indian, trained Castaneda in the traditional technique for becoming an Indian *brujo* (sorcerer), and Castaneda may well be the first white man in history to have obtained this training. The chief teaching devices were peyote, or *lophophora williamsii,* a psychedelic cactus discussed elsewhere in this book; an unidentified "magic mushroom" (probably *psilocybae Mexicana*); and, of course, jimson weed (*datura noxia,* to be technical).

In the course of the training, Castaneda was turned into a crow, flew through the air, and saw colors as (according to don Juan) crows actually do see them. Or, at least, that's what *seemed* to have happened. When Castaneda insisted that it had only *seemed* so, don Juan was amused and indignant and thought it quite typical of a white man to believe ideas from scientific philosophy rather than trust his own experience. Castaneda finally broke off the training because he was beginning to believe don Juan's version of what was happening instead of the officially materialistic version of traditional Western science.

He later returned, however, and underwent further training with don Juan, told in the first sequel, *A Separate Reality.* A note on the wording of this title is quite charming:

> I have used the word "reality" because it was a major premise in don Juan's system of beliefs that the states of consciousness produced by the ingestion of any of those three plants were not hallucinations, but concrete, although unordinary, aspects of the reality of everyday life. Don Juan behaved toward these states of nonordinary reality not "as if" they were real but "as" real.

One detects some conflict between Castaneda's scientific restraint and the intensity of his experiences of that "separate reality"—his own backdoor to Eden, as it were. The same conflict, magnified, was evident in Dr. Timothy Leary who once resolved it by frankly junking science and setting up shop as a high priest of a new church, then decided religion was always bunk and returned to science. Traces of this, as we will see, appear in anyone who has had a strong dose of a mind-expanding chemical.

A Separate Beauty

The same issue appeared as early as the Fourth Century BC, in Euripides' *Bacchae,* mentioned earlier. As a rationalist, Euripides seems to sympathize with King Pentheus as that tragic hero denounces the superstition and gullibility of those who think they see the god Dionysus after drinking these chemicals. As a poet, however, Euripides gives all the best and most lyrical lines to the chorus of bacchantes who sing the praises of that god, whose "loveliness shall be loved forever."

And it is loveliness—at least in the majority of trips—that breaks down the line between "reality" and "hallucination." Charles Darwin said, quite correctly, that the sense of beauty is a development of the sex drive—that is, it is a function developed as part of mating rituals. Certainly, we would not be aware of beauty at all if we were sexless creatures. (Note how the early Christian ascetics, who became as sexless as it is possible for beings of mammalian nature to make themselves, lost all sense of natural beauty and raged against the earth as "dark," "diabolical," "foul," and "putrid.")

Merely to see Dionysus—or Mescalito, the god of don Juan—or any divinity—would mean nothing to any person of normal skepticism or scientific training. One knows that one is hallucinating, and that's all there is to the matter. But to see Dionysus glorified—to see a beauty that transcends anything one had ever imagined possible before—is not so easily dismissed. Where did this wonderful experience—this back door to Eden, this "loveliness that shall be loved forever"—come from? Not from one's conscious mind, which has never conceived such wonders. (It is precisely their shocking sense of being alien that gives them their conviction.) From the unconscious then? Not from Freud's unconscious, certainly; these heavenly creatures do not inhabit that hellhole. Where then? Perhaps from Jung's conjectured "collective unconscious," that seedbed of timeless wisdom and art; or, as Dr. Leary suggests, from the DNA molecule that is coded in our genes along with the chemical triggers that make us white or black, tall or short, male or female, and so on.

But, even if this explanation be granted, the wonder and the beauty of some of these images continue to haunt the drug experimenter. As Jung himself has said, "It is pointless to deny the gods, when confronted with forces that act just as the gods are supposed to act."

To say that these beings are not gods but timeless genetic archetypes is merely to juggle with semantics, to replace one large mouthful with another. Ultimately, *what* they "are" is less striking than the power they possess.

And, if they are beautiful, we have Darwin's authority to believe that they are connected somehow with our sexual drives.[1]

---

[1] Before dropping witchcraft and the solanaceae drugs, it is worth mentioning that John Dickson Carr has written a detective thriller, called *The Crooked Hinge,* revolving around a revival of witchcraft in which the members drink belladonna and imagine they are flying around on broomsticks or copulating with demons. Carr cooked this plot up before the current occult revival—his book was published in 1937! It's still reprinted frequently in paperback and is worth your time. The surprise ending is a lulu.

Divorce Psychedelic Style: The Story of Tom & Jerri

It is a lie, this folly against self...
Thou hast no right but to do thy will...
— *The Book of the Law*

Tom and Jerri were the only middle-class sharecroppers I ever met.

Tom had a Ph.D. in aeronautical engineering and a good career at one of our biggest defense industries when he got hit by Marxism and religion in 1959. He caught them both at the same time and they made a strange blend. He actually quit his job, took his wife, Jerri, and their two children, and became a sharecropper in Alabama. It was some sort of penance for having spent several years designing intercontinental ballistic missiles for the capitalists.

Curiously, it was Dorothy Day, "the grand old lady of the peace movement" as Ed Sanders sardonically calls her (she's the co-founder of the Catholic Worker Movement and the most uptight puritan in left-wing politics), who inspired Tom's rupture from straight society. I say this is curious, because Tom's break was to escalate steadily throughout the 1960s and to take him much further from the means and norms of American society than Dorothy Day has ever been.

Jerri went through the same conversion process, although having had a liberal arts education she was already much closer to the norm than any Ph.D. in science could ever be. Tom, you must always remember, started his rebellion from a framework in which the following theories are held: The length of an object is not *in* the object but in its relationship to the observer (Einstein); light is basically waves but is also basically particles (Bohr); the shortest distance between two points is not a straight line (Fuller); and some particles get from one place to another place without passing through the places in between (Planck). It is not hard for a modern physicist or mathematician to believe in the LSD world.

But LSD comes later in this story; in 1959, Tom and Jerri had just found socialist Christianity and were determined to act out Debs' famous declaration, "As long as there is a lower class, I am part of it" by becoming sharecroppers.

It is easy to overestimate the "simplicity" of such persons. Anyone seeing Tom and Jerri in the early 1960s, toiling at the menial tasks of Southern sharecroppers, pathetically trying to distribute radical newspapers to their hostile or indifferent neighbors, blandly aloof from the possible economic advantages of their college educations, would have regarded them as hopeless innocents in this wolfish world. It is well to remember that Leo Tolstoy, who, for a time, lived as a serf, was not so naive and childish as "tough-minded realists" like to think; his *War and Peace* is one of the most probing psychological examinations of human motivation ever attempted.

Those were the years of the Freedom Riders, but they were also the years of infatuation with Fidelismo among radical youth. Somehow, by slow stages, Tom and Jerri moved away from the Christian socialism of Dorothy Day and embraced the revolutionary socialism of Castro and the charismatic Che Guevara. Their "martyrdom" as voluntary sharecroppers now seemed as romantic and pointless to them as it probably does to the average straight American, although for different reasons. They returned to the big city to work with other *Fidelistos* and create a revolution in America.

I had met them while I was writing a piece on the revival of the Ku Klux Klan, and now I helped them find a pad in the kind of neighborhood where they would have fellow-radicals as neighbors.

In the mid-1960s, that meant a neighborhood where they would also have hippies as neighbors.

Of course, this was initially an irritation to them. Your *Fidelisto* of that era regarded the dope cult with no more affection than did J. Edgar Hoover, and for the same reason: it was a distraction from the real problems of the world, all of which concern the acquisition and retention of power. Tom would lecture his neighbors on the subject:

"You kids are really playing Wall Street's game," he would say with the shrewd expression and soft drawl he had acquired or affected since his sharecropper days. "They want you to stay high all the time. The last thing they want is for you to sober up and start doing the real hard work of making a revolution."

"Revolution sucks," one of them would reply, and the others would break into helpless giggles.

Tom would shake his head in grief at the infantilism of these kids who were, on the whole, quite bright and could have been hard-working activists of socialism if the damned dope hadn't ruined them. Of course—as I sometimes pointed out to him— they might also have been Wall Street lawyers, "if the damned dope hadn't ruined them."

But *Yippie* was already a gleam in Abbie Hoffman's eye; some hard SDS theoreticians were already smoking a joint now and then with the dopers, hoping to become closer to them and gradually lead them into the correct Marxist paths; and the potheads who were busted and spent some time in jail tended to come out with more willingness to listen to radical agitprop, especially if it had a strong anti-cop bias to it. The Black Panther Party's polemical panchreston, "pig," was even beginning to appear in some white vocabularies. And then, Eldridge Cleaver, who was a god in those days, announced that although heroin was rejected by the Panthers, they had no objection to marijuana.

The dopers and the politicos began their honeymoon, which wasn't to end until Cleaver placed Dr. Leary under "revolutionary arrest" in Algiers in 1970.

And in the late 1960s, as the dopers became radicalized, many of the Marxists began sampling various drugs. My friends Tom and Jerri, formerly Christian radicals and now dialectical materialists, were part of this weird chapter in the history of American socialism.

Things had certainly changed since the days when John F. Kennedy was President. In those romantic Camelot years, radical students thought that a few more demonstrations would force the government to reform and abandon its evil ways, and my friend Jane was spending weeks trying to find LSD in Manhattan. Now Lyndon Johnson glowered above us like some Moloch, radicals talked constantly of "taking up the gun," and acid was no harder to get than a haircut and far more common in youth-kulch or red-rad circles.

Tom's first acid trip was a fizzle. He took only a psycholytic dose (100 micrograms—"mikes," everybody was saying by then) and, when he told me of his experience, it was obvious that his mind had been expanded no further than if he had smoked a joint of marijuana.

This no longer surprised me. I had seen other such cases since Jane had toiled her way upward through hashish and peyote in desperate search of *feelings.* I even had a rule-of-thumb about it: Frigid women and Marxist men were the ones who required the heaviest doses to turn on. I assumed that this had some connection with the chronic muscular tensions holding back emotions that the Reichian and Gestalt psychologists discuss.

"Acid is bad for some people," I warned him. "Especially for people with a lot of morality, like you. But," I added, wondering why I encouraged him, "if you really want to have *the experience,* take a stiffer dose." (The adjectives "psychedelic" or "peak" had disappeared by then and people were merely saying *"the* experience.")

The thought of a psychedelized Tom probably intrigued me. I had been with him once when he had tried to take Jerri and their five-year-old son into a movie theater that only admitted children over six. Joey could easily have passed for seven or older, but when the ticket-seller asked the boy's age, Tom said "five." Joey cried all the way home; he had wanted to see the movie.

"We revolutionaries must have the highest ethic in the world if we're going to inspire the masses," Tom had explained to me, in thoroughly humorless fashion. "There can be no exceptions."

Pity, for even his own son could not interfere with such rectitude.

I would hate to have him as an enemy.

Tom's second trip was a success. I walked in while it was in progress and, as is always the case with a good acid scene, I found that the trippers seemed much more beautiful than absurd. Tom, Jerri, a young revolutionary named Simon who was temporarily crashing in their pad, and a girl from across the hall were all laughing, crying and laughing again every few minutes.

Tom blew my mind, and perhaps his own, by shouting suddenly, "You know, Rockefeller can keep all the fucking *oil* and *money*. This makes even Marxism seem trivial to me." He looked guilty immediately afterward, and then laughed again.

I have never forgotten that moment. Tom had reverted to Marxism and revolution by the next morning (although that moment of heresy was a harbinger of things to come, as we shall see), but the experience was a shocking example of the power of LSD to alter consciousness. I have seen two successful "middle Americans" announce, while on acid, that money isn't so important after all, but this was the only time I ever heard a Marxist make that statement.

The next occasion on which I met Tom (at an automat), he was full of enthusiasm, new ideas, wild plans and general euphoria. He and Jerri were tripping fairly regularly and smoking a lot of grass as well.

"I used to be so *mental*," he said, tapping his forehead disapprovingly. "Now I'm beginning to *live*."

I had heard that from other acidheads. I pointed out that American Indians and others who regularly employ psychedelics in religious rites tend to restrict such inner space voyages to four times a year (the solstices and equinoxes) or, at most 13 times (the full moons). "There's probably more than astrology behind that," I said. "People who do acid every week tend to get a bit weird. It shouldn't be overdone."

"Bullshit," Tom said cheerfully. "Leary does acid every weekend and he's in fine shape."[1]

---

[1] Nobody can take an acid trip more than about once a week, whatever you may have read in the tabloids. This is because LSD has an

I had heard that before, too. Some of the people I had heard it from were no longer in fine shape, although, to tell the truth, I had yet to see anybody utterly destroyed by LSD in the manner pictured in government propaganda. Nevertheless, some of them did become peculiar after several months on the trip-a-week plan.

One advertising copywriter had confided to me, after six months of relentless tripping, that he was now in daily communication with the flying saucer people from outer space. Then he added cautiously, "But don't tell that to anyone else. They might think I'm crazy."

(Is that a psychotic delusion? When I asked him how sure he was that his messages were coming from outer space and not inner space, he answered, "Man, I'm not sure of *any*thing anymore!" Was that expression of universal agnosticism a proof that he had retained some skepticism and therefore sanity? Or does it just show that he had a "defended psychosis" as some psychiatrists would say? To me, such questions are less interesting than the actual effects of such mental processes. He, like most acidheads, eventually abandoned his career; and, like many of them, he is now successful in a new career. He's directing movies.)

The upshot of Tom and Jerri's acid voyaging was not long in arriving. Typical of acidheads and of the general "upfront" ethos of the counterculture in those years, they were talking about it frankly to all their friends.

"We never did dig each other sexually," Tom might say. "It was all an intellectual relationship, because we had the same *ideas,* dig? The same *ideas*! Christ, what a lousy way of relating!"

"I was a virgin when we got married," Jerri would add, with a trace of anger. "God! How baroque!"

"But now we know *who we are,*" Tom would break in, "and we know *what we want.* And we're way outside all that *personal property* horseshit. She doesn't own me, and I don't own her."

---

unusual "tolerance" effect, which comes on quickly and goes away just as quickly. In general, anyone who takes a dose of acid within three or four days after his last trip will get no effect at all. A waiting period is, therefore, built into the drug.

Anarchist books had begun popping up on their shelves between the Marxist classics; anarchist phrases began to appear in their conversation, sandwiched between samples of Marxist jargon.

"The important thing," Jerri would clarify further, "is that *you can't do good unless you feel good.*"

"Stalin fucked up socialism in Russia because he didn't understand that," Tom might add at this point. "And all the old lefties with tight assholes are fucking up the movement in this country for the same reason. There can be no political revolution without a sexual revolution." Obviously, they'd been cracking the works of Reich and Abbie Hoffman as well as those of the anarchists. Acid had an odd way (it sometimes seems) of directing people toward those ideologies compatible with the acid experience itself.

What it all came down to, minus rhetoric, was that their *commitment to each other,* and their children, was keeping them together. Sexually they were living like two bachelors (or a bachelor and a bachelorette). It seemed to me that they were doing, as a married couple in their early thirties, what less dedicated people do as swinging singles in their early twenties. In short, what the altruistic ethics of Christianity and socialism had kept them from enjoying in youth, they were now recapturing desperately.

My good friend Joel Fort, M.D., a rare bird who is both a psychiatrist and a sociologist, repeatedly tells me, when I recount such tales to him, that there is no scientific proof of cause-and-effect LSD influence in these transformations. "There is no proof," he repeats, "that a drug alone causes such changes. All the evidence suggests, rather, that the *ideas* that are fashionable in the drug-using world are the causative factor in such conversions."

I am inclined to agree. A different view, however, is put forth by Dr. Andrew I. Malcolm, a Canadian psychiatrist who claims that LSD is an agent that specifically inclines people toward "alienation." According to Dr. Malcolm, if you give enough acid to anybody, he will tend to enter "an altered state of consciousness" and will find the counterculture more attractive than the majority culture. Timothy Leary, Ph.D., as is well-known, agrees with Dr. Malcolm, except that he emphatically thinks this change is for the better, and Dr. Malcolm inclines to think it is for the worse. (He calls LSD "illusionogenic," apparently thinking that "hallucinogenic" is not pejorative enough.)

The working hypothesis of Czechoslovakian psychiatrists who have been using LSD in therapy for several years is that this chemical (at least temporarily), destroys conditioned reflexes. That is, if you have been conditioned (trained) to hate Mexicans, or to repress your sexual drives, or to feel inferior to any male taller than yourself, these reflexes will, at least temporarily, vanish during a session with a heavy dose of LSD. Thus, if you want to change one of these reflexes, the chemical will—according to this theory—at least give you a head start in that direction.

The reader can decide for himself which, if any, of these four theories best accounts for the subsequent, post-acid career of Tom and Jerri.

Once having embarked on the Sexual Revolution, these serious-minded sensualists proceeded with the relentless dedication of de Sade himself, although without his perversity.

One day, about a year after all this began Tom was telling me how much his life had improved since he had discovered acid and free love.

"How many women have you balled in the last year?" I asked curiously.

"Seventy-three," he said promptly. It didn't surprise me that he had the exact number in the forefront of his consciousness. I felt sure that he would hold a special celebration when the number reached 100.

"And how many were there in your life before acid?"

"Two," he said, a bit embarrassed. "Jerri and one other before her."

"Well," I said thoughtfully, "there's no doubt that in your case LSD was an aphrodisiac, of sorts."

"It was for my sister, too," he said. "She was a virgin when I balled her. Twenty-four and still a virgin! She might have ended up frigid if it weren't for LSD."

"Oh, you balled your sister?"

"Yes," he said proudly, "and she was the best lay I've ever had." He stared straight into my eyes, daring me to reveal middle-class hangups by looking shocked. "It did her a world of good," he added. "She might have ended up a Republican, like the rest of my family."

I wasn't at all sure that LSD and incest would always prevent people from becoming Republicans, but I didn't express my skepticism. Like most 1960s radicals, Tom was firmly committed to the dogma that everybody in the Establishment or straight culture, from J. Edgar Hoover down to each and every person who dared to live in a suburb, was hopelessly sunk in Victorian taboos. He never would believe that many of them talked that way only in public, but behaved much the same as he did in private, with a few minor changes, such as replacing LSD with bourbon.

It was after about two years of this program (with Jerri participating as eagerly as he), that Tom told me, reflectively, that sexual freedom had really helped his marriage.

"We're closer than ever," he said flatly.

I had heard that before—and usually, in my observations, the marriage broke up completely shortly thereafter.

"Closer in what sense?" I asked.

"Oh, you're going to put me in one of your books," he said in his sharecropper's twang. Writers' friends are always suspecting that—and they're usually right.

"Maybe," I said. "But I *am* curious. How do you feel that you and Jerri are closer?"

"We don't quarrel at all anymore," he said proudly. "Never. We have a complete understanding of each other's needs, and there's nothing to quarrel about."

"Are you sexually more compatible?" I prompted.

"Well, not exactly. Fact is, I haven't been in the same bed with her for five or six months now. But," he emphasized, "we like each other, we don't fight, and the kids are having a fine home life.

Divorce psychedelic style, I thought. But it seemed to be satisfactory to them, so how was I to judge it from outside? It was none of my business, really. Probably it was better than the normal divorce with its associated rages, hostilities and lingering grudges.

The years passed, I took my family to Mexico for a while, and then one day I was in the editorial of office of a prominent magazine for men and on the desk of a friend who worked there I saw an outline of a proposed article—by Tom of all people. He was the last man on earth I would have expected to blossom forth as an author. I asked if I could look at it, and the editor pushed it over to me.

The article was a plea for Sexual Revolution, but with a difference.

Tom's old scientific training, so long repressed by politics, had come back in a curious form, and he demonstrated that with normal sexual functioning over a lifetime every man could be linked with (I think) 5000 women and every woman with 50,000 men and the "amative ties" between any two people in our three-and-a-half billion world population would, by 2000 AD, be reduced to about four. That is, very concretely, if everybody followed his program, in the year 2000 any man or woman in, say, Peoria, Illinois, would be part of a four-person chain of sex that should include somebody, in, say, Canton, China, or Paris, France. The "extended family" found in some communes today would then be virtually planet-wide. There were demographic and sexological tables to prove the mathematical soundness of this, but behind it was the huge unproven assumption that people would not kill other people who had balled with somebody who had balled with somebody who had balled with somebody that they had balled.

This remarkable piece of religio-statistical sexology was datelined from "The Church of One Flesh," whose address was given as the boardwalk in Coney Island. Obviously, the church was a reconverted grocery store or hardware shop. I wondered how many followers the Reverend Tom had and how long it would be before the cops started harassing him.

There was not a word in the whole article about capitalism or socialism or anarchism or even Yippieism. *Good sex and plenty of it will solve all humanity's problems*—that assumption, which is half-stated and half-believed in a good share of recent radical sociology—was here taken with a mathematician's literalness and carried out to its logical conclusion. All other panaceas or reforms were studiously ignored. This was the Sexual Revolution at its apotheosis.

LSD was, I think, an intellectual aphrodisiac in this case.[1]

---

[1] I later encountered Jerri again; she was living in a rural commune in New Jersey. She told me that she and Tom were still friendly and that he visited her and the children frequently. As for his religion, she was tolerant but seemed more interested in traditional hatha-yoga for herself.

3

The Smoke of the Assassins

High Thats Hight Uberking Leary his fiery grass-belonghead
all show colour of sorelwood herb-green...
— James Joyce, *Finnegans Wake*

When Marco Polo returned to Europe after his epic journey
across Asia to China, he brought with him the three products that
seem to define the modern world: gunpowder, paper and spaghetti. He also brought many colorful yarns, and one of the most
bizarre of all concerned Hasan i Sabbah, the founder of the Order
of Assassins (in Arabic, the word means "under the influence of
hashish") which he ruled from his mysterious fortress, Alamut,
high in the peaks of Afghanistan.

By all accounts, Hasan, born in the middle of the 11th Century, was a remarkable man even in his youth. At college, he had
impressed all with his intelligence, and, while still a student, he
struck up a friendship with Omar Khayyam, who was later to become an astronomer and poet of great fame. Hasan went into the
government and rose to an important position—but was then disgraced and forced to flee, evidently because of strong evidence
that he had been embezzling funds. (One account—not sympathetic to Hasan—states flatly that this was a frame-up by other
government officials, jealous of Hasan's rapid advancement.)
After this, he embarked on a series of journeys that were to lead
him all over the Middle East. He eventually sailed from Palestine

to Egypt, arriving in Cairo in 1078. There he enrolled in one of Islam's most famous colleges. It was a school of mental-spiritual training run by the Ismailian sect, who were generally regarded as heretical and were often persecuted by more orthodox Moslems. The knowledge that Hasan i Sabbah gained there probably played a large role in his subsequent bizarre career, for it seems that he became—900 years before Dr. Timothy Leary—*a skillful programmer of other people's drug trips, especially erotic trips.*

The Ismailian sect, at that time, had nine degrees through which the candidate for wisdom had to pass. Details on all of them are not available, but those facts that we do know indicate that at one stage the candidate was induced to grovel in utter gullibility, believing everything his *imam* (teacher) told him, while at a later stage he was led to suspect that everything the *imam* said was a flat lie. There was also a stage at which the Koran was explained as an allegory and Allah Himself, Supreme God of All, was described as a mere symbol of the awakened or illuminated human mind at its peak of development.

This method of training, in which the student is forced into absolute subjugation and infantile dependence on the teacher at various intervals, but is finally catapulted into total self-realization and independence, is not unlike that often used in yoga, in Zen Buddhism, and even by American Indian *brujos* like don Juan Mateus, mentioned earlier. Behind it is a notion that (as Ezra Pound once said) "a slave is a man waiting for somebody else to free him." The subject must eventually issue his own "declaration of independence"; until he does, the teacher makes his slavery as miserable as possible, so as to encourage that act of creative rebellion.

Hasan i Sabbah junked this entire system when he became *imam* of the Ismailian movement. In its place he put—but let Marco Polo tell the tale:

> In the centre of the territory of the Assassins there are deli-cious walled gardens in which one can find everything that can satisfy the needs of the body and the caprices of the most ex-acting sexuality. Great banks of gorgeous flowers and bushes covered with fruit stand amongst crystal rivers of living water. About them lie verdant fields and from the shaded turf burst bubbling springs. Trellises of roses and fragrant vines cover

with their foliage pavilions of jade or porcelain furnished with Persian carpets or Grecian embroideries.

Delicious drinks in vessels of gold or crystal are served by young boys or girls, whose dark unfathomable eyes cause them to resemble the Houris, divinities of that Paradise which the Prophet promised to believers. The sound of harps mingles with the cooing of doves, the murmur of soft voices blends with the sighing of the reeds. All is joy, pleasure, voluptuousness and enchantment.

The Grand Master of the Assassins, whenever he discovers a young man resolute enough to belong to his murderous legions, invites the youth to his table and intoxicates him with the plant *hashish.* Having been secretly transported to the pleasure gardens, the young man imagines that he had entered the Paradise of Mahomet. The girls, lovely as Houris, contribute to this illusion. After he has enjoyed to satiety all the joys promised by the Prophet to his elect, he falls again into a lethargy and is transported back to the presence of the Grand Master. Here he is informed that he can enjoy perpetually the delights he has just tasted if he will take part in the war of the Infidel as commanded by the prophet.

The Peak Experience

Considering that hashish does not generally work in the fashion suggested here—in which sleep or unconsciousness evidently supervenes between the administration and the transportation to the Eden-like garden, the typical hashish high occurs then, and sleep supervenes once again before the youth is returned to the *imam*—one must assume that Marco Polo knew only part of Hasan's secret. As Dr. Michael Aldrich has written, the Ismailian college in Cairo was known to pursue the most advanced alchemical studies of the time, and there is good reason to suspect that Hasan had learned there how to combine hashish with other chemicals to produce this unique sequence. Specifically, Dr. Aldrich suggests that the candidates were given a *time-release capsule* that first released soporifics or narcotics, producing the original period of sleep; the hashish followed later, and, much later, another soporific produced the second sleeping period.

It is also likely that Hasan had calculated the whole program, including his exhortations to the candidate, and probably every word and action of the lovely houris in the garden, to leap up to a "peak experience," as suggested in Figure 2 of Chapter One.

Many writers have ignored these points and have treated the whole story as an example of the gullibility of the Arabs of that time. This is hardly historical; the Moslems, who were far ahead of the West in science and philosophy then, had known about hashish for centuries before Hasan (perhaps since the Stone Age) and were not to be taken in by any confusion between a mere administration of that drug and a genuinely transcendental experience. Hasan, we must assume, anticipated modern psycho-pharmacology in realizing that control of *set* and *setting*—i.e., environment and the mental attitude of the subject—was necessary to provoke a true "peak" or "psychedelic" experience.

This kind of knowledge has traditionally been possessed by various European occult groups, as we shall see, and has been traced by them back to the Knights Templar, the order that the Catholic Church attempted to destroy for heresy in 1307. (The Crusaders had come into contact with a Syrian branch of the Assassins as early as the 12th Century.) Since contemporary sources accuse the Templars of being secret allies of the Assassins—it was this rumor that led to the investigation that disclosed the Templars' strange forms of sexual worship and pagan dogma—I suggest that it is more plausible to consider the primary source to be Hasan i Sabbah, who had a clear link with hashish and alchemy before the Templars appeared on the scene.

It is worth mentioning in this connection that much of the alchemical literature of Europe now appears to be a coded tradition of drug-and-sex programming. It was Freud's old rival, Carl Gustav Jung, who first suggested that the alchemical texts, nonsensical in terms of modern chemistry, make sense as psychological manuals written in a special symbolism; but Jung never penetrated to the roots of that symbolic language.

This code is especially notable in *The Chemical Marriage of Christian Rosycross* (1615), which forms the visible link between traditional alchemy and modern Rosicrucianism. The mystical rose and cross from which the Rosicrucians take their name are, in fact, no more or less than the vagina and the penis, respectively—as Henry Miller must have suspected when he entitled his sexual autobiography *The Rosy Crucifixion.* Dark sayings like, "It is only on the Cross that the Rose can bloom" are understood when this code is understood.

(For the curious, here is the rest of the traditional symbolism, as given by Louis T. Culling in his *Manual of Sex Magick*: *cucurbit*—the vagina; *retort*—the same, during copulation; *eagle*—the vagina, or the female mouth, depending on the context; *lion*—the penis; *transmutation*—the sexual "peak experience"; *elixer of life*—the semen; *quintessence*—the semen as transmuted by ritual and ecstasy.) With this code, most traditional alchemical works immediately make sense. Here, for instance, is a passage from Valentine's 1642 *Chariot of Antimony,* on how to accomplish the "Great Work":

> Let the Lion and the Eagle duly prepare themselves as Prince and Princess of Alchemy—as they may be inspired. Let the union of the Red Lion and the White Eagle be neither in cold nor in heat... Now then comes the time that the elixer is placed in the alembic retort to be subjected to the gentle warmth... If the Great Work be transubstantiation, then the Red Lion may feed upon the flesh and blood of the God, and also let the Red Lion duly feed the White Eagle—yea, may the Mother Eagle give sustainment and guard the inner life.

If the last part of this passage still seems obscure, it means that the man should obtain some of his own semen by performing cunnilingus after coitus has been completed. Some of this he himself swallows and some he transmits to the lady, who swallows it via a kiss. This curious rite, which goes back to the Gnostics c. 300 AD, has always been highly regarded by European occultists. Modern psychology might suggest that it is a particularly vivid way of communicating a love that forcibly transcends the sex disgust and loathing of the orthodox Christian.

Occultists insist that there is nothing "symbolic" about this semen eating, however. They claim that the elixer, as they still call it, contains a real spiritual substance that is beneficial when consumed. Aleister Crowley even argued by analogy with another custom that will disturb some readers: the Epicurean habit of eating live oysters. Anyone who has tried this, Crowley insists, will agree that one feels a sense of energy and power that is never experienced when eating cooked meat. This is because the "life force" is still in the oysters he claims. Similarly, the semen contains this "life force" and gives one the extra energy needed to reach Illumination.

Whether this is true or false, the spermophagia (as we might call it) is a booster of the basic effect, which depends really on prolonging the sexual act and concentrating the attention more totally upon it than we usually do. As will be seen later, the cannabis drugs are especially likely to cause this kind of concentration—in which one may even become totally identified with the sex organs and lose all other awareness entirely.

And even that will not inevitably trigger a "peak experience" unless it is accompanied by ritual, self-hypnosis, autosuggestion or some combination of the three.

The Assassin Ethic

Hasan i Sabbah was an original thinker in more ways than one. For instance, he evidently also invented the "sleeper agent" so important in modern espionage. This is a person who enters a given government, works diligently and avoids all connection with the foreign power that he is really serving. After 10 or even 20 years of such exemplary conduct, in which he is slowly promoted and trusted more and more by his nominal superiors, this agent is "activated" by a message from home, and goes to work for his true boss.

The signal used to "activate" one of Hasan's agents, incidentally, was a parchment bearing the symbol:

On receiving this, the agent would immediately kill the man who had been his target throughout those years—the particular shah, prince or general whose personal staff he had been assigned to infiltrate. The weapon was always the same—the celebrated flame dagger that identified the killing as an Ismailian job (which, in current Mafia language, is known as "letting the other guys know where it came from"). It was placed precisely in the throat, while the recipient was asleep. Usually, the agent disappeared like smoke before the body was found.

Such behavior may seem unethical by our standards, but it seemed even worse by the standards of Hasan's own time. In those days, both orthodox Christians and orthodox Moslems believed that the most unpardonable of all sins was to deny your religion verbally; it was for this reason that, even under torture, they would not convert to another faith. Thus, the murders committed by Hasan's agents were less shocking than was their habit of passing themselves off as believers in the faith of whatever court they had been sent to infiltrate. Since Machiavelli, we have all learned to live with such duplicity—especially on the part of governments and their agents—but it definitely seemed beyond the pale to the men of the late Middle Ages. It meant that you literally couldn't trust anyone and that any passing paranoia that flitted through your head might well have a basis in fact.

Hasan made modernists and even post-modernists out of his contemporaries, and they didn't like it at all.

Curiously, there are even some traces of gallantry, or at least restraint, in certain legends of Hasan. One general, for instance, on being ordered to march into Afghanistan and capture Hasan in his mountain stronghold, Alamut, immediately surrounded himself with six men who had earned his total faith through years of service and refused to have anyone but them sleep in his tent. The first morning, he awoke with two flame daggers in his pillow, one on each side of his throat. He wisely resigned his commission and refused to march into Afghanistan.

Novelist William S. Burroughs, an unabashed admirer of the tricky Sabbah, insists that Hasan was strictly a counterpuncher, who only attacked those who were prepared to invade his own territory—chiefly the orthodox Moslems, who couldn't abide Ismailian theology, and the crusading Christians, who couldn't abide any non-Christian theology. Furthermore, Burroughs says, the assassinations, while unnerving and destructive to social confidence, possessed a kind of morality of their own. They saved Hasan from ever sending an army into the field, and thus followed the injunction often put forth by pacifists, that the legitimate target in war is the enemy *leaders,* and not an entire people.

In any event, Hasan's methods worked. The Ismailian sect still exists—still small but now nonviolent—within the community of Moslem sects. Its current leader is the Aga Khan, who is the 47th direct descendant of Hasan i Sabbah himself.

Hasan died in 1124 at a ripe old age. The only person in the room was his favorite disciple, Buzurg Umid, and, according to the contemporary Moslem historian, Juvaini, it was to him that Sabbah spoke his last words: "Nothing is true. All is permitted." Immediately thereafter, says the shocked Juvaini, "Hasan's soul plunged straight to Hell."

The Drug, Hashish

Hashish is, of course, the resin of the Indian hemp plant, technically called *cannabis sativa.* The flowering tips of the same plant, when dried and smoked, are known in our part of the world as marijuana or pot (from Portuguese *potiguaya,* intoxicated, via the earlier name of the plant, which was *potiguaya bush*).

Hash is not the same as pot, however—no more than vodka is the same as beer or a blow on the head from a rock is the equivalent of one from a feather. There are differences of degree, and hash is to ordinary weed as three double martinis are to one small glass of malt liquor.

Hashish is usually smoked but sometimes (as was evidently the case with Hasan i Sabbah) eaten in food. Marijuana is also usually smoked and less often eaten (it tastes especially good in brownies or fudge, in curried dishes, or in spaghetti sauce). A third way of taking cannabis is popular in India and is called *bhang.* This is a kind of milkshake (made of buffalo milk and ice cream) into which a spoonful of the local grass is mixed. In all of these cases, the cannabis product must be cooked before it is eaten or drunk; if it is not cooked first, it will have no effect.

It is traditional, in all books on cannabis, to begin by saying that this drug was first described in a medical work written by the Chinese Emperor Shen Neng in 2737 BC. In it, he recommended the drug for gout, constipation, and absentmindedness. Some specialists in Chinese history believed, for a long time, that Shen Neng was one of the mythical or non-historical emperors. Nevertheless, the only book on drugs that I consulted in researching this tome that did *not* invoke the "imaginary" Shen

Neng was *The Pursuit of Intoxication,* by Dr. Andrew I. Malcolm.

As we mentioned earlier, knowledge of cannabis goes back to at least the New Stone Age, when our ancestors in the Near East buried their dead with specimens of marijuana—perhaps to keep them happy on the voyage to the "other side," or perhaps to bargain with the denizens upon their arrival. This shows the same religious awe for this plant that, according to U.S. government officials, was only invented in the 1960s as an excuse to smoke it.

The *Vedas,* the most ancient Hindu writings, are full of praise for a plant or drug called *soma,* which was said to cure a variety of diseases and to enable the practiced yogi to see God face-to-face. Dr. Michael Aldrich, the most erudite of all historians of cannabis, believes that soma was some form of cannabis drug. It is only fair to add that John Allegro, English philologist, is equally convinced that soma was actually the hallucinogenic mushroom *amanita muscaria* or "fly agaric", and R. Gordon Wasson, the Chairman of the Board of the Morgan Guaranty Trust Co. of New York, who also happens to be one of the world's leading authorizes on mycology (the study of mushrooms), agrees with Allegro.

But whether or not soma was cannabis, it is probable that many other mythical drugs were. Aleister Crowley, the poet-mystic-magician-mountain climber-explorer-hoaxer-big game hunter-homosexual-heterosexual eccentric whom we have several times quoted already, probably knew as much about drugs and mysticism as any man of our century, and the cause of his interest, as told in his essay "The Psychology of Hashish," is worth recounting here.

> In 1898–1899 I had just left Cambridge and was living in rooms in Chancery Lane, honoured by the presence of Allan Bennett (now Bikkhu Ananda Meteyya) as my guest.
>
> Together for many months, we studied and practiced Ceremonial Magic, and ransacked the ancient books and MSS. of the reputed sages for a key to the great mysteries of life and death. Not even fiction was neglected, and it was from fiction that we gathered one tiny seed-fact, which (in all these years) has germinated to the present essay.

Through the ages we found this one constant story. Stripped of its local and chronological accidents, it usually came to this—the writer would tell of a young man, a seeker after the Hidden Wisdom, who, in one circumstance or another, meets an adept; who, after sundry ordeals, obtains from the said adept, for good or ill, a certain mysterious drug or potion, with the result (at least) of opening the gate of the Otherworld. This potion was identified with the Elixer Vitae of the physical Alchemists, or one of their "Tinctures," most likely the "White Tincture" which transforms the base metal (normal perception of life) to silver (poetic conception), and we sought it by fruitless attempts to poison ourselves with every drug in (and out of) the Pharmacopoeia.

Like Huckleberry Finn's prayer, nuffin' come of it.

Eventually, however, Crowley got to the Near East, discovered hashish, and "something came of it." He became convinced that hash was the royal road to these expanded mental states that all mystics seek (and, as we shall see later, he found it especially useful for sexual yoga). His argument against the scientific skeptic, although written in 1907, sounds exactly like the debate that is still going on today:

My dear Professor, how can you expect me to believe this nonsense about bacteria? Come, saith he, to the microscope; and behold them!

I don't see anything.

Just shift the fine adjustment—that screw there—to and fro very slowly!

I can't see—

Keep the left eye open; you'll see better!

Ah!—But how do I know? ...

Oh, there are a thousand questions to ask!

It is fair observation to use lenses, which admittedly refract light and distort vision?

How do I know those specks are not dust?

Couldn't those things be in the air?

And so on.

The Professor can convince me, of course, and the more sceptical I am the more thoroughly I shall be convinced in the end; but not until I have learned to use a microscope. And when I have learned—a matter of some months, maybe years—how can I convince the next sceptic?

Only in the same way, by teaching him to use the instrument.

And suppose he retorts, "You have deliberately trained yourself to hallucination!" What answer have I? None that I know of. Save that microscopy has revolutionised surgery, &c., just as mysticism has revolutionised, again and again, the philosophies of mankind.

The analogy is a perfect one. By meditation we obtain the vision of a new world, even as the world of micro-organisms was unsuspected for centuries of thinking—thinking without method—bricks without straw!

Just so, also, the masters of meditation have erred. They have attained the Mystic Vision, written long books about it, assumed that the conclusions drawn from their vision were true on other planes—as if a microscopist were to stand for Parliament on the platform "Votes Fur Microbes"—never noted possible sources of error, fallen foul of sense and science, dropped into oblivion and deserved contempt.

I want to combine the methods, to check the old empirical mysticism by the precision of modern science.

Hashish at least gives proof of a new order of consciousness, and (it seems to me) it is this *prima facie* case that mystics have always needed to make out, and never have made out.

But to-day I claim the hashish-phenomena as mental phenomena of the first importance; and I demand investigation.

I assert—more or less *ex cathedra*—that meditation will revolutionise our conception of the universe, just as the microscope has done.

Then my friend the physiologist remarks:

"But if you disturb the observing faculty with drugs and a special mental training, your results will be invalid."

And I reply:

"But if you disturb the observing faculty with lenses and a special mental training, your results will be invalid."

And he smiles gently:

"Patient experiment will prove to you that the microscope is reliable."

And I smile gently:

"Patient experiment will prove to you that meditation is reliable ."

So there we are.

Aldous Huxley, Dr. Timothy Leary, Dr. John Lilly, philosopher Alan Watts and several other recent theorists have used this metaphor and this argument, usually without knowing that they were echoing Aleister Crowley.

Varieties of Hashish Experience

An early 19th-Century Englishman, whose adventures are recounted in David Evin's *The Drug Experience,* overdosed himself on hash and quickly developed the illusion that he was a locomotive. Chugging around the room and pumping his arms like pistons, he made his friends nervous and they asked if he might not like a drink of water. "God, no," he cried, "it might blow my boiler!"

More typical was the experience described by French poet Charles Baudelaire, a member of the famous Haschischin Club that met in the Hotel Pimodan in Paris in the 1850s to sample the Arabian drug and compare their experiences. Writing in the third person, in an essay titled "The Artificial Paradise" (our back door to Eden, again!), Baudelaire says:

> None now should be astonished by the final, the supreme thought born in the dreamer's mind—"I have become God!" That ardent, savage cry bursts from his lips with so intense an energy, with so tremendous a power of projection, that, if the will and belief of an intoxicated man had effective virtue, the cry would topple the very angels scattered about along the roads of heaven: "I am a god!" But soon this hurricane of arrogance becomes transformed. A mood of calm, muted and tranquil, takes its place; the universality of man is announced colorfully, and lighted as it were by a sulfurous dawn. If perchance a vague memory reaches the soul of this poor happy man that possibly there is another God, be certain that he will rise up and question *His* commands and that he will face him without terror. Who is the French philosopher who said, with the intention of mocking modern German doctrines, *"I am a god who has dined poorly"*? This irony would not touch a man intoxicated by hashish. He would reply: *"Perhaps I did dine poorly, yet I am a god."*

A friend of mine once described a very similar feeling about food, although it didn't quite give him the sense of becoming God. While under the influence of hashish, he suddenly got the "munchies" well-known to all cannabis users and remembered that there were some delicious donuts in the pantry. Alas, when he went to look for them, the donuts were all gone, having been eaten by his house guests earlier in the day. He thereupon sat down and began chewing on flat, ordinary white bread—the dullest food in the world—and, since the milk had also been used up, he drank water with it. Suddenly he realized that he was enjoying this repast immensely, incredibly, ecstatically—more than he had ever enjoyed any food in his life. "For the first time," he told me, "I understood the saints who said that they could live on bread and water and be happier than the millionaire dining on caviar, fava beans and cognac."

(A contemporary theory, developed by Dr. Robert DeRopp, Dr. Humphrey Osmund, Dr. Abraham Hoffer and others, holds that the great mystics—and some varieties of psychotics, or persons diagnosed as psychotic—are manufacturing the equivalent of a psychedelic drug in their own glands. It is suspected that "pink adrenaline"—a mutation of ordinary adrenaline, which is produced under prolonged stress—may be the agent involved, although a further mutation after "pink adrenaline" is assumed by other investigators. This substance, also called adrenochrome, bears a distinct chemical resemblance to LSD and, even more, to mescaline, the active drug in the peyote cactus. The natural consequence, which is the possibility of becoming high on the plasma of schizophrenics, is imaginatively and bizarrely explored in Terry Southern's short story, "The Blood of a Wig," in which the hero tries this novel form of vampirism, turns on with blood siphoned out of a patient in Bellevue Hospital's schizo ward—one "Chin Lee," formerly a famous "symbolist poet"—and has a vision of Lyndon Baines Johnson performing necrophilia on the neck wound of the corpse of John F. Kennedy. According to stand-up comic and editor Paul Krassner, this story was suggested by the experience of a *Newsweek* reporter, who actually did have that gruesome vision while tripping on LSD.)

Returning to hashish, another member of the Parisian Haschischin Club was the poet Theophile Gautier. Here's a sample from his account of a memorable trip:

> A certain numbness overcame me. My body seemed to dissolve and I became transparent. Within my breast I perceived

the hashish I had eaten in the form of an emerald scintillating
with a million points of fire. My eyelashes elongated indefinitely, unrolling themselves like threads of gold on ivory spin-
dles which spun of their own accord with dazzling rapidity.
Around me poured streams of gems of every color, in ever
changing patterns like the play within a kaleidoscope. My
comrades appeared to me disfigured, part men, part plants,
wearing the pensive air of Ibises. So strange did they seem that
I writhed with laughter in my corner, and overcome by the
absurdity of the spectacle, flung my cushions in the air, making them turn and twist with the rapidity of an Indian juggler.

The first attack passed and I found myself again in my
normal state without any of the unpleasant symptoms that
follow intoxication with wine. Half an hour later I fell once
again under the domination of hashish. This time my visions
were more complex and more extraordinary. In the diffusely
luminous air, perpetually swarming, myriad butterflies rustled
their wings like fans. Gigantic flowers with calyxes of crystal,
enormous hollyhocks, lillies of gold or silver rose before my
eyes and spread themselves about me, with a sound resembling that of a fireworks display. My hearing became prodi-
giously acute. I actually listened to the sound of the colors.
From their blues, greens and yellows there reached me sound
waves of perfect distinctness. A glass inverted, the creak of an
armchair, a word pronounced in a deep voice vibrated and
rumbled about me like the reverberations of thunder. My own
voice seemed so loud that I dared not speak for fear of shatter-
ing the walls with its bomblike explosion. More than five hundred clocks seem to announce the hour in voices silvery,
brassy or flutelike. Each object touched gave off a note like
that of a harmonica or an aeolian harp. Floating in a sonorous
ocean like luminous islands, were motifs from *Lucio* and the
Barber of Seville. Never has greater beauty immersed me in its
flood. I was so lost in its waves, so separated from myself, so
disembarrassed of my ego, that odious appendage that accom-
panies us everywhere, that for the first time I understood the
nature of existence of elementals of angels and spirits separated from the body. I hung like a sponge in the midst of a
warm sea; at each moment waves of happiness traversed me,
entering and emerging by my pores. Because I had become
permeable my whole being became tinged by the color of the
fantastic medium in which I was plunged. Sounds, lights, per-
fumes reached me through tendrils fine as hairs in which I

heard magnetic currents vibrating. By my calculation, the state lasted about three hundred years for the sensations which followed one another were so numerous and pressing that any real appreciation was impossible. The rapture passed... I saw that it had lasted just a quarter of an hour.

A third rapture, the last and most bizarre, terminated my Oriental soiree. In this one my vision doubled itself. Two images of every object were reflected on my retina in perfect sympathy. Soon the magic ferment began once again to act with power on my mind. For a full hour I became completely insane. In Pantagruelian dreams I saw passing by me creatures of fantasy, owls, sea storks, satyrs, unicorns, griffins, vultures, a whole menagerie of monsters trotting, gliding, vaulting, yelping about the room... The visions became so baroque that a desire to draw them took hold of me. In less than five minutes I made a sketch of Dr. X ... who appeared to me seated at the piano, dressed as a Turk with a sunflower on the back of his waistcoat. My drawing represented him emerging from the keyboard in the form of a corkscrew of capricious spirals. Another sketch bore the legend "an animal of the future," and represented a living locomotive with the neck of a swan terminated by the jaws of a serpent from which emerged billows of smoke and monstrous paws composed of wheels and pulleys. Each pair of paws was accompanied by a pair of wings and above the tail of the animal hovered the antique god Mercury, who advanced upon it victoriously in spite of its talons. By the grace of hashish I had been able to draw a "farfardet" from nature.

There was a hashish club in New York City at the same time—a little-known fact recently unearthed by that prodigious researcher of drug history, Dr. Michael Aldrich—but none of the members left behind any literary accounts of their adventures. All one can say with certainty, since the members lived in the United States when cannabis drugs were known only to a small percentage of the populations, is that they would be quite astonished to see that, a hundred years later, their diversion had become a federal crime.

Hashish & Sex

It stands to reason that a drug that will magnify sensation and externalize one's fantasies, as we have seen hashish do, will be a most powerful enhancer of the sex act if the experimenter's mind is open to its possibilities in advance. Such is indeed the case.

Some writers try to deny this, evidently fearful that any admission of the "aphrodisiac" properties of hash will encourage further usage of an illegal chemical. The best that such people can do to rebut the obvious facts is to make a highly artificial distinction between experience and impression. If the hashish user says that he saw brighter colors, they correct this to "he imagined brighter colors"; should he say that his sense of touch was more acute, they will write that "he imagined his sense of touch was more acute"; if he experiences a cosmic vision, they become especially arch and tell us "he imagined he was having all sorts of mystical insights."

This sort of skepticism cuts a hair so fine that it makes Einstein look bald. In ordinary language and by ordinary philosophy there is no such distinction between one's experience and one's impression of that experience. Certainly, I may imagine that I have a million dollars when I do not—and that is certainly an illusion, and a dangerous one if I start writing checks while still in its grip. But is there any sense in saying that if red looks brighter to me, then I am only imagining that it looks brighter to me? Or that if my orgasm seems more intense to me, then I am only imagining that it is more intense? Or that I have a delusion that I'm happy, or am hallucinating that I feel great?

Something is wrong when language is stretched to such a breaking point. If a man believes that he is happy and hilarious and grooving on everything around him, the only sane description of his state is to say he's euphoric, not to say that he imagines he is euphoric.

What the skeptic really seems to be claiming is that he knows what the subject feels better than the subject knows—i.e., that the subject doesn't feel what he feels but feels something else. This is the kind of verbal metaphysics that made the medieval theologians become the laughing-stocks of Voltaire and other rationalist critics.

If a man says his orgasm is better, he may be lying, of course, but if he is not lying, then there is no further dissent that can be offered against his declaration. He must be presumed to be the best observer of his own subjectivity.

I have spoken to users of cannabis drugs in virtually every state of the union, in Mexico and in Canada. I have yet to find one user who would definitely contradict Norman Mailer's famous assertion that "sex without pot is never quite as good as sex with pot."

In 1968, the *American Journal of Psychiatry* published "The Marijuana Problem: An Overview," by Dr. William H. McGloth-lin and Dr. Louis Lolyon West. When a study group of users was asked why they continued to smoke the weed, 73 percent of them said to "increase sexual satisfaction."

Barbara Lewis, an Associated Press reporter, interviewed 208 *middle-class adult* users for her book *The Sexual Power of Marijuana,* emphasizing professional and successful persons who were not part of the belief system and fads of the youth culture. Despite all the talk about seeing brighter colors and hearing music better, these people emphasized again and again that pot was valuable to them because it enhanced their sex lives.

Here's the verdict of a 33-year-old woman who works as a laboratory technician:

> Grass helps you get into sex—you are totally uninhibited... You do things that otherwise you might feel very uptight about. You can make love for *an hour and a half* before actually screwing and I don't think you'd do that "straight." [Italics added]

A 31-year-old male research scientist said:

> With pot, sexual intercourse becomes more pleasurable, more relaxed. It makes you a better lover. You feel closer to your partner than you would otherwise. I can feel myself actually fusing with the other person—it is difficult to know even anatomically what part of myself is me and what part is the woman.

A 37-year-old New Jersey computer programmer gave similar testimony:

> With pot, you can feel things you never felt before, like a girl's orgasm. You can feel her vagina spasming. Right from the beginning there's a good awareness of how far along toward orgasm the other person is, so you can get to the same point, go at the same speed. And feeling her orgasm is sensa-

tional. It makes you understand what it's like to be a woman—you can empathize, rather than fantasize.

All of this, of course, is also true of the far more potent form of cannabis known as hashish. Yussef el Masry says emphatically in his *The Sexual Tragedy of the Arab Woman* that "the principal reason" for the popularity of hashish in the Middle East is its "aphrodisiac" properties—although a more complex phrase such as "sex-enhancing" would undoubtedly be more accurate than "aphrodisiac."

As we have suggested earlier, this is part of the key to the enduring popularity of underground "occult" movements such as the witch cult, the alchemists, the Illuminati, various brotherhoods of the Rosy Cross, and so on, which have appeared, disappeared and reappeared throughout European history. The more recent mystic societies (since the mid-19th Century) such as the Order of Paladins, and Ordo Templi Orientis (which guided Wagner in the writing of *Parsifal*) and the super-mysterious A∴A∴[1] are especially *apropos* here. What is called "ritual," "invocation," "evocation," etc., and presented with great mystic mumbo-jumbo and mystery, consists largely of what Dr. John Lilly and Dr. Timothy Leary call "programming" and "metaprogramming"—that is, directing a consciousness-expansion experience to go in a particular desired direction. It is feeding into the 2 1/2 pounds of goo that we call the brain (and which modern psychologists, to show how up-to-date they are, prefer to call the *biocomputer*) precisely those chains of words and images that will trigger the appropriate response.

I am not asserting that there is nothing in the occult tradition other than drugs; on the contrary, there are many techniques of inducing the consciousness expansion trip. Among them are fasting, isolation, sensory withdrawal, sensory over-stimulation, and *pranayama* (slowed breathing, as taught in hatha-yoga). All

---

[1] Only members are allowed to know what those mysterious initials mean. The three dots signify direct descent from Egyptian magic of the dynastic period, and are part of the Illuminati eye-in-the-triangle symbolism (see the back of a U.S. one dollar bill). As part of the same tradition, Masons salute each other with "greetings on all points of the triangle."

these methods are part of occult history—the modern sensory withdrawal tank as used by Dr. John Lilly and other recent researchers, for instance, improves little on the "witch's cradle" of medieval days, which also blots out most of the sensory input and leaves the mind confronting nothing but itself. In all these methods, however, ritual and invocation do help to program the trip; and in some of these schools—following Hasan i Sabbah through various underground traditions—this ritual is superimposed upon a hashish foundation.

For instance, consider the following definition, written in the 19th Century by Kenneth R.H. Mackenzie, a leading English freemason who did much to lead London freemasonry into occult explorations:

> Magic is not a necromanteia—a raising of dead material substances endowed with an imagined life—but a psychological branch of science, dealing with the sympathetic effects of stones, drugs, herbs, and living substances upon the imaginative and reflective faculties—and leading to ever new glimpses of the world of wonders around us, ranking it in due order of phenomena, and illustrating the beneficence of The Great Architect of the Universe.

Considering that Victorian England had the same prejudice against drugs as Nixonian America, but was less paranoid about every reference thereto, one can only admire the careless tone with which Mackenzie drops "drugs, herbs" into the middle of that sentence.

It might be worthwhile to quote, also, a few words from Dr. Michael Brodie-Innes, who, along with Mackenzie, helped organize the Hermetic Order of the Golden Dawn among high-ranking freemasons in England. (Through William Butler Yeats and his circle, the Golden Dawn was to influence the imagery of modern poetry and literature more than any other single source of ideology.) Says Dr. Brodie-lnnes:

> Whether the Gods, the Qlipothic forces or even the Secret Chiefs really exist is comparatively unimportant; the point is that the universe behaves as though they do. In a sense the whole philosophy of the practice of Magic is identical with the Pragmaticist position of Pierce the American philosopher.

I take it that this should persuade the thoughtful reader that at least some of the occultists of the past were conscious that the rites worked on the mind as programs and that to use these rituals did not at all require one to believe that such beings as the Holy Guardian Angel or the various gods had any objective existence. The Mackenzie/Brodie-Innes position, in fact, despite its occult terminology, is virtually identical with that presented, in hyper-modern cybernetic terminology, in Dr. John Lilly's manual for LSD-tripping, *Programming and Metaprogramming in the Human Biocomputer:*

> ... if one plugs the proper beliefs into the metaprogrammatic levels of the computer ... the computer will then construct (from the myriads of elements in memory) those possible *experiences* that fit this particular set of rules. Those programs will be run off and those displays made which are appropriate to the basic assumptions and their stored programming.

In other words, for those who took mind drugs in ancient Athens, with rituals to invoke Dionysus, the experience would have been Dionysian and included a "display" (vision) of a horned or bull-like God. If you took it in a 1960s commune of nature mystics and ecology freaks, you would have experienced the harmony and beauty of nature as deity. And, if you took the same drug in a 1990s research lab, with a warning that it produces a psychotic reaction, you would have the experience of going mad for a few hours.

The Rose & The Cross

From *somewhere* in the dim past, via certain alchemists and Illuminati, the tradition has come down that the best usage for hashish is to invoke a goddess, and that this works especially well if one copulates with a woman one actually loves while performing the ritual mentally. The woman is then transubstanti-ated into the goddess. This is the secret teaching of several occult schools, and it appears that the violent death meted out to sup-posed witches during the Holy Inquisition is the chief reason that the secret has been so closely guarded for so many centuries.

For example, Aleister Crowley writes rather cryptically in his *Confessions*:

Now the [Ordo Templi Orientis]] is in possession of one supreme secret. The whole of its system at the time when I became an initiate of the Sanctuary of the Gnosis (IX°) was directed toward communicating to its members, by progressively plain hints, this all-important instruction. I personally believe that if this secret, which is a scientific secret, were perfectly understood, as it is not even by me after more than twelve years' almost constant study and experiment, there would be nothing which the human imagination can conceive that could not be realized in practice...

It is interesting to recall how it [the secret] came into my possession. It had occurred to me to write a book, *The Book of Lies,* which is also falsely called *Breaks,* the wanderings of falsifications of the one thought ... which is itself untrue... One of the chapters bothered me. I could not write it... In the midst of my disgust, the spirit came upon me and I scribbled the chapter down... When I read it over, I was as discontented as before, but I stuck it into the book in a sort of anger against myself as a deliberate act of spite toward my readers.

Shortly after publication [the Outer Head of the Ordo Templi Orientis] came to me. (At that time I did not realize that there was anything in the O.T.O. beyond a convenient compendium of the more important truths of freemasonry.) He said that since I was acquainted with the supreme secret of the Order, I must be allowed the IX° and obligated in regard to it. I protested that I knew no such secret. He said, 'But you have printed it in the plainest Language.' I said that I could not have done so because I did not know it. He went to the bookshelves and, taking out a copy of *The Book of Lies,* pointed to a passage in the despised chapter. It instantly flashed upon me. The entire symbolism, not only of freemasonry but of many other traditions, blazed upon my spiritual vision. From that moment the O.T.O. assumed its proper importance in my mind. I understood that I held in my hands the key to the future progress of humanity... As soon as I was assured by experience that the new force was in fact capable of accomplishing the theoretically predictable results, I devoted practically the whole of my spare time to a course of experiments.

The secret is hinted at constantly in Crowley's "occult" manuals. For instance, in *Magick in Theory and Practise* (which can best be considered a manual for programming drug trips), we find the traditional rosicrucian rigmarole:

The Cup is said to be full of the Blood of the Saints; that is, every saint or magician must give the last drop of his life's blood to that cup in the true Bridal of the Rosy Cross... *It is a woman whose Cup must be filled...* The Cross is both Death and Generation, and it is on the Cross that the Rose blooms... [Italics added]

Dr. Israel Regardie, writing on behalf of a branch of the Hermetic Order of the Golden Dawn, uses a more traditional alchemical symbolism to hide the same secret:

Through the stimulus of warmth and spiritual fire to the Athanor there should be a transfer, an ascent of the Serpent from that instrument into the Cucurbite, used as a retort. The alchemical marriage or the mingling of the two streams of force in the retort causes at once the chemical corruption of the Serpent in the menstruum of the Gluten, this being the *Solve* part of the general alchemical formula of *Solve et coagula.* Hard upon the corruption of the Serpent and his death arises the resplendent Phoenix which, as a talisman, should be charged by a continuous invocation of the spiritual principal conforming to the work in hand. The conclusion of the Mass consists in either the consumption of the transubstantiated elements, which is the Amarita, or the anointing and consecra-tion of a special talisman.

By some authorities it is roughly estimated that from the preliminary invocation, with the binding of the forces in the elements, to the act of taking the Communion itself from the consecrated Chalice, the operation should not take less than an hour. Sometimes, indeed, a much longer period is required, especially if it is required that the charging of the talisman be complete and thorough.

Dr. Regardie adds the helpful comment that the procedure is "no harder than riding a bicycle." Thanks a lot, doc.

Whether or not one drinks the elixer from the "consecrated Chalice," this basic concept is always the same as the Roman Catholic Mass, except that one is seeking communion with a goddess, not a god, and the physical body of the beloved female partner forms the "magical link" through which the divine pres-ence begins to manifest itself. The ultimate is not merely com-munion with the divinity, but actual *union,* and (no matter how skeptical one may be in advance, or think that one is) this hap-

pens fairly easily with the right programming (ritual) and especially with a good grade of hashish.

(Incidentally, if the reader is wondering what chapter in *The
Book of Lies* contains the passage that caught the attention of the
Ordo Templi Orientis and led them to invite Crowley to join, I
would suggest that it is probably the mysterious, and appropri-
ately named, Chapter 69. Behind the religious symbolism of the
Pentecostal miracle—The Gift of Tongues, Bible commentators
call it—Crowley seems to me to be describing a real incident in
which he had a religious vision while engaged in mutual oral
genitalism with his mistress, Leila Waddel, the violinist. Evidently this was when he first realized that his religious and sexual
interests could be combined and need not be separated. The
chapter number is a typically Crowleyan clue to this secret.
Another is the chapter title, which is a gorgeous pun: "How to
Succeed—And How to Suck Eggs.")

I refer the cynical reader back to the 31-year-old scientist
quoted earlier who said "I can feel myself actually fusing with
the other person—it is difficult to know even anatomically what
part of myself is me and what part is the woman." He was not
even using ritual programming to get that result; the drug alone
led him there, and it was only comparatively weak marijuana,
not the stronger hashish.

Forerunners of Masters-Johnson

This "sexual magic" derives from the Sufis, according to
Louis T. Culling, who as a member of the Great Body of God
and the Order of Paladins and a former member of the Ordo
Templi Orientis probably knows as much of the inner tradition as
anyone living. (The Sufis, like the Gnostics, had an ascetic wing
and a sex-yoga wing.) Religious historians alternatively attribute
it to the Sufis or the Assassins, and quarrel over the question of
whether it came into Europe via the Knights Templar or via the
Albigenses, the heretical movement whose destruction in the
12th Century is generally considered the most bloody episode in
the Middle Ages. (Kenneth Rexroth ironically called it "the
worst atrocity in history, before the invention of Progress.") In
either case, the original orthodox Christian reaction was one of

such murderous hostility that the sex cult had good reasons to go underground and stay there for several centuries.

Behind the Arab influence, it is now agreed by historians of mysticism, was an Indian tradition known as Tantra—the yoga of touch, which includes the yoga of sex and inspired the famous erotic temples that every American tourist photographs to astonish his friends. It is within Tantrism that we must seek the transformation by which this sexual mysticism evolved from naive fertility magic (a rite to make the crops grow) and became a form of consciousness expansion.

The Tantrists, evidently dissatisfied with the asceticism of orthodox hatha-yoga, and perhaps also seeking a quicker path to consciousness elevation, discovered that strange mental results occur when the sex act is deliberately slowed down. They grew so entranced with this process—which does, indeed, lead to peak experiences much more quickly than the other yogas—that they made it central to their cult, and also included a rule against orgasm that has baffled and bothered most commentators. The Sufis and the European occultists relaxed this rule, although still postponing orgasm as far as possible, and through this latter development we can see what the Tantrists were aiming at.

Masters and Johnson, as is well-known, also use a "no orgasm" rule in their therapeutic work, which is intended for couples in which one or both parties suffers from "sexual dysfunction"—that is, conditions popularly called impotence, frigidity or premature ejaculation. (These latter terms are all frightening and degrading to patients, Masters and Johnson have found, so they prefer not to use them.) The essence of their technique, as employed at the Reproductive Biology Research Foundation in St. Louis, is virtually classic Tantrism. That is, the couple is instructed to go to bed, attempt to enjoy each other, but strictly avoid any effort toward orgasm or any position that might lead to orgasm.

The results are astonishing. Over 70 percent of all dysfunctioning couples—where one or both have not had an orgasm in years—often achieve climax within two weeks after starting this Tantric program. The explanation, according to Dr. Masters, is that anxiety about orgasm is the principal cause of failure, and once the anxiety is removed, the natural happens by itself, spontaneously—*tsu-jan*, "of its own nature," as a Taoist would say.

This similarity of the Masters-Johnson therapy to Tantrism is perhaps not so surprising, if we accept the radical notion of the strict Freudians and the disciples of Wilhelm Reich that most people in patriarchal civilizations are somewhat dysfunctional sexually. That is, normal orgasm—D.H. Lawrence's "sneeze in the loins" or the "momentary trick" as it was mournfully called by none other than William Shakespeare—may, in itself, be a sexual dysfunction. This, at any rate, was the opinion of the arch-heretic of modern psychology, Wilhelm Reich, who insisted that the general psychosomatic disease of civilized humanity was "orgastic impotence," the inability to achieve total orgasm, caused by the anxieties implicit in our anti-sexual religions and patriarchal institutions.

Suggestively, Dr. Reich's description of the natural orgasm places great emphasis on certain "pulsations" of "orgone energy," which sounds very much like the "astral vibrations" described by the occultists. We have heard a great deal about "the vibes" ever since psychedelic drugs and the Sexual Revolution swept through the youth of the 1960s.

Masters of Tantric yoga are said to be able to continue the act of love for seven or eight hours or longer. This has nothing at all to do with supposed "secrets of muscle control" allegedly known only to the master yogis, or similar rumors and myths that are published in occult magazines. It is just a mental set, based on the "no orgasm" rule and the attitude taught by Masters and Johnson to their therapeutic subjects. According to Louis Culling, practitioners of traditional sex rituals of European occultism easily learn to prolong the act to two or three hours before allowing the orgasm to take place. (Culling admits that a little cannabis helps in acquiring the proper meditative or trance-like attitude.)

Aleister Crowley, who mastered most of the other techniques of Western occultism and Eastern yoga in his youth, became convinced, after he discovered this sexual yoga in 1906, that it was the quickest and easiest way to consciousness expansion for the average person (who, after all, is not likely to quit his job and enter a monastery for several years while hatha-yoga slowly does its work). It is, therefore, appropriate to terminate this section with some quotations from his *Book of the Law.* The goddess, Nuit, speaks in this passage and what she says is probably the best "invocation" or "program" anyone could need for embarking on sexual experimentation with hashish:

> Every man and every woman is a star... Come forth, o children, under the stars & take your fill of love! I am above you and in you. My ecstasy is in yours. My joy is to see your joy... And the sign shall be my ecstasy, the consciousness of the continuity of existence, the omnipresence of my body...
>
> Be not animal; refine thy raptures. If thou drink, drink by the eight and ninety rules of art: if thou love, exceed by delicacy; and if thou do aught joyous, let there be subtlety therein. But ever unto me—unto me...
>
> For I am divided for love's sake, for the chance of union. This is the creation of the world, that the pain of division is as nothing and the joy of dissolution all...
>
> Do what thou wilt shall be the whole of the law. The word of Sin is Restriction. O man! refuse not thy wife if she will! O lover, if thou wilt, depart! There is no bond that can unite the divided but love: all else is a curse...
>
> Invoke me under my stars! Love is the law, love under will... I give unimaginable joys on earth, certainty not faith while in life; upon death, peace unutterable, rest, ecstasy; nor do I demand aught in sacrifice...
>
> But to love me is better than all things: if under the night-stars in the desert thou presently burn incense before me, invoking me with a pure heart, and the Serpent flame therein, thou shalt come a little to lie in my bosom.
>
> Pale or purple, veiled or voluptuous, I who am all pleasure and purple and drunkenness of the innermost sense, desire you. Put on the wings, and arouse the coiled splendor within you: come unto me... Sing the rapturous love songs unto me! Burn to me perfumes! Wear to me jewels! Drink to me, for I love you! I love you! I am the blue-lidded daughter of Sunset; I am the naked brilliance of the voluptuous night-sky. To me! To me!

From India, with Love

Crowley always claimed that he did not compose these passages as he composed his other books—that they were literally

dictated to him by the goddess, Nuit. Be that as it may, he was
certainly on speaking terms with her, and the ancient Egyptian
concept of this divinity is a clear-cut example of how ancient the
union of sex and religion actually is. Nuit is pictured, in many
surviving frescoes, as the goddess of the sky (hence the starry
imagery Crowley associates with her); and she is frankly shown
in the oral-genital (69) embrace with the god of earth.

This is hardly an oddity in Egyptian religion. Atem, the god
who created the universe, is pictured by them performing that
notable feat in a manner we prudish moderns might find surprising. To be frank about it, he is masturbating, and his semen, as it
spurts forth, is crystallizing into the universe we know. Isis, the
goddess who is invariably compared to the Virgin Mary by students of comparative religion, is best known for the "magic rite"
by which she brought her husband (and brother) Osiris back to
life after Set had foully murdered him. This rite, as shown in
various frescoes, was quite in the Gnostic, alchemical and
Crowleyan mode. She is fellating him—just as if he were President and she an intern.

In this context, I can't resist quoting Sir James Frazer's nice
wording of the rites associated with the yearly celebration of
Osiris' resurrection (which became the Christian Easter). Osiris'
statue was carried through the streets and it showed, says Dr.
Frazer, "in the clearest manner imaginable" that "the generative
power of the god" was still in good working order.

None of this tradition has been lost completely; through the
Manicheans, Gnostics, Albigenses, Knights Templar and various
others, it has always coexisted with Christianity in an underground fashion. The real forerunners of Masters and Johnson,
however, were, as we have indicated, the Hindus, especially
those of the Tantric and Shivite sects.

The famous erotic carvings in certain Hindu temples are acts
of worship. The purpose of the whole gamut of positions is the
same as in Western occultism—union with the goddess, called
Shakti rather than *Nuit* by the Hindus but still the same archetypal figure.

It is hard to resist the conclusion, considering the parallels we
have already noted between Tantrism and the recent studies of
Masters and Johnson, that a great deal of this variety—the

countless positions, far more than the legendary 69 of European reckoning—is in service to the Tantric "no-orgasm" rule. As with Masters and Johnson, this rule may have been intended, originally, to be temporary, until the proper control could be achieved. In any case, the same variety (which Freud once humorlessly called "polymorphous perversity," God save the mark!) almost invariably appears in Occidental sex magic and in those who experiment with sex and hashish.

It might as well be stated frankly that this variety is the largest part of the art of prolonging sex, for most practitioners. The Tantrists also use the tricky "double lotus" and the woman superior position—the man flat on his back, the woman mounted upon his upright penis—and both parties then remain totally unmoving, all sensation depending on her ability to dilate and contract the vaginal barrel rhythmically. (This art, curiously, is known as "the Cleopatra" among New York prostitutes.) But for those who have not mastered this Tantric gimmick, variety is the actual road to the higher ecstasies.

This is where the peculiar properties of hashish seem— according to users—especially noteworthy. *All* sexual dalliance is enhanced (when the drug, the set and the setting are all working together properly). Acts that are usually considered "foreplay" or "variations" are no longer performed only "for the woman" or only "for the man." They become delights to both, and all desire to rush on to coitus appears quite absurd. Not only are oral-genital acts more enjoyable for both the oral and the genital partner, but any oral act is transformed into new dimensions of rapture. This is true not only of ordinary kissing ("For one kiss then, thou wilt gladly give all," Nuit says in *The Book of the Law*) but of such Japanese sports as toe nibbling or even finger sucking. In a word, all bodily contact then becomes sexual— just as it is in the visions of Hieronymous Bosch and Jacob Bohme. One is literally living in the timeless ecstasy suggested by those famous Hindu statues.

The power of this kind of self-programming is indicated by a story about Sinan, the third successor to Hasan i Sabbah as ruler of the Order of Assassins. A visiting ambassador said that his king inspired fervent loyalty in his citizens. "You speak of fervor?" said Sinan. "Watch this!" And he spoke to the nearest guard on the wall of the fortress where this conversation was occurring. Without a word of protest, or a moment of hesitation, the guard threw himself from the wall, over the cliff, into the abyss below. "That is fervor," said Sinan calmly. And that was the result of the backdoor to Eden that Hasan i Sabbah opened with the keys of sex and hashish.

Drug of Choice: The Story of Bill

> I would be far happier if my own teenage children would, *without breaking the law,* smoke marijuana when they wished, rather than start on the road of so many of their elders to nicotine and ethyl alcohol addiction.
>
> — An English Doctor, quoted in *Drugs: Medical, Psychological and Social Facts,* by Peter Laurie

Bill used the word "pig" regularly, but he wasn't a radical. Nor did he mean "policeman" when he said it. "Pig" was his charming way of referring to women.

I met Bill during one of the low points of my life, when I was toiling on Mad Avenue and applying my talents to what I called "pop poetry"—which is a euphemism for advertising copy. Bill had been writing that strange variety of prose for some years and was a master of its peculiar preliterate rhythms. ("This is the new Blotz. It's different. And better. You need a new Blotz. You need it today!") "There's nothing to it," he told me, "it's just Gertrude Stein without the wit."

Bill was a reformed idealist, according to his own description of himself. And, of course, just as the reformed alcoholic can never resist heckling the man who still drinks, Bill was a constant critic of any manifestation of altruism or humanism that came before his attention. "A good deed never goes unpunished," he would warn. "People *stink*. They really do, baby. Stick your neck out for nobody. Take care of Number One."

Like most people with that cast of mind, Bill drank. Since he was a New Yorker and an intellectual of sorts, this was ritualized: He drank only martinis, made exactly to his own specifications, and he enjoyed nothing so much as nagging the bartenders who slipped and offered him what he would indignantly call "an effeminate martini." He would ask sadly if he looked like a little old lady from New Rochelle, or if the bartender had an interest in the vermouth company, or, more melodramatically, if he had stumbled into the house of the Borgias. Sometimes he would even clutch his throat and pretend a toxic reaction. All this was carried out in a very funny imitation of the great W.C. Fields, but Bill was serious about it. If the martinis did not improve, he would take his business to another bar.

He was a bachelor and detested nothing so much as the Women's Liberation movement. "The fuck-heads," he elegantly called them. "When a woman puts a lock on her pussy," he would explain, "all the repressed sex goes up into her head and fucks up her brain. It's like having come in the cranium. Impossible to think straight until some of it gets drained off in orgasms. That's what's wrong with these pigs." To hear him expound on this subject you would imagine that he had been divorced seven times and was paying the heaviest alimony in legal history.

Other women, who were not members of Women's Lib, were not spared Bill's venom, either. They were still pigs. "A woman," he would explain at the slightest provocation, "is constitutionally a parasite. It's been bred into them. They have this little radar that smells money and marriage licenses, and that's all they ever want from you. Can't blame them," he would add philosophically, "they're too dumb and too lazy to support themselves." His greatest pride was that none of them had gotten a marriage license, or much money, out of him. "I know how to handle the pigs," he would say.

Bill's technique of handling the pigs, I soon discovered, was simplicity itself. His sex urge bothered him once a week, no more, and he would then shift his post-five o'clock drinking to a "single's bar," where he could easily pick up a youngish woman who was also cruising for companionship. He never saw any of them a second time. Whether he insulted them roundly before leaving at the end of the night, or whether he simply gave them a false name and phone number, I don't know. Whatever his method, they remained one-night stands.

I would hear about it at a coffee break. "Picked up a lovely little pig last night," he'd say. "Lovely, lovely. Great in the hay. Of course," he would add, "her conversation was stupid, like all women."

A parlor psychoanalyst adding together Bill's drinking, his bachelorhood and his misogyny would form a theory about latent homosexuality. Bill was no fool and he undoubtedly had some awareness that this surmise followed him around like tracks behind a muddy wheel. He was *(the best defense is offense)* the harshest critic of psychoanalysis I have ever met. If he happened to meet a professional analyst, his conversation would turn particularly intellectual and urbane but would revolve monotonously around variations of "Doctor, heal thyself." With people who quoted analytical theories in his presence, he was merciless. "I'd find it easier to believe in the tooth fairy," he'd growl in his best W.C. Fields style; or, "The psychoanalysts in Europe are all starving. Only Americans are dumb enough to believe that Mother Goose theory of motivation." The *bon mot* I most treasure was: "Freud was the Nietzsche of the nursery."

Bill's favorite victims were people who were themselves in psychoanalysis. He had no mercy. "Try a chiropractor," he'd suggest. "They're cheaper, and every now and then they help a patient." Or: "How much are you paying that bandit to rob you? Twenty dollars a session! And you've been at it for four years! Hey, fellow, I've got a nice bridge I'd like to sell—it runs from Manhattan over to Brooklyn..."

Occasionally, in spite of timidity, one of these poor souls would be goaded into replying that Bill might profit from some form of psychotherapy himself. "That's a hot one," Bill would come back, "four years at two sessions a week and you're still too screwed up to get along without a shrink, and you have the arrogance to think *somebody else* is crazy!" They would retreat into their timid shells—and, probably, another six years of analysis.

I don't suppose I've made Bill seem like an attractive person. Actually, his wit was quite amusing (when you weren't the particular target of it) and I suppose he considered himself to be one of those lovable drunks you used to see so often in the movies. He played that part, within the limits of his own notion of lovability, and I actually enjoyed his companionship most of the time. He was quite willing to be helpful when I was learning how to write Mad Avenue English. ("Just pretend you're writing for your four-year-old son," he told me the first day; and that's as good a guide to ad prose as I've ever heard.)

And nobody was particularly likable as the 1960s ground toward their miserable end. The flower children had grown thorns; the Weathermen contingent of the old SDS was planting bombs hither and yon; movies like *Joe* or *Easy Rider* seemed to underscore the mood of genocide or civil war that was in the air just as the joyous and hilarious *Skidoo* and *I Love You, Alice B. Toklas* had echoed the open-ended optimism of the early 1960s. Freaks I had known who had been on acid once and had been quite charming in a fey sort of way, were now often enough on speed (methamphetamine) and not at all charming any more; heroin was appearing in high schools, outside the ghettos—in *white* high schools, dig, a fact that really shook the Establishment. We were all, I suppose, half consciously waiting for Kent State to mark a period at the end of that epoch and move us on into the strange silence and graveyard quietude of the Nixon era. As I said, *Joe* and *Easy Rider* had already warned us that Middle America was armed and dangerous.

In that context, Bill's misogyny and misanthropy hardly seemed extreme or neurotic. After all, the radicals who had sung Dylanesque hymns to love at the beginning of the decade were now defending not only violence but, in the wake of Fanon's studies of the psychology of the repressed, were speaking of the socially valuable functions of hatred, rage and fury. Had anybody quoted the flowery slogans of the Kennedy years at this point, he would have seemed as quaint as an alchemist walking into the chemistry labs at Dupont seeking a job.

"People stink," Bill would say emphatically, whenever politics was discussed in his presence, and it was hard to be entirely sure that he was utterly wrong.

My stay on the Avenue of the Mad wasn't long—perhaps I am not really cut out to write for four-year-olds—and I have only one story to tell about Bill and the Drug Revolution. It occurred just a few weeks before I quit that job and embarked on my latest attempt to survive as a freelance writer. The catalyst was a young Ivy League copywriter whom I shall call Danny.

Danny was some strange survivor, or late blossom, of the Kennedy world; he even looked a little bit like John or Bobby. He was liberal through and through, which meant, among other things, that he smoked pot without scorning alcohol, worked on the Avenue of the Mad without guilt (and was amused by the radicals who considered him a prostitute), and still believed that America could be a great country, if only the Democrats would nominate the right candidate again. Revolution and reaction he despised, but he never really believed that either extreme had much of a chance in America and, hence, he was not afraid of them. His was the last *innocent* soul I knew during this paranoid and bullying epoch. If he never actually said it, I kept imagining that he was ready, at any moment, to declare: "If Roosevelt were still alive…"

When Danny came to work at Beelzebub, Belial, Devil and Ogre (as I shall call our agency), Bill immediately elected him as chief target for his blasts of cynical wit. There was something about Danny's innocent, optimistic face that provoked people to say shocking things to him—but he was, behind that bland exterior, as shockproof as a Swiss watch. It seemed impossible to anger or depress him; he would always understand, and (worst of all), he would forgive, with a wry smile, reminding me of Pat O'Brien playing a priest. It was enough to bring out the latent cynicism in anybody less innocent than Danny himself, and it brought out the Iago and Claggert in Bill.

If Danny mentioned an aunt who owned houses in Boston, Bill would ask, "Slum properties?"—and then hurriedly add, "If you don't know, don't try to find out. Better you shouldn't face it." If Danny had something complimentary to say about the Kennedys, Bill would recall having heard of Joe Kennedy's (real or alleged) links with the Mafia and rum-running during prohibition; if Danny praised FDR, Bill remembered what he had heard about FDR's grandfather's interest in the opium trade; if he dared to say that "blacks, after all, are just like us," Bill would inform him that "nobody who's been shit on for three hundred years is just like you; don't kid yourself. They want to cut your balls off and feed them to their dogs. Look at the Mau Mau; look at any colonial uprising. That's what our black revolution is going to be when it comes."

It was like Rousseau arguing with de Sade—the eternal liberal versus the eternal misanthrope.

Danny never lost his cool, in any of this. Once, though, he came close. "If I believed what you do," he said, "I'd have a drinking problem, too."

"At least I'm not a dope fiend," Bill retorted.

I thought Danny would reply that alcohol is listed under "drugs" in any pharmaceutical text, but he didn't answer at all. He was gazing into the distance thoughtfully. I didn't realize it then but a solution to the problem of Bill's nihilism had occurred to him. It was a solution out of the early 1960s but Danny still believed in it. He was going to turn Bill on.

Some while back a female copywriter had come to the office one day after a night-long acid trip, thinking she was back to planetside reality. She wasn't, and she began to freak out. Danny was afraid that she would either do a Steve Brodie out the window or at least make her state sufficiently conspicuous to the hierarchy to get herself fired, but I had taken her into my office, sent my secretary to the drugstore for niacinamide (Vitamin B-3) and talked to her for two hours. The niacin (see Chapter One) and my gift of gab finally quieted her. She kept her sanity and her job.

Danny was impressed, although he needn't have been. Long ago I had financed my college tuition by working nights as an ambulance attendant, and I saw a good share of psychos on that job, under tight situations. No government propaganda has ever been able to convince me that acidheads are as far out as psycho patients or that they can't be dealt with.

Danny's interpretation of that incident was that I had to be some kind of expert in treating bad trips; and, of course, everybody knows that a bad acid trip is much, much worse than a bad pot trip (it isn't, necessarily; it depends on the persons involved). So, when he finally persuaded Bill to try a joint of marijuana and the situation immediately became spooky, he called me at my apartment.

"Dr. Wilson," he said cryptically (despite his innocence, he had the standard New York assumption that all phones are tapped), "we have an emergency case here. Just like Miss X," he added, naming the lady with the acid jimjams at the office. "Can you come right away!?"

"Oh, shit," I said inelegantly. "I'll be right there."

"What is it?" Arlen asked.

"I'm now a psychiatrist for all the nuts on Madison Avenue," I said morosely. I have never hated our drug laws more than I did at that instant. I knew that I could handle the problem, whatever it was, but I loathed the responsibility, and I longed to live in a free country where Danny could have summoned professional help without risking prison.

When I arrived at Danny's, I found five very subdued and worried-looking potheads—and Bill, sitting apart from the others and glowering.

"Why'd they call you?" Bill asked immediately. "To dispose of my body?" There was no jocular W.C. Fields in his delivery now. This was Rod Steiger playing a cornered Nazi—trapped by his enemies, but still nasty and dangerous. I gave him a cheery laugh and pretended to take the hostility for humor; in his case, the two were always close anyway.

I passed on to the kitchen, as if Bill were not a major item of interest at the moment. That was step one; everybody, I was sure, had been treating his symptoms as a grave problem, and I wanted to give him back his sense of perspective. There were nearly three billion people on earth who didn't know and didn't care about his mental states and I was standing in for all of them.

When Danny followed me to the kitchen, I asked if he had niacinamide in the house. Naturally, he didn't. People who take drugs are frequently almost as ignorant as the legislators who pass laws against them.

I asked if he had Thorazine, Librium or any other tranquilizer. He had nothing of that sort.

"Okay," I said, "we'll bail out without a parachute this time. How long has this been going on?"

"About three-quarters of an hour."

"How much did he smoke?"

"We only passed around two joints when he started getting scared."

"Okay. Take me to my patient." I was remembering one psycho case, back in my ambulance riding days, who had announced, halfway down a flight of stairs, that he didn't want to come to the hospital. He was over six feet tall, had shoulders like the Parthenon, and I was two steps below him. Bill was not going to be as difficult.

I dragged a chair behind me in the living room and sat facing Bill, our faces only about a foot apart.

"Got the fear?" I asked cordially.

"Don't play games with me," he said tightly. "They gave me some bad stuff just to see this happen, and you know it."

"In a pig's ass," I said. "They were smoking the same joints as you. That's part of the courtesy in the pot world, just to prevent crazy ideas like that. Think about it—didn't the joints go from mouth to mouth?" I didn't wait for his answer. "What you've got," I said, "is the one-hour willies. It frequently happens to novices the first time they smoke weed, and it's called the one-hour willies because it always ends in an hour. How long has it been going on?"

"Christ," he said in a dry, cracked voice, "it seems like days."

"How long has it been?" I asked Danny again.

"Three-quarters of an hour," he repeated.

"Well," I said brightly to Bill, "it's almost over. The worst of it is, anyway. Give me your hand." I took it before he could get the fag terrors and held it firmly for a minute. "Just as I thought," I said. "You're not even shaking. The worst is over."

All of this was sheer fiction. The pot horrors, when they come, can last four hours, eight hours or longer—far longer than the drug itself. When the usual armors against anxiety collapse, the accumulated repressed terrors of decades can come out, and long after the drug has left the bloodstream the momentum can continue to build. However, it is fairly easy to short-circuit the process *(which usually happens only to novices and is probably a result of autosuggestion produced by anti-pot propaganda combined with ignorance)* by telling the smoker a convincing yarn—as I had done. Government propaganda and Bill's ignorance had produced this bad trip, and I was going to use *my* propaganda and his ignorance to convert it into a good trip.

"One nice thing about the one-hour willies," I went on blithely, "is that the second hour is always great. Honest to God. Somehow, getting all this out at the beginning is like a purge, and in the second hour you're able to really swing." I went on with the yarn, bringing in the usual good effects of pot—the colors, the rushes of energy, the hilarity—and trying to "suggest" him into picking up some of them.

"That isn't always true," he interrupted. "I've read of cases where people flipped out and spent months in a nuthouse."

"They also can't talk," I said. "They're too scared and confused to talk. Now, you're not in that state, you're getting better minute by minute—I can see the color coming back to your face—and you're not trembling—and *you're arguing with me,* as usual. Nah, you're not confused and panicky at all anymore. You're just sulky and hostile. And that's ending, too," I rushed on. "I can tell by the color of your skin. You're really starting to turn on now…"

Half an hour later I was still talking to him, telling him that the one-hour willies were about to end. He was still glowering, not quite in a panic any more but very far from being turned on or even comfortable. The one sign that he was on weed and not in the middle of an angry drunk was that fact that he hadn't taken a swing at me yet.

"I need a drink," he said suddenly.

I could have kicked myself. I should have had Danny mix him a martini right away, as soon as I got there. It was obviously the right therapy in this case.

Danny quickly mixed up a martini in the kitchen and brought it to Bill. "Just the way you like it," he said.

Bill took a sip and made a face. "Brooklyn," he said with distaste. "This is the way they mix them in Brooklyn."

"There!" I shouted, "You're back to normal!"

Everybody laughed, including Bill. When everybody else stopped, he continued to laugh. On and on. And on.

"*There,* that's the second-hour laugh," I said. "You're finally turning on."

He took another quick gulp of his drink. "I sure am," he said, still but with a touch of nervousness creeping back.

An hour later, however, he was thoroughly relaxed and having a fine time. A third joint was finally circulating in the room, which he sipped very carefully, not inhaling much—and he was also on his third martini. He was regaling the assembly with one of his diatribes against sentimentality but with more humor and less hostility than usual. I left, feeling satisfied.

Months later, after I had departed from Mad Ave for good, I met Danny in a bar and had a chat about old times.

"Bill still comes to my pot parties," he said with a dry smile.

"Really?"

"Yeah—and he brings his own bottle now." At my inquiring gaze, he went on: "He smokes a little of the grass, not much, and then when he starts getting turned on, he drinks a lot to bring himself down again. Then he smokes a little bit more, and drinks a lot more."

"You mean he's just smoking to be one of the crowd?"

"That's about it. Booze is still his real drug of choice."

I shook my head in amazement. "What a strange guy."

"Oh, that's the least of it. I guess the pot has had some effect on him, even mixed with booze."

"What do you mean?"

"These days," Danny said, draining his glass and smiling a Leary smile, "Bill is as gay as a tree full of parrots."

4

The Mexican Weed

Crime thrives in many places, and has increased by leaps and bounds through the past years; much of it, and the majority of it, caused by the drug user, addicted by his own volition... Such dereliction and destructive use of narcotics can only lead to the tragedy of death...

Our youth, by nature, are curious, unafraid to experiment... They think too much about themselves—subjectively—instead of about doing for others—objectively. When they are under the influence of drugs, they find themselves either atop the pinnacle of exhilaration, unafraid, and ready to go beyond the limits of law and decency—or—they find themselves at the bottom of the pit of depression, and ready to take their own lives. In between lies, seduction, pregnancy, assault, theft and even murder...

Vice is everywhere.

— *Drug Abuse Is an Escape to Nowhere* Greene County Sheriff's Department (Ohio), Revised 1972 edition

Vice, indeed, is everywhere. Seventy years ago the Mexican laborers in Texas and Louisiana began introducing the weed from their own country, and now it has spread like a plague, and the great republic of our founding fathers is being undermined by sex and sin.

That is the way cops and clergymen generally look at it.

The truth is somewhat more complicated. Vice has always been around, in heavy doses; it is mankind's most fervent interest, and differentiates us sharply from our closest relatives in the ape family, none of whom are in heat all year long as we are. Indeed, if man were not the most relentlessly sex-oriented animal alive, there would not be so many of us on this small planet.

Nor has marijuana been introduced from Mexico to corrupt the high ideals of our founding fathers. Rather, this plant, which is of Eurasian origin, was first imported to this continent by our founding fathers (especially George Washington) and then, later, taken up by the Mexicans. If there was any seduction across the Rio Grande, the first families of Virginia were the seducers, and the innocent Mexicans were the seduced. *There seems to have been no marijuana on this continent before the 18th Century, and the chief cause of its wide dissemination was the enthusiasm of George Washington.*

This curious fact, which was called to my attention by Dr. Michael Aldrich, is well-documented in the *Writings of Washington,* U.S. Government Printing Office, 1931. Here are some of the citations:

Volume 31, page 389, October 1791, letter from Mount Vernon to Alexander Hamilton, Secretary of Treasury: "How far ... would there be propriety, do you conceive, in suggesting the policy of encouraging the growth of cotton and hemp in such parts of the United States as are adapted to the culture of these articles?"

In the next three years, Washington evidently settled the matter in his own mind, and we don't know what Hamilton thought of the "proprieties." Volume 33, page 279, finds him writing from Philadelphia to his gardener at Mount Vernon to "make the most you can of the India Hemp seed" and "plant it everywhere," an injunction that could almost be construed to suggest that he was abandoning all his other crops. Waxing even more enthusiastic on page 384, he writes to an unidentified "my dear Doctor," telling him, "I thank you as well for the seeds as for the Pamphlets which you had the goodness to send me. The artificial preparation of the Hemp from Silesia is really a curiosity..." And on page 469, he again obsessively reminds the gardener about the seed of the India Hemp: "I desire that the seed may be saved in due season and with as little loss possible."

The next year the general was even more preoccupied that the seeds be saved and the crop replenished; Volume 34, page 146, finds him writing (March 15, 1795) to the gardener again: "Presuming you saved all the seed you could from the India Hemp, let it be carefully sown again, for the purpose of getting into a full stock of the seed."

Volume 35, page 72, an undated letter of the spring of 1796 shows that the years did not diminish this strange passion; he again writes to the gardener: "What was done with the seed saved from the India Hemp last summer? It ought, all of it, to have been sown again; that not only a stock of seed sufficient for my own purposes might have been raised, but to *have disseminated the seed to others, as it is more valuable than the ordinary Hemp.*" [Italics added] On page 265, he is still nagging that poor gardener about the seed (what the gardener thought of all this is not recorded) and on page 323, he writes to Sir John Sinclair proclaiming that his experiments have definitely proven that "the Indian Hemp is for all purposes superior to the New Zealand variety."

It has been proposed by some conservative admirers of the general that he was interested only in the use of hemp for *rope* (it was used in hangmen's nooses). This, of course, is considered much more admirable than any interest in the plant for its recreational purposes, but the rope theory simply doesn't hold water. As early as August 7, 1765, Washington wrote in his diary *(The Diaries of George Washington,* Houghton Mifflin Co., 1925): "Began to separate the Male from the Female hemp at Do— rather too late." The separation of hemp by sex is not required and never practiced when rope manufacture is intended, but it is essential if one wants to use the unfertilized flowering tips of the female plant for marijuana.

Some writers who have accepted this inevitable conclusion from the evidence still try to argue that George Washington could not possibly have smoked weed for recreation. Rather, they suggest, he was probably using the marijuana for its analgesic properties, to kill the pain of his frequent toothaches. (Considering the passion shown in these records, the toothaches must have been *very* frequent.) Even if this was so, he was still stoned fairly often, no matter what his principal intent. And his obsession for "disseminating the seed to others" partly accounts for the fact that, unknown on this continent at the time of his birth, it could be found throughout the states and in Mexico a century later.

Pot: From Prehistory to the Present

The plant, of course, had a long history before that, some of which we have touched on already in Chapter Three on hashish. *Cannabis sativa* seems to have originated in Asia, perhaps around the Caspian Sea, and its cultivation began during what might be called the First Drug Revolution, that is, at least as early as 15,000 BC. Our ancestors in Eurasia at that time were mostly hunters, and their religion was shamanism, which is based not on dogmas or teachings but on actual visions or "spirit experiences." The quest for such experience (the backdoor to Eden) had always been part of shamanism, and had always been sought by various methods, probably including a variety of drugs, but mostly self-hypnosis, isolation, sadomasochism (human sacrifice, self-torture), melohypnosis (trance induced by singing rhythmically), etc. Some time before 15,000 BC the first Drug Revolution began when it was discovered that drugs were the royal road to these altered states.

This information seems to have journeyed west and south to Europe and Africa very quickly, and up across Siberia and down through North and South America almost as rapidly. According to Peter Furst, Professor of Anthropology at the State University of New York, it is now fairly certain that shamanistic use of some drugs goes back to at least 15,000 BC in parts of Asia; the fly agaric mushroom (the soma of the Hindus, according to recent theories) was discovered around 5000 BC, the magic mushrooms of Mexico by at least 2000 BC and peyote probably around 1000 BC.

(Psychedelic mushrooms seem to have been central to this early Drug Revolution, and, according to John Allegro in *The Sacred Mushroom and the Cross,* it is this which explains the sex rites that were conspicuous in religion at that time, since the mushroom looks like a penis and suggests sexual symbolism to its worshippers. Allegro also believes that many gods, including Dionysus, Osiris and Jesus, are based on the mushroom. He attributes the virgin birth of these gods to the fact that the generation of mushrooms has traditionally been a mystery that evaded understanding, no sexual pattern could be found by either primitive cultures, classical civilizations or Western science itself until *the mid-19th Century.* Until that time, the magic mushroom really did seem to be virgin born and miraculous— especially when one "ate its flesh" or "drank its blood" via the fermented juices that catapulted one directly into the divine or timeless realm.)

As part of this process, which may have been the most important single step in the evolution of religions, the cannabis plant was carried across Europe and Asia and down into Africa. The Chinese, as mentioned previously, were familiar with cannabis in their very earliest periods. They used a staff carved of its stem to cure various illnesses. This staff was in the shape of a serpent coiling around a rod—very similar to the still-existing symbol of the physician, or the caduceus of Mercury—and clearly indicates a magical and religious attitude. By early Han times (200 AD) the famous physician Hua-T'o was using cannabis resins and wine to anesthetize patients for surgery.

Halfway around the world, Democritus (460–370 BC) described the visionary states (and "immoderate laughter") that followed the ritual use of this plant, which was evidently burned with myrrh and frankincense over a brazier and inhaled by worshippers sitting in a circle, in several of the ancient civilizations around the Mediterranean. It has been suggested that Democritus himself was a devotee of this custom, and this might explain his reputation as "the laughing philosopher." (R. Gordon Wasson, incidentally, has suggested that Plato along with many of his fellow Greeks was initiated in the Eleusinian mysteries, or some similar rite that involved the use of a "magic mushroom." Wasson argues that the mushroom experience inspired Plato's ideas that there is a timeless world above or alongside our ordinary universe.)

Cannabis was well-known to the Arabs by the time the tales of the *Thousand and One Nights* (10th Century) were compiled. One of these yarns concerns a sultan who (while mingling with his people in disguise to learn what they are thinking—a traditional theme) falls asleep on a floor and is urinated upon by a fisherman who is stoned on hashish. In the morning, the fisherman is called to the palace, where the sultan reveals himself as the person he had pissed upon. "What of it?" says the fisherman boldly. "You are in your palace this morning, I was in *my* palace last night." The sultan was a philosopher to whom "truth was the sweetest noise in his kingdom" and he immediately forgave the fisherman, saying, "We are both sultans!"

Another Arabian yarn concerns three men who arrive at a city after dark when the gate is closed. The first, an alcoholic, takes an aggressive stand at once and shouts, "Let's batter the damned gate down!" The second, an opium addict, is typically passive in accordance with the drug of *his* choice. "Let's sleep on the ground until morning," he says. The third is a cannabis smoker, and he takes a characteristically cannabis view of the matter. "Let's sneak in through the keyhole," he suggests thoughtfully...

In India, recreational use of cannabis seems to go back to around 500 BC and one myth claims it was given to mankind by Shiva, god of sex, intoxication and mysticism; in other versions of this legend, Shiva is actually incarnate in the Indian hemp plant. From about that time to the present, Indian doctors have prescribed cannabis extracts for dysentery, sunstroke, indigestion, lack of appetite and other conditions. Shivites use it in their religious worship, and other sects believe it is useful as spiritual preparation for reading holy writings or entering sacred places.

The cannabis drugs penetrated many parts of Africa in prehistoric times, but had their greatest popularity in more recent days, due to the conqueror Kalamba Moukenge, who defeated most of the tribes of the Congo in 1888 and tried to unite them into a nation. Borrowing an idea from earlier conquerors, Moukenge decided that the local tribal gods should be subordinated to "one God" who would hold all of them together. For this "one God" suitable to all, he chose the cannabis plant.

In those lands of North Africa that have been civilized since ancient times, cannabis has always played a large role. Paul Bowles, composer and writer, has pointed out that the hemp drug has influenced "music, literature and even certain aspects of architecture" in that area.

The hemp plant entered Mexico, as we have seen, after Washington and other Virginia planters enthusiastically spread it around the southern United States. As early as 1902, anthropologist Carl Lumholtz observed that some of the Indians in northwestern Mexico were using its leaves in religious rites whenever the peyote cactus was unavailable. They called it *rosa maria* (Rosemary) but whether they anthropomorphized it and considered it a goddess (like Peyote Woman) is not clear. In the Tepehua region, *rosa maria* became *santa rosa* (Saint Rose), but elsewhere it became *maria juana* (Mary Jane)—and, hence our modern name, marijuana. Under the latter title it was celebrated in the famous marching song of Pancho Villa's rebels during the Mexican Revolution of 1910–1920:

> La cucaracha, la cucaracha,
> Ya no puede caminar,
> Porque no tiene, porque no tiene,
> Marijuana que fumar.

("The cockroach, the cockroach, he cannot walk about, because he doesn't have, because he doesn't have, marijuana to smoke." This might be the origin of the current slang use of *roach* to mean the end of a marijuana cigarette.)

An interesting Mexican ritual involving marijuana is described in Peter Furst's *Flesh of the Gods,* concerning the Tepehua Indians. They regard the plant as potentially dangerous (just like our solons in Washington) but control it by ritual rather than by law, dedicating it to the worship of the three most powerful local gods, Jesus, the Virgin Mary, and the sun. Praying, sometimes laughing, they get high amid song, speeches, ringing of bells, dancing, chanting and whistling. The ceremony not only allows each worshipper to confront his god directly, but is believed to cure any illnesses the children of the village might have.

Comedian Flip Wilson, on a late-night television talk show discussing marijuana, described a similarly syncretic religion (involving pot, Christianity and African folk religion, this time) which he had observed on one of the Caribbean islands.

An elderly jazz musician once told me about a cult, unknown to anthropologists, which flourished in Chicago in the 1930s. The single time that he was allowed to attend one of their ceremonies, there were six worshippers present, all of them musicians, some white and some black. Each marijuana cigarette was lit by the priest or shaman and then passed around in the circle, in the manner still traditional among potheads. There was no ceremony, just meditation and occasional "testimony" in the manner of the Society of Friends (Quakers). Each member had a holy name, and when testimony was sparse, the priest would occasionally ask for some.

"How does it go with the Lord Krishna?" he might enquire.

"The Lord Krishna is at peace on the second level," might be the reply.

"How does it go with the Lord Shiva?" the priest might ask next.

"The Lord Shiva is in bliss on the fifth level," would come the reply.

My friend has no information about the origins of this cult, how it hit upon Hindu names, the mysterious (cabalistic?) language of (astral?) levels, and so on. I include this here not only for its intrinsic interest but in hopes that some knowledgeable anthropologist or jazz historian might be able to shed further light.

An even more modern marijuana cult, on traditional shamanistic lines, was shown on "CBS News" in 1970, featuring some American G.I.s in Vietnam. The soldiers used a shotgun—regarded religiously and named "Ralph"—to inhale large quantities of the weed and become thoroughly stoned. The squad leader, acting like a Stone Age shaman, ejected the shells from the shotgun, inserted the grass into the breach and then blew the smoke into the mouth of each of the men in turn. Professor Peter Furst, an anthropologist, has commented that such "spontaneous ritualization" almost seems to be innate in the use of psychedelic drugs (cf., the story immediately above, and the tradition of passing the joint in a magic circle among even the most casual smokers) and that the use of a weapon of death is strangely similar to the way in which some South American Indians use tubes similar to deadly blowguns in psychedelic religious rites.

Pot & Sex

Marijuana has long had a reputation as "the most powerful aphrodisiac in the world," to quote John Dickson Carr's detective novel, *Below Suspicion.* Modern authorities dispute this and claim that neither pot nor any other drug is a true aphrodisiac. That is, neither pot nor any other drug will provoke passion in an otherwise neutral situation.

There can be little doubt, however, that marijuana definitely tends to enhance sex, for many users, when the situation is propitious.

Under hashish we have already quoted a few typical reports by users interviewed by Barbara Lewis in her book *The Sexual Power of Marijuana.* Here is further testimony from the same source:

A 38-year-old radio announcer:

> A woman's body becomes a cafeteria. You want to eat every part of it. No part of it is sacred, yet everything is sacred.

A 31-year-old housewife:

> It lasted forever. Everything, the foreplay, the actual act, the orgasm. I'm sure that marijuana prolongs sex beyond the ordinary span. It gives you more endurance.

A 22-year-old coed at the University of New Mexico:

> I know that marijuana really isn't an aphrodisiac. But for me it is. Because when I smoke with my boyfriend, the sensations go right to my genitals. He can be in another room, and I will feel it in the vagina. It's almost an independent thing.

A 26-year-old housewife told of trying marijuana alone in the afternoon:

> I became so horny that I called my husband at the office and insisted he come home immediately. When he couldn't oblige ... the feeling was so intense that I actually went in to the bedroom and masturbated.

Former U.S. Commissioner of Narcotics Harry J. Anslinger:

> In the earliest stages of intoxication, the will power is destroyed ... moral barricades are broken down, and often debauchery and sexuality result.

Dr. James Fadiman, psychologist:

> Marijuana helps you listen to your senses. Anything that makes you more aware makes sex better.

The usual references by enthusiasts are to increased sensitivity, more empathy, and so forth. By contrast, the publisher of a medical journal told Barbara Lewis that marijuana had improved his sex life by making him more brutal:

> Why am I a better lover? Because I find myself fucking a hell of a lot harder than it would have occurred to me before. I'm able to accept the fact that some women like to be fucked violently.

Echoing our remarks concerning the feats of sexual yoga, a Berkeley coed said:

> You actually make love for an hour, an hour and a half. Without marijuana you'd get into the actual fucking part much faster and then it would be over faster.

A 22-year-old coed from Long Island had an experience that devotees of sexual yoga will also recognize:

> After smoking there are times when I literally feel as if I'm a huge cunt. And that he's a large penis. In your mind's eye, this is how you see yourself.

A 32-year-old California pharmacist reported the same traditionally occult experience:

> I sometimes feel like a huge sexual organ, like I'm duplicating the thrust of the penis. And that the woman's body has the proportions of one large vaginal tract. It's an exciting sensation, it has an intrinsic rhythm, movement and music of its own.

Dr. Louis Jolyon West, psychiatrist:

> It's been published repeatedly that marijuana is not an aphrodisiac. But I think it's a fair generalization to say that marijuana stimulates the appetites, *all* the appetites, including the sexual appetite, and that it takes less psychosocial stimulation to get a person in the mood if he's had marijuana than if he's cold sober.

Of course, there are some persons who report no sexual effects at all from marijuana. This should not surprise us. There is no real aphrodisiac, as we have noted several times—none, at least, in the traditional mythical sense of a drug that has the same sexually provocative effect on all users. The first law of psychopharmacology is that the action of any drug depends partly on the drug itself and partly on the *set* and *setting*—the mental attitude of the user and the forces at work in his immediate environment. With these cautions carefully in mind, it is probably safe to say that the evidence to date indicates fairly conclusively that, for an overwhelming majority of users, marijuana is a decidedly safe and pleasant enhancer of sexual experience.

Perils of the Weed

Of course, there are many who still proclaim that the weed is terribly dangerous. Their arguments are becoming increasingly unconvincing. Scientific data that will support them are hard to find and there is almost an embarrassment of riches available when one looks for scientific evidence proving that pot is no more threatening to civilization than bubble gum.

In 1892, the English government appointed a Hemp Drug Commission to investigate the cannabis habit in India, where it is generally consumed in the milk drink *bhang* or smoked in the form of *charas,* usually considered stronger than marijuana. (Some estimates say that *charas* is even stronger than hashish.) After interviewing thousands of doctors and users all over India and checking out every story of "addiction" or of "psychoses" resulting from abuse, in an investigation that required two years, the commission concluded that cannabis was not addicting, that "moderate use" is the rule, that overuse or abuse is rare, that the stories of "psychoses" were unfounded and that the drug represented no menace; they recommended that no law be passed against it, and no law was ever passed, until India ratified the United Nations Hemp Drug Act over 50 years later—which they did, according to Dr. Joel Fort, who was drug consultant to the World Health Organization at the time, only because they were bullied into doing so by the American delegation. Even then, India did not ban the flowering tips of the hemp plant from which marijuana is made.

In 1923, the U.S. Army, not a notably liberal organization, also investigated the use of marijuana among American soldiers in the Panama Canal Zone. Again, the report concluded that the habit was harmless and did not need to be prohibited; it pointed out that alcohol created more problems for the soldiers who used it.

In 1942, the LaGuardia Commission investigated the marijuana habit in New York, and also concluded that the weed is not addictive and does not produce any clear-cut bad effects even in users who have had the habit for a matter of decades. (It is often said, by conservatives, that the American Medical Association rejected the LaGuardia Report. This is not strictly true. *One* writer for the *A.M.A. Journal* rejected the report.)

In 1968, Drs. Zinberg and Weil, in Boston, completed the most intensive scientific investigation of marijuana made to date. They, too, found no clear-cut harmful effects. I subsequently interviewed Dr. Zinberg and he mentioned that he *has* seen temporary psychosis-like conditions in some users, although not in the control group used in the study. He emphasized that these conditions were always temporary and only appeared in persons who had no previous experience with the drug—usually, he said, in parents who had been turned on by their own children. Tranquilizers calmed them down quickly, in a matter of hours, he added.

The Presidential Commission on Marijuana (March 22, 1972), as is well-known, came to the same basic conclusions, and recommended that jail sentences for use of the weed be discontinued. President Nixon, however, disagreed with the commission, saying, in effect, that their evidence did not support the conclusions he had formed before their evidence was collected. As was the case in his rejection of the previous Pornography Commission, the President seemed to think that scientific evidence should guide legislators only when it supported his own intuitive judgments; many other people seem to have that attitude toward science but few are so refreshingly frank in stating it as Mr. Nixon was.

Non-Medical Use of Drugs, the Interim Report of the Canadian Government Commission of Inquiry, comes to the same general conclusions, and recommends the abolition of criminal penalties for blowing the weed.

To believe that pot is really harmful, at this point, one must posit an 80-year-old conspiracy of M.D.s, chemists, psychologists, psychiatrists, government officials and military officers, in several nations on four continents, deliberately distorting their evidence to hide all alleged bad effects. Members of the John Birch Society may believe in such conspiracies, but for all others it would seem that, at a minimum, the verdict on marijuana's harmfulness must be: not proven.

In addition, there is considerable evidence that marijuana may be beneficial. Dr. Ted Mikuriya, a San Francisco psychiatrist, has collected literally hundreds of citations from 19th-Century American medical journals in which cannabis preparations were recommended for the treatment of toothache and other pain, for melancholy and depressive states, and even for antibiotic purposes, including the alleged cure of gonorrhea. Some of these claims were probably true, Dr. Mikuriya argues, since they were, after all, written by responsible medical men, and they are worth further investigation. After all, he adds, Dr. Morton discovered *ether* for anesthesia after observing medical students at Harvard bombed out of their minds in an *ether frolic*—the 19th-Century equivalent of a pot party; we should not let recreational use of a drug blind us to its other possible uses.

Dr. Solomon H. Snyder has followed up on Dr. Mikuriya's lead and, in his *Uses of Marijuana,* has documented widespread use of cannabis preparations in 19th-Century medicine, which was abandoned only because the crude chemistry of the time made standard doses of this volatile drug difficult to prepare. Dr. Snyder points out that this is no longer true since THC, the active principle, has been isolated, and he also calls for further research, especially on the weed's analgesic action against such painful conditions as migraine headache and menstrual cramps. (Some of his citations, involving the use of cannabis in treating opium withdrawal, suggest that it might also be worthwhile to try *special* cannabis preparations in heroin withdrawal, even though addicts all insist that ordinary street marijuana does not help with these symptoms. Dr. Lloyd J. Thompson, an English psychiatrist who, in the 1940s, worked with parahexine, a high-potency cannabis derivative, found that it helped greatly with various depressive psychoses that did not respond to ordinary tranquilizers.)[1]

Doctors in India, as we mentioned earlier, have long believed that cannabis is useful in treating a wide variety of diseases. Dr. Joel Fort, who has made first-hand observations in India and other parts of the Orient where this medical usage is common, concludes that the weed "may be helpful in treating depression, stimulating appetite,[2] alleviating headaches, lowering high blood pressure and producing sedation or relaxation." He adds that "marijuana may be better for some mental patients than any tranquilizer currently in use." (Barbara Lewis, in the *Sexual Power of Marijuana,* claims that "a surprising number of marijuana users ... told me that their therapists actually encouraged and explored their marijuana experience." One woman told Ms. Lewis that when she asked her psychiatrist for tranquilizers, he told her that, in his opinion, marijuana is safer.)

Even the U.S. Army, it turns out, has found curative properties in the "vile hemp." In this case, however, the scientific evidence was deliberately concealed for more than ten years—evidently for fear of embarrassing other government agencies that were proclaiming that pot had no medical uses and was totally destructive. The data was gathered in 1955–1959, and only released in 1971, after one of the scientists on the project virtually forced its declassification. This report indicated so many possible uses of cannabis derivatives that one commentator suggested that

---

[1] See David Solomon's *The Marijuana Papers* for similar citations of marijuana derivatives as therapy in mental illnesses.

[2] This is mentioned so often in marijuana literature that some readers in the United States, where overeating is endemic, may wonder why it is important. Here's why: Many pre-psychotics and psychotics actually do themselves considerable harm by complicating their mental problems with cases of malnutrition, due to a distaste for food. Getting them to eat again is often an important part of their therapy. (It is even believed by some advocates of the nutritional theory of psychosis that the loss of appetite is the *modus operandi* by which a disturbed person graduates to psychosis; the malnutrition may start the chemical processes that lead to paranoia or hallucination.) Others who need to have appetite stimulated include heroin addicts and "speed freaks" (abusers of the amphetamine drugs).

grass may replace penicillin as the most useful all-around "wonder drug" of our age. Its achievements include the following: THC (tetrahydrocannabinol) has put dogs into "hibernation" or deep sleep for eight days, after which they were awakened and showed no ill effects. If this could be applied to humans, for example, people who have been injured and are unable to obtain extensive treatment (e.g., in an air raid, on a battlefield, in jungles, on mountains, etc.), might be placed in states of suspended animation while being moved to treatment centers.

Since marijuana usage has reached at least 50,000,000 in the United States, according to Professor William McGlothlin and other authorities—Dr. Michael Aldrich, admittedly a pro-pot crusader, sets the figure at 70,000,000—the present laws must, eventually, be doomed. There is no way to enforce a law when that many citizens oppose it, as we should have learned during alcohol prohibition (1920–1933). The only remaining question, then, is: How long will the government resist the inevitable, throw harmless citizens into jail, and hold back the research that might confirm the many possible and probable benefits of this herb? Considering the government's record, the only answer to that question must be: longer, far longer, than any rational person would expect.

As of 1998, the principle conditions that seem to benefit most from marijuana are cancer and AIDS. This has become so widely known that the voters of two states (California and Arizona) have voted to legalize medical use of the Devil Weed for those diseases; but, as noted earlier, the Federal government has threatened any doctors who dare to prescribe marijuana or its derivatives for these or other conditions. Most doctors seem terrified, but a few are brave enough and humane enough to write prescriptions for those whose acute pain obviously decreases or vanishes with cannabis. President Clinton and his Justice Department still make threatening noises, but it is estimated that in San Francisco alone over 3000 AIDS and cancer patients are receiving the drug quasi-legally through the Cannabis Healing Club. How the Feds ever acquired the power to decide how much pain a sick person must suffer before dying remains legally obscure. The Constitution certainly never granted such sadistic power to any part of the government.

Marijuana & Frigidity

Among the benefits of marijuana hardly ever discussed in medical and psychiatric literature, but widely claimed in the drug culture, is its alleged curative effect in some cases of frigidity. It is very hard to evaluate this properly. Jane, whose story was told in the Prelude, had a problem so severe that drugs as strong as hashish and peyote could not open her up and only LSD finally helped her (at the cost, seemingly, of sending her to a mental hospital for a few months). Another woman I know, admits to being frigid and has been smoking the weed for 12 years now. (She has also tried LSD and mescaline, without any effect on her sexual problem.) I have, however, heard countless stories of *young* women who had suffered frigidity problems for only a few years and who were helped to orgasm by marijuana (or by *the hope and faith* that marijuana would help them, as skeptics would say).

Dr. Louis Jolyon West told Barbara Lewis, "I have talked with young girls who have had some sexual experience, as well as with older women who have been having intercourse for some time. All were capable of sexual pleasure and arousal, but had never had orgasm. Under marijuana, they did." Dr. West adds that he favors the explanation that this effect is psychological rather than medical. Almost certainly, he is right. Nearly all frigidity is psychological, and therefore all cures for it (which will vary from woman to woman) must, necessarily, be psychological, including those that involve physical retraining *a la* Masters and Johnson.

Ms. Lewis' book, *Sexual Power of Marijuana,* contains three case histories of women who were cured, seemingly, of frigidity while on marijuana. Subsequently, all of them were able to achieve orgasm even without the weed.

Here is one of Ms. Lewis' case histories, as told by a woman identified as "Heather," who had been frigid for 12 years and then began experimenting with marijuana and other aids:

> "We used a vibrator at first to help me reach orgasm, clitoral orgasm, and this was a tremendous step for me. At twenty-six, I had never experienced one! But it wasn't quite as big a moment as three weeks ago when I had my first vaginal orgasm."

Despite the frankness with which Heather talked about herself, she found it embarrassing to describe how it happened. "My mind says I should be able to talk about it, but emotionally it's difficult" she admitted. But it is characteristic of these new marijuana people, I found, to seek to be as open as possible. "Honesty" was a quality they strove for, and Heather was no exception.

"Well—Pete and I talked about everything. We had no secrets from each other. I had told him about one of my fantasies—about being tied down while fucking. I wanted to act it out. I thought both of us might learn something from exploring this so-called 'perversion.' We turned on, and I can tell you, I've never been so turned on in my life. I was *really* turned on. I was spread-eagled on the bed, lying on my back, my arms and legs tied to the four posters. It was a very slow thing at first. We spent two hours at love play, the most intense love play, just letting it happen. Then, for a while, Pete lay down beside me, not doing anything, just talking to me, reminding me he was doing what he wanted to, that there wasn't anything to worry about. Because one of the things that always brought me down was worrying about stupid things, like whether or not I was responding the right way, worrying about how 'well' I was making love.

"Finally, I went out of control—my facial muscles were twitching. My arms began to tingle, and I couldn't move my hands—they felt as if they were paralyzed. I remember feeling like it was just too much, as if I would explode. I just couldn't stand it. I started to cry somewhere along the line, but Pete became very frightened, so I brought it under some control.

"Then, when he got on top of me and we started fucking, I knew it was going to happen and that nothing could stop it. It sounds silly, but I felt out in the universe—there's this spiritual thing that happens on grass—and I saw myself out there surrounded by stars. Then I became more aware of what my body was going—it began to convulse, up and down, in waves. I was half-crying and half-choking. Finally I had this incredible orgasm. My whole body was involved. When I 'came to' I assured Pete that I was okay, and then he did his own thing."

This is definitely an area deserving of more investigation, since, according to Kinsey's figures, two out of five American women have difficulty reaching orgasm during the first two years after commencing sexual intercourse. *But, perhaps, this research has already been done, and favorable results have been found. That is, science may not know about it because the researchers have no degrees after their names and are all, by act of Congress, criminals.* This hypothesis, which is not intended as a joke, would explain how marijuana grew from a habit of a few hundred thousand blacks and Mexican-Americans in the 1930s to a passion shared by somewhere between 30 and 70 million Americans today.

Undoubtedly, there are many other factors to explain the astonishing growth of the marijuana habit. It has long been associated with jazz and rock musicians, and everybody has a tendency to imitate his artistic heroes; it produces many amusing and interesting perceptions of a non-sexual nature; it is (usually) cheaper than an alcohol high. (This last undoubtedly has a lot to do with the weed's popularity in the ghettos.) Nevertheless, the growth trend is one of the most astonishing success stories of our time, which any businessman would be delighted to claim for his product—it amounts to around 6000 percent over a 60-year period—and only some very dramatic and strong appeal can account for that. Seventy-three percent of the pot users in the McGlothlin-West survey mentioned earlier stated that the chief reason they smoked the weed was to "increase sexual satisfaction" and I am inclined to believe them. More than psychoanalysis or Masters and Johnson, marijuana has shown millions of Americans that the sex act need not be the "momentary trick" scorned by Shakespeare, but can become an event of cosmic grandeur.

INTERLUDE

Behind Suburban Doors: The Story of George & Martha

But to others, ever say, " 'Tis foolish to talk of Witches flying through the air. To do so they must be light as thistledown. And men say that Witches all be so bleared-eyed, old crones, so what pleasure can there be at a Witch meeting such as folks talk on?"

And say, "Many wise men now say there be no such creatures." Ever make it a jest and in some future time, perhaps, the persecution may die and we may worship our Gods in safety again.

— *The Book of Shadows*

George is an engineer with one of the largest consulting engineering firms in the United States. He is balding, fiftyish and a conservative dresser. He and his wife, Martha, live in a suburb of Philadelphia, so conservative in its reputation that radicals sometimes use its name as a joking synonym for everything stodgy, timid, boring and repressive.

George arises every morning, brushes his teeth, shaves carefully—although beards worn on men his age and of portly build are becoming quasi-respectable again, he does not care to give even the appearance of moderate individualism—and drives to Philadelphia. All day he toils at the technical details involved in producing new war toys for the Pentagon to terrorize its competitors and murder its enemies. At home, Martha does the housework, perhaps goes out to a bridge game with the other ladies of the neighborhood or writes occasional nature poetry that is published often in the nice pre-*Cosmo* sort of women's magazines.

They seem like the ideal "middle Americans," and they are accepted as such by all their neighbors.

Naturally, there is more to George and Martha than appears on the surface (or they wouldn't be in this book). They have been smoking pot longer than anybody I know. Martha was turned on by a former beau, and she turned George on shortly after they were married.

"He was a jazz musician," Martha said, when telling me of that almost antediluvian initiation. "I was very artsy in those days. It was so long ago we didn't even have the word 'beat generation.' We just called ourselves bohemians."

Whatever fears George may have had about the weed initially, he has been converted thoroughly over the years.

Generally, George and Martha smoke alone, in their own bedroom, late at night. "And I spray with three different air-fresheners afterwards," Martha adds with a smile.

Before the 1960s, George and Martha never worried much about being caught. Nobody up in that suburban nest of Republicans and sinners would ever have suspected that such an exotic, non-Caucasian vice was being practiced in their midst—not in the age of Truman and Eisenhower. "Those were the good old days," Martha says. "It was our little secret, and as long as the windows were tightly closed we never worried about a thing."

With the advent of the 1960s, things changed. "Kids were getting busted on all sides of us," George says. "The cops even bought a pot-sniffing dog. They'd walk around the streets at night, and he'd bark when he smelled the fumes. Then they'd crash in. It was unconstitutional, of course, but up here anybody who mentions the Constitution is regarded as a Communist.[1] We kept our mouths shut, and I bought all sorts of tricky locks and

---

[1] By the 1990s, of course, the U.S. government no longer considered people who showed respect for the Constitution to be suspected *Communists*. Instead, such people were considered suspected *Terrorists*.

designed some cute gimmicks of my own." George may be, for all I know, the inventor of the self-destruct stash box; at least he designed one model. Nobody who breaks down their doors—knock or "no-knock"—will ever find tangible evidence.

Some carefree potheads I know would regard George as paranoid—but they don't have jobs like his to protect.

For instance, George and Martha always open a bottle of whisky and take one small sip before turning on. Should the cops crash in some night, any arrest will hinge on how "high" George and Martha appear to be since there will be no physical evidence of marijuana's presence. They, therefore, plan to spill the whisky on the floor and act drunk to mask the real cause of their glow.

George also made a substantial contribution when the local police force solicited citizens to pay the printer's bill on an anti-drug pamphlet to be distributed in the town high school. "I felt kinda shitty about that," he admits. "The pamphlet was full of the most idiotic old 1930s mythology—the kids were bound to laugh at it—but at least it gave me an avenue to meet the local narcotics officers and impress myself on them as a real straight citizen." George knows the value of image, and expects that the impression he laid on them at that time will slow them down as much as his tricky locks—if they ever do decide on a bust.

In one minute and forty seconds—he tells me, having timed it—he can burn all the grass in his self-destruct box, and Martha can have sprayed Pine, Trade Winds and Lysol all over the room. The bedroom has its own special bolt lock to slow the cops down after they get through the front door. It looks cool.

Yet, George is not satisfied. A methodical man, he likes to approach every challenge in a scientific way. He experimented for a while with cooking the weed up in fudges or brownies—"no fumes, no telltale odors for that damn dog of theirs"—but the self-destruct box, which reaches 1000° F. in 30 seconds, still leaves traces behind when confections like fudge or brownies are rammed into it. And he has purchased "guaranteed drug-free urine" from a place in Boulder, and learned enough stage magic to escape the Piss Police.

George, curiously, does not believe marijuana should be legalized. For that matter, he doesn't believe alcohol prohibition should have been abandoned entirely.

"The best system for *all* drugs," he says, "is the way the Canadians handle booze. It keeps abusers from becoming a menace to the rest of us, and it allows mature, responsible people to make their own decisions without the state playing Daddy-knows-best with them."

Under the Canadian system, alcohol is only available in state stores, and you need a license to buy it. If you are arrested for being drunk and disorderly on the street, or if you have an auto accident while inebriated, the license is suspended for a time. With repeated infractions, the license may be taken away permanently.

"That's the sane way to handle all drugs," George says. "If people want to get stoned in their own homes, that's their business and society has no legitimate concern in the matter. If they come out on the streets and make themselves obnoxious or cause accidents, then society should stifle them. That's a simple, practical, intelligent distinction that even a five-year-old can understand. Private, non-invasive behavior is nobody's business. Invasive or disruptive behavior is everybody's business. What could be more clear?"

Our society currently classifies an intoxicated individual as criminal or non-criminal entirely on the basis of which drug he used to get high, irrespective of whether he's done any harm. George has to live under the present laws, and he is taking good care not to be caught in their web.

"No wonder so many kids are alienated and angry," Martha says. "It's like living in an occupied country. I honestly don't feel that anybody in power—the cops, or the Congress or whoever—is my representative. Sometimes I feel like I'm living in one of those old movies about Occupied Europe from the 1940s."

That is precisely how the majority of pot smokers feel. If there are actually 60,000,000 of them, as some estimates suggest, they are the largest minority group in the country (there are only 20,000,000 black Americans, by comparison) and, yet, they are living in a weird scenario straight out of the French Underground.

(Their phone conversations can be hilarious:
"Uh, Sam? This is Bill."

"Oh, hi, Bill. What's happening?"

"Uh, Charlie just got back from uh Texas and he's bringing over some interesting Mexican *cooking utensils.*"

"Cooking utensils?... *Oh! I* see. Yes, I'd be interested in getting some for my *pot*tery collection."

"You got the message, baby."

"I'll be right over.")

Martha and George have solved the supply problem in a manner typical of their cautious approach to lawbreaking. Their current dealer is a university student whose college is in a town several miles from their own suburb. Thus, among the myriad pot-smoking young people in their own town, there is not one who has ever sold to them, or has any other way of knowing that they blow the weed. No matter how many busts take place on blocks north, east, south or west of them, their name will never appear in anybody's confession.

George was both proud and shy when he ran down this list of precautions for me. He was proud of the meticulous care for detail that he and Martha exhibited, but he was shy for fear that I might have regarded him as paranoid.

I didn't. It is my feeling that the federal government has grown to such leviathan proportions since FDR that anybody who isn't paranoid must be on heavy tranquilizers.

George and Martha have never tried LSD or any of the psychedelics. "I don't care much about God and that mystic stuff," George says bluntly when asked about this. "I get far enough out on grass," Martha adds—and quotes one of her nature poems to prove it.

George has other reasons. "A junkie," George says, "has no choice. He's hooked. But somebody who isn't an addict, somebody who has the freedom to say 'yes' or 'no,' has to be crazy to take a pill or powder admittedly manufactured illegally and put it in his mouth. There is just no way of knowing what you're getting."

In short, George and Martha are the ideal, well-adjusted couple of folklore—except for their marijuana.

And one other secret.

It took me a while to discover this—just as, earlier, it had taken a year of friendship before the private pot habit was revealed. (To this day, I am convinced that they told me about that because they had hopes that I, a writer with a beard, might also be dealing on the side.)

One bright, fine Saturday in April, about the middle of the second year of our friendship, I happened to drop by their house and sat and had a few beers with George. After a while, the beer having undergone its usual chemical transformation in passing through the Wilson gut, I excused myself and went upstairs to the bathroom. On my way back, I got turned around and started in the wrong direction. I found myself in George and Martha's bedroom.

There, on the wall, twice as big as life and painted in the most garish colors imaginable, the countenance of the current pope glared down at me. He also looked down, I noticed, directly upon the bed. He had a testy, disapproving expression—such as is often found in Catholic paintings of saints—as if he were about to explain for the thousandth time that, no, you can't use contraceptives even though you already have 12 kids, Mrs. Murphy. And—I noted for the second time—he seemed to be staring straight at the bed.

"Are you a Catholic?" I asked George later that day.

"Ex-Catholic," he said. *"Very* ex. I don't give a damn for all that misty-mystic blah-blah. I go to the Episcopal church here occasionally, but just for appearances. The atomic theory explains all the philosophical questions *I* ever wanted to ask."

Well, there you have his word for it. If I had pressed him about the picture of the pope, he probably would have said he bought it at an auction or a rummage sale or something like that, just because it seemed humorous or campy in its horrible colors and sanctimonious expression. Oh, yes, I'm sure that's the explanation—at least the conscious one.

But the pope stares down at the bed, and his pious face witnesses whatever varieties of pot-inspired, acrobatic sex George and Martha may enjoy. I thought of the theme of the parents witnessing and approving sexual intercourse—a theme very common in pornography and risqué jokes. ("What you and Marie doing in the living room, Benito?" "We're fuckin', Ma!" "That's-a nice, don't fight.") Freudians tell us that this theme is so popular because the desire to perform sexually in front of these authority figures is actually quite widespread, but on a sub-conscious level.

And there are those charges, mentioned again and again in the witch trials of medieval Europe (and in Huysman's novel of 19th-Century diabolism, *La-Bas*), that the witches would use Christian images in their rites and employ them as sexual receptacles in their orgies. Some of these confessions were extracted by torture, but some of them must have been genuine. The witches also used drugs (the henbane and belladonna mentioned earlier) that bring buried subconscious material up into the conscious mind. Every small boy who has written "fuck you" on a fence was acting on the same impulse, to force the authorities to confront that which they claim to hate, that which (we all secretly believe) they lust after just as hotly as the rest of us.

And so, out there behind suburban doors, George and Martha run through the gamut of Kama Sutra positions (or so I imagine it, in my own undoubtedly lewd mind) and the smoke of Shiva fills the air, and the pope looks down on all of it, but cannot speak or object in any way. And, then, his rebellion acted out and cathartically discharged for a few days or a week, George rises in the morning, dresses in his middle-class uniform, and joins the terrapin multitude of other cars driving toward the city and the daily tasks of conformity and responsibility.

Take away the pot and the picture of the pope and who knows what other form of rebellion (political? cultural? psychotic?) George and Martha might attempt next, to prove to themselves that they are individuals with free wills and not just actors in a bourgeois script authored by Dr. Laura Schlessinger.

5

Powders White & Deadly

— So this was the dope that woolied the cad that kinked the
ruck that noised the rape that tried the sap that hugged the
mort?
— That legged in the hoax that joke bilked.
— James Joyce, *Finnegans Wake*

Cocaine has the most licentious reputation of any chemical,
and probably deserves it. Users talk more of a "flash" than a
"high" and all attempts to describe the "flash" sound very much
like a description of orgasm. In fact, cocaine has been used as an
enhancer or booster of sex since at least the 1890s. Aleister
Crowley wrote of it, with self-mocking rapture:

> Stab your demoniac smile to my brain
> Soak me in cognac, cunt and cocaine
>
> Heart of my heart, come out of the rain
> Let's have another go of cocaine
>
> Always go on till you have to stop
> Let's have another sniff? Over the top!

The effects are almost invariably described in orgasmic language by users, and it is tempting to believe that cocaine is, in
some way, a stimulator of the same centers that respond to sexual
charge and discharge. For instance, the black author who writes

under the name "Iceberg Slim" describes his first injection of coke as follows, in his book *Pimp: The Story of My Life*:

> I shivered when it daggered in... It was like a ton of nitro exploded inside me. My ticker went berserk. I could feel it clawing up my throat. It was like I had a million "swipes" in every pore from head to toe. It was like they were all *popping off* together m a nerve-shredding *climax...*
>
> It was like I had been blown apart and all that was left were my eyes. Then *tiny prickly feet of ecstasy* started dancing through me... I felt a superman's surge of power. [Italics added]

The same orgasm-like sensations, and the same sense of superhuman power, are reported, almost monotonously, in cocaine literature the world round. The Peruvian Indians say of *erthroxylon coca,* the bush from which this potent potion is derived, "God is a substance!" The Mexican dealer in the film, *Easy Rider,* when he sells the white powder to Peter Fonda, says proudly: *Esta es la Vida!"* (It is the Life!) William S. Burroughs, the poet of psycho-pharmacology, says with simple awe, "It is the most exhilarating of all drugs."

In essence, the cocaine user feels, after the orgasm-like flash, a long afterglow (sometimes three hours long) during which it seems almost impossible to be frightened, depressed or in any way defeated. Some cokeheads hit again in a half hour, or even sooner, to magnify this afterglow. Whatever happens, the user is, at this stage, master of the situation. Hence, in ancient Peru, the coca leaf was the symbol of the royal family, the Incas, and myth claimed that the children of the sun had given this plant to humanity "to cause the unhappy to forget their misery."

With chronic use, as we shall see, the effects are not quite so lovely. It is worth mentioning, however, that cocaine can be an extremely dangerous drug even without overuse or habituation. Large doses may have a direct, toxic action on the heart muscle and result in immediate death from cardiac failure. Remember that (write this 1000 times before you start experimenting) *death in such cases comes too rapidly to permit any effective counter-therapy to be administered.* (If you *must* try this kick, memorize a table of weights and measures and learn how to use them. Your life may depend on it.)

The effects of cocaine abuse have already been described, briefly, in Chapter One, and will now be discussed further. One of its most characteristic side effects, curiously, is the well-known "coke bugs" renowned in underground lore for at least 90 years. These are tiny spots in the visual field, moving in a peculiarly "swarming" fashion, and regarded as insects by most people suffering their presence. In acute cases, the "bugs" are not only seen but felt, and seem to be *under the skin* of the victim. Curiously, heavy use of Benzedrine or other amphetamine compounds sometimes produces the same vision. Truck drivers, who often hit the Benzedrine trail very hard on long trips, know that it is time to stop by the side of the road and recuperate when the "spiders" suddenly appear on the windshield.

It is possible that these specks are inside the eye and usually ignored (one can see them in a clear sky without any drug if one relaxes the body and looks upward long enough); these stimulant drugs seem to bring the specs into sharper focus. Even more curiously, patients who have completed prolonged Reichian psychotherapy often see them without drugs, and they appear blue in this context but move in the same "swarming" pattern; in this case, they are identified with the "orgone" energy postulated by Dr. Reich. Finally, students of yoga often see them while doing *pranayama,* the heavy breathing used in hatha- and raja-yoga. Why they appear as benign whorls of energy in the Reichian or yogic context, and as maddeningly irritating insects in the context of cocaine or amphetamine, is still a mystery.[1]

---

[1] These "bugs" or "orgones" seem to be relatives of the geometric light displays witnessed by people on peyote or its derivative, mescaline. They also appear in sensory withdrawal experiments, in which the subject is submerged in a tank of water and isolated from all outside stimuli; indeed, one stage of sensory withdrawal is called 'mescaline" by the researchers because of this similarity. Alan W. Watts has suggested that what is happening in these cases is that the electrical patterns in the brain itself are being projected outward. Perhaps; but see, also, the lady in the last chapter, who found herself amid "the stars" while having an orgasm under the influence of marijuana. The vision of Nuit, the Egyptian goddess of the night sky and the stars, is the goal of Aleister Crowley's sex magic, and he recorded in his most emotionally satisfying vision that the universe was "Nothing, with

There are worse effects than "coke bugs" for the cocaine abuser. Symptoms very similar to those of paranoid schizophrenia—almost identical with them, in fact—often appear. William S. Burroughs, for example, tells of a friend who got the copper horrors (visions of policemen) while sniffing too much coke. Just like a madman in a joke, this fellow ran into the alley and hid *his head* in a garbage can, evidently convinced that this made him totally invisible. (Again, the logic of amphetamine is similar. DeRopp, in *Drugs and the Mind,* tells of a truck driver who took so much Benzedrine that he became convinced "Benny" was driving the truck and therefore crawled into the back to have a nap. "Benny" drove him into a ditch, but he survived to tell the tale.)

The Epic of Cocaine

The most memorable account of cocaine as both a provoker of ecstasy and a stimulator of madness is undoubtedly Aleister Crowley's *The Diary of a Drug Fiend,* which was the subject of a campaign of incredible vilification in the English press when it was published in 1920. *John Bull* and similar right-wing moralistic tabloids denounced Crowley in terms that have clung to his reputation permanently; some of their charming headlines were "A Cannibal at Large," "A Man We'd Like to Hang," "The Wickedest Man in the World," and (in something of an anticlimax) "A Pro-German and a Revolutionary." The novel, in today's context, hardly seems to deserve such a sharp response, although it is still somewhat controversial. As an underground favorite since it was written, it has played a decided role in developing the philosophy or mystique of the Drug Revolution.

Crowley's protagonist is named Sir Peter Pendragon, a name which implies that he is descended from the original royal family of King Arthur of the Round Table. A young man who once wanted to be an engineer, Sir Peter received his knighthood and

---

twinkles—but *what* twinkles!" Through such odd reports we might eventually trace an understanding of how bioelectricity converts into thought and mind.

a small fortune when his uncle died. The money turned him into an empty-headed wastrel.

In the first chapter, Sir Peter drops in on a London nightclub, meets a middle-aged jet-setter who offers him some cocaine, and decides to sample the drug. Just as the flash hits him, a beautiful young woman named Lou enters and chants a Gnostic hymn typical of Crowley's odd religiosity:

> O Thou red cobra of desire, that art unhooded by the hands of girls! I adore Thee, Evoe! I adore Thee, IAO!
> O Thou burning sword of passion, that art torn on the anvil of flesh! I adore Thee, Evoe! I adore Thee, IAO!
> O Thou snow-white chalice of Love, that art filled up with the red lusts of man! I adore Thee, Evoe! I adore Thee, IAO!
> O Thou naked virgin of love, that art caught in a net of roses! I adore Thee, Evoe! I adore Thee, IAO!
> O Thou sparkling wine-cup of light, whose foaming is the heart's blood of the stars! I adore Thee, Evoe! I adore Thee, IAO![1]

Sir Peter, fortified by a few more sniffs of cocaine, dances with the beautiful Lou as she sings several more choruses of this highly erotic and highly mystical chant. As they whirl across the floor in a dance of courtship (they haven't spoken to each other yet; she is still singing the Gnostic hymn), the cocaine hits again and again. "I had exploded," Sir Peter writes:

> I was the slayer and the slain!... We were the only two people in the Universe—she and I. The only force that existed in the Universe was the attraction between us... We went up and down the floor of the club; but, of course, it wasn't the floor of the club, there wasn't the club... One was the Universe, eternally whirling. There was no possibility of fatigue...

Within a few hours, picking up some more cocaine on the way, Sir Peter and Lou are off on a trip to France in his private

---

[1] The name *Evoe* is also used for the horned god (Pan?) in the contemporary witch cult, but this is because Crowley wrote their rituals for them (and was handsomely paid for it, by Gerald Gardner). *IAO* is the Gnostic name for the supreme divinity, who created Jehovah and all the other gods in the archetypal world, who thereupon created the material world.

airplane. He has no idea whether he can fly while under the influence of the drug, but he sees no reason not to try:

> For the first time in my life I was being absolutely myself, freed from all inhibitions of body, intellect and training…. I seem to remember asking myself if I was insane and answering, "Of course I am—sanity is a compromise. Sanity is the thing that keeps one back."

His mystical identification with Lou spreads to include the airplane and the sky: "I could hear the beat of my heart. It was one with the beat of the engine… I could not bear the weight of the air. Let us soar higher, ever higher. I increased the speed…"

Sir Peter soon discovers that, in his cocaine enthusiasm, he had forgotten to check the fuel. Even when the engine stalls, however, his only thought is that he can handle the situation—superman that he is—if only he takes another snort of cocaine first:

> As we swooped down toward the sea in huge wide spirals, I managed to extract my bottle. Of course, I realized instantly the impossibility of taking it by the nose in such a wind. I pulled out the cork, and thrust my tongue into the neck of the bottle.
>
> We were still three thousand feet or more above the sea. I had plenty of time, infinite time, I thought, as the drug took hold, to make my decision. I acted with superb aplomb…

He manages a quite creditable landing at sea, still high and euphoric. They are then picked up by a French fishing boat and rush on to Paris, where they are married and embark on a honeymoon, after obtaining some more cocaine, of course.

After several weeks of ecstatic sex and cocaine (treated in euphemisms; Crowley was writing for British publications in 1920), the coke bringdown begins to hit. At this point, a kindly friend introduces them to heroin—just the perfect sedative for cocaine nerves. Besides, Sir Peter and Lou are quite convinced by now that all the warnings about cocaine being addictive are just nonsense, so why should they believe the same fuddy-duddy medical authorities when they say that heroin is addictive?

The first part of the book is labeled "Paradise"; we now enter Book Two, which is called "Inferno." Sir Peter realizes one day that they have used up his year's annuity on his fortune; he has to face the humiliation of borrowing ahead on it from the lawyer who manages the estate. He also realizes, shortly, that he and Lou are quite definitely addicted to heroin, just as the fuddy-duddy doctors had warned.

The decline thereafter is dizzily swift. In a few chapters, Peter and Lou arrive at a kind of mole-like existence on his country estate, stretching out his money to pay for ecstatic cocaine trances to cheer them up (and stave off the growing horror of their situation), together with a steady diet of heroin (to calm them down and hold back the agonies of withdrawal that they have already experienced a few times). There is little additional cash for food or similar distractions. Lou is soon prostituting herself, and Sir Peter, under the influence of the cocaine, has become convinced that German agents are skulking about the huge house plotting against them. Both are very close to the clinical status of pure paranoid schizophrenia.

Eventually, in a moment of terrible clarity, they realize exactly where they are at. They attempt suicide—unsuccessfully.

In the third, and most controversial part of the book, "Purgatorio", Peter and Lou attempt a cure under the auspices of a mysterious magician named King Lamus—a thinly disguised portrait of Crowley himself. At the Abbey of Thelema (based on an actual religious retreat once run by Crowley in Sicily), Peter and Lou are put in a situation where all the cocaine and heroin they can possibly want is immediately and easily available to them. King Lamus tells them, using Crowley's favorite slogan, "Do what thou wilt shall be the whole of the law."

There is a gimmick, of course. In fact, there are several gimmicks. The abbey, although hardly as austere as a Christian monastery, is quite isolated from civilization; Peter and Lou are soon confronted with the most underrated but powerful force in the world—boredom. There are no movies, nightclubs or other distractions. When they complain, King Lamus tells them again, "Do what thou wilt shall be the whole of the law." They soon discover that, in spite of their hedonistic existence, they have never actually done their "will" in a profound sense, but have only followed momentary whims. Isolated at the abbey, they are forced to ask themselves, again and again, what they truly do "will" for their subsequent lives.

Meanwhile, although Lamus refuses to ever speak a word against cocaine or heroin, and uses a variety of drugs himself at various times, Peter and Lou are required, as a condition of membership in the abbey, to keep careful records of their psychological and spiritual progress. Specifically, they can use as much dope as they want, but on each occasion they must write in their record book *why* they used the drug on this particular occasion. A genuine and quite rational distaste for drug excess begins to grow in them, although Lamus refuses to allow them to experience this as a moral guilt, and endlessly repeats his slogan about "Do what thou wilt," sometimes varied to "Find your True Will and follow it."

Crowley provides, incidentally, a bitterly brilliant insight into the mind of the addict in the list of reasons for continuing to take heroin. Among them are:

1. My cough is very bad this morning...
3. I can't sleep without it.
4. I can't keep awake without it.
5. I must be at my very best to do what I have to do. If I can bring that off, I need never take it again.
6. I must show I am master of it—free to say either "yes" or "no." And I must be perfectly sure by saying "yes" at this moment. My refusal to take it at the moment shows weakness...
8. It is dangerous to stop too suddenly...
10. It is very bad for the mind to be constantly preoccupied with the question of the drug. It is better to take a small dose and rid myself of the obsession...
19. Most of us dig our graves with our teeth. Heroin has destroyed my appetite, therefore it is good for me.
20. I have gotten into all sorts of messes with women in the past. Heroin has destroyed my interest in them...
25. I am feeling very, very rotten and a very, very little would make me feel so very, very good...
26. We can't stop while we have it—the temptation is too strong. The best way is to finish it. We probably won't be able to get any more, so we take it in order to stop taking it.
27. ...Suppose I take all this pain to stop drugs and then get cancer or something right away, what a fool I shall feel!

The only drug I have ever been addicted to was nicotine, which I have quit five times in the last 20 years. Speaking from experience, I must say that Crowley has great understanding of the addict mentality and the way the biological need for the drug can generate "reasons" that almost seem rational at the time. Writing down the reasons for taking another cigarette, Crowley fashion, I have found is a real help in recognizing their self-deceiving quality and really quitting.

The climax comes when Sir Peter, driven into extreme stress by boredom in unrelieved doses, and finding himself less and less enjoying his drugs as the hollowness of the above reasons becomes clearer and clearer, wakes up one afternoon to realize he has been designing a new airplane engine all day. Lamus then tells him that he didn't speak to anybody during lunch and that he was almost in the same sort of trance as any "holy man" in the Orient. According to Lamus (and Crowley), this is the meaning of "doing one's will," and it is not always a religious experience as we are usually told. Not only a scientist, but a businessman or virtually anyone who is truly "entranced" by a project achieves some variety of the same mental concentration and transcendence of the usual ego hang-ups.

Sir Peter, in short, had the "true will" of an engineer, but the inheritance that made him rich gave him negative, upper-class attitudes toward learning a profession. Ergo, isolated from his own will, he drifted from one pointless pleasure to another, until heroin got its hooks into him and then he drifted toward self-destruction. (The same, Crowley would probably insist, accounts for people who are born with the true will of an engineer but are too poor to afford engineering school; they, too, can become addicts easily.) Having found his true will, Sir Peter does not need heroin.

Lou, women's liberationists will be enraged to hear, also finds her true will, but it consists of being a good wife to her previously simple-minded husband in his new guise as scientific genius.

King Lamus draws the moral of the story, quoting from Crowley's own *Book of the Law,* in which the goddess Nuit says, "To worship me take wine and strange drugs whereof I will tell my prophet and be drunk thereof. They shall not harm thee at all." After admitting that this might "tempt people to be foolhardy," Lamus says:

> ... if you read it carelessly and act on it rashly, with the blind faith of a fanatic, it might very well lead to trouble. But nature is full of devices for eliminating anything that cannot master its environment... The only excuse for using a drug of any sort, whether it's quinine or Epsom-salt, is to assist nature to overcome some obstacle to her proper functions. The danger of the so-called habit-forming drugs is that they fool you into trying to dodge the toil essential to spiritual and intellectual development. But they are not simply man-traps. There is nothing in nature which cannot be used for our benefit, and it is up to us to use it wisely... And every man and every woman is a star. The taking of a drug should be a carefully thought-out and purposeful religious act. Experience alone can teach you the right conditions in which the act is legitimate, that is, when it will assist you to do your will.

This is, of course, the approach taken in those societies that have sought to control drugs by making them sacred and putting them in a religious context, as distinguished from those cultures that seek to control them by passing laws against them. Paradoxical as Crowley's reasoning may sound to most of us, many anthropologists have agreed that drugs are actually less of a social problem in the former context than in the latter.

At the end of the book, Sir Peter and Lou return to England where he plans to build a laboratory and continue his researches and experiments on airplane motors. They have no more desire for heroin, but, typical of Crowley's attitudes, they continue to use cocaine occasionally in a religious-erotic context.

John Bull and other tabloids denounced this novel as an attempt to seduce England into irresponsible drug abuse, and implied that Crowley was paid for this dirty work by the German High Command. (Actually, the first oath required of candidates for the Ordo Templi Orientis, Crowley's "magick" freemasonic society, was "I will never allow myself to be mastered by any force or any person," and it was explicitly stated to the novice that this oath included drink and drugs.) Crowley's idea, however, lives on. Responsible use of drugs in a religious setting, as an alternative to prohibitive laws that are violated widely, is still urged by persons as diverse as poet Robert Graves, philosopher

Alan Watts, Dr. John Lilly, Dr. Humphrey Osmund, Dr. Huston Smith, novelist Ken Kesey, and many others; and the conservatives still reply that to adopt such a policy will lead to reckless abuse and chaos. They seem not to have observed that the prohibitive laws they support have already produced precisely those results along with more crime, more violence, and more police corruption.

Heroin: Treacherous Antidote

Heroin inspires more superstitious terror than any other drug, and—although there are good reasons for staying far, far away from it—we must admit that much of the terror is based on mythology. For one thing, there are very few heroin addicts around, and, being afraid of them is, literally, being afraid of a group that we outnumber by odds of 400 to 1. To put it mildly, that is not very brave of us. It is especially old-maidish since, of all drug users, heroin junkies tend to be the most passive, lethargic and non-aggressive. They are, in a word, much more afraid of us than we are of them.

The relations between the junkie and the straight citizen are, in fact, rather like the old comedy routine in which two frightened individuals keep trying to terrorize each other while actually backing away from a fight. Weird mythology about heroin addicts is believed widely, and part of it (as Dr. Robert DeRopp has pointed out) is based on confusion between heroin and cocaine. Both are white powders; both are sometimes called "snow", both can be sniffed or injected with a needle; both provide a quick hit followed by a slow afterglow. On this basis, a legendary composite "dope fiend" has been created to haunt the nightmares of the straight citizenry.

The only real link is that cocaine is, *sometimes,* a kind of "stepping stone" to heroin, for reasons discussed earlier. (In actual fact, however, heroin seems more closely allied to alcohol, in that heavy booze drinkers, according to a University of California study, are more likely to become heroin addicts than are heavy abusers of cocaine, marijuana or any other drug; and recent New York studies have shown that a significant minority of heroin addicts, after a methadone withdrawal program, become alcoholics. Alcohol and heroin are *turn-off* drugs, tending to move the user toward torpor or oblivion, whereas cocaine, pot, the amphetamines, and even the LSD-type psychedelics, whatever their other qualities, all tend to be *turn-ons,* moving the user toward excitation or even hyper-excitation.)

The cocaine user is often sexually stimulated; the heroin user never is. The cocaine user almost always sniffs, although he can inject; the heroin user almost always injects, although he can sniff. The cocaine *ab*user, as his habit becomes chronic, turns quasi-paranoid and hostile; the heroin *ab*user, as his habit becomes an addiction, turns increasingly passive, torpid, withdrawn or "on the nod," in addicts' jargon. Above all, the cocaine user, however heavy his habit, suffers no true physiological withdrawal if he discontinues the drug—although he is often depressed and, sometimes, hallucinatory; the heroin addict suffers such a hideous withdrawal syndrome—including muscular convulsions, vomiting and diarrhea—that to cause a man to become addicted and then cut off his supply is the cruelest torture imaginable.

Even here, however, the element of mythology tinges our picture of the junkie. Heroin withdrawal is, indeed, terrible, but it is not necessarily the worst form of drug withdrawal. Some authorities suspect that withdrawal from barbiturate addiction is even more stressful, and this is indicated by the fact that there are hardly any records of heroin junkies actually dying of withdrawal syndrome (although they often wish for death). Barbiturate addicts, however, often die in the same circumstances, unless they receive careful medical attention. (William S. Burroughs has noted that his one barbiturate withdrawal was more agonizing than his 11 heroin withdrawals.)

Some lower-level criminals have been known to sniff cocaine before going out on a hold-up, to boost their nerve; in popular lore this has been transferred, very inaccurately, to the heroin addict. In fact, a shot of heroin would probably induce the mood to lie around in his pad and postpone the robbery indefinitely (or until he needs money for another fix). Similarly, cocaine abusers are often irrationally violent and attack their friends, or total strangers, without apparent motive. (This is because they *know* that the victim has actually been plotting against them.) Heroin addicts are about the most nonviolent citizens around outside of the Quakers.

> As the heroin hit home, a bolt of energy shot through him. All fear was gone; he was a God, and nothing could stand in his way. Across the street, a young girl walked toward the park. Lurching to his feet, he headed for the door, unable and unwilling to control the lust that had surged through him at the sight of her...

That kind of cliché, which used to be endemic in true-detective magazines and tabloids, is utter rubbish. *Heroin addicts are always impotent;* or, if there are any exceptions to this rule, they are few and far between. They never become "high" in the sense that pot smokers, speed freaks, cokeheads or even boozehounds become "high." Basically, they behave like nobody so much as your Aunt Matilda since the doctor put her on heavy tranquilizers. Heroin is, indeed, a heavy tranquilizer itself.

Heroin & Sex

As Dr. Hoffman notes in his *Comprehensive Psychology*:

> Over and over again one hears addicts describe the effects of their injection in sexual terms. One addict said that after a fix he felt as if he were coming from every pore. Another said that he used to inject the solution in a rhythmic fashion until it was all used up, and said this was akin to masturbation albeit much better.

In fact, the rhythmic manner of injection is actually called *jerking off* in American addict circles, according to Rabbi Joseph Rosenbloom, writing in *The Reporter* in 1959. I once knew a young woman from San Francisco who, in describing to me how two male addicts she knew used to inject each other, said, "The way they played with the needles and clucked and fussed, it was just like a sexual act. As if they were a pair of fags."

The Freudians, of course, assume that some variety of sexual misery is what causes addiction in the first place. Like most Freudian theories, this is undoubtedly oversimplified, since it ignores the fact that, epidemiologically, addiction is a disease of exposure, just like malaria (that is, if you are born in Harlem, you will more likely become a junkie than somebody born on Park Avenue). Nevertheless, sex and junk have some symbiotic relationship, if only because junk destroys physical sex and leaves the addicts with no eroticism except in their fantasy. This probably explains their sexual games with their needles.

It is not that addicts aren't people with histories of sex problems; rather, they are people with so many problems that sex is hardly conspicuous among their hang-ups. For instance, there is some experimental evidence that the *pleasure* of heroin, which varies widely among different subjects, is almost nonexistent for the person who isn't abnormally troubled. Opiates are "not inherently attractive," as the Chien study in England concluded; even earlier, in 1925, Kolb had published a study showing that "the intensity of pleasure produced by opiates is in direct proportion to the degree of psychopathy of the person who becomes an addict."

In other words, heroin seems to affect the more normal individuals in the same way that a tranquilizer does—the effect is hardly perceptible to consciousness—but produces a definite "hit" and afterglow for the seriously disturbed. The only theory that can account for these facts is that (a) heroin innately produces no pleasure, (b) the pleasure experienced by the mentally disturbed user is equivalent to that felt by normal people, most of the time and (c) it appears as a bolt of joy to the user because his ordinary state is one of acute misery. More simply, heroin, which was invented as a pain killer originally, acts as a psychological pain killer to those who are potential addicts. It makes life bearable, which is all they ask.

There is even evidence, summarized in Peter Laurie's book *Drugs,* that heroin addicts are people who were, before addiction, well on the way to becoming schizophrenic. The addiction has, in some chemical fashion not quite clear, staved off the schizophrenia. "It is even possible," as Laurie comments ironically, "that the incipient psychotic who chooses drugs is in a better position than one who tries to cope alone." Many doctors today are putting schizophrenics on heavy tranquilizers which have the same sedative action as heroin, with the overt intent of lessening a nervous or mental breakdown. The addict is, if this theory is true, one who had elected this preventive therapy against insanity as a kind of prescription for himself.

He loses his sexuality; he loses that mysterious faculty called freedom, for he is henceforth enslaved to the drug; he becomes a scapegoat and a victim of society's most irrational sadisms (at least in America); but he has escaped from terrors that were slowly escalating and undermining his very identity. Only those who have passed through that nightmare of eternal[1] duration called "a psychotic episode" can empathize fully with this decision.

The cost of continuing to treat these born losers as criminals is absolutely staggering. There are, approximately, 1,600,000 addicts in the U.S., and the average habit costs $150 per day. The addicts, therefore, need 87.6 *billion* dollars per year to pay for their dope. A few of them are doctors, and can steal opiate drugs to keep themselves going; a number are attractive young women and have the dubious privilege of prostituting themselves; but the rest must steal. Since it generally takes about $300 worth of merchandise to pry $150 loose from an underworld fence, the addicts who are stealing are not stealing $150 a day but $300 a day—from all the rest of us. That's where your television went when your apartment was robbed. That's where your car went when it was heisted. That's where most stolen property goes nowadays. If even half of the addicts (a conservative estimate) are stealing to support their habit, it's still costing us around a trillion dollars per year to maintain these laws.

If the addicts were given a daily supply of junk *free* it would cost, by comparison, only around 292 *million* dollars per year for the whole country, because, without the black market, heroin can be manufactured at a cost—per addict per day—of approximately 50 cents—one *three hundredth* of the street price. (To satisfy the possible complaint that giving the addicts free junk would corrupt their morals, the addicts could be required to work a few hours a month to cover the $15 cost for that month's supply.)

Would addiction spread further under such a system? The answer seems to be: not much. As we have already seen, most normal people get *no* kick at all from heroin. Any heroin that got

---

[1] There is no time in the psychotic's world. Three months of schizophrenia is longer than the average reader's life.

into general circulation would still be competing with drugs of less frightening reputation: alcohol, barbiturates and tranquilizers. Probably, most addict personalities—those who are not of low educational level and not under especially acute stress— would continue to choose these "more acceptable" depressants. And, of course, any decriminalization of addiction could still retain the laws against sale, to discourage any addict from selling part of his day's ration to a curious non-addict.

One additional fact about heroin has been observed by the very distinguished Dr. Joel Fort and is worth quoting here. It should give us a bit more perspective on this much-sensationalized problem. Says Dr. Fort:

> Heroin is a hard drug only in the sense that the addiction is very strong: it's much softer than many other drugs in the dimension of actual physical harm to the body. Chronic excessive use of heroin produces no permanent damage at all except for the addiction itself—which is, of course, a form of slavery. Chronic excessive use of alcohol, by comparison, would inevitably create irreversible and often fatal destruction of the liver and brain.

Chronic excessive use of amphetamines also produces a situation, in a matter of months, much worse than that of any heroin addict—except, of course, for those junkies who have been through "cold turkey" withdrawal in a city jail and never quite recovered from it.

You are wise if you fear heroin—it is a bad trip in the long run. But fearing the *heroin addict is* one of the most absurd prejudices of our time. Even under our present laws, which makes it necessary for most of them to steal to get their junk, few are armed robbers; true to their passive and defeatist personality type, they generally become sneak thieves striking only when a house is empty, evidently feeling that even with a gun they couldn't terrorize anybody into surrendering property to them knowingly. William S. Burroughs has commented that, in his years as a junkie, he hardly recalls an addict who committed a crime of violence.

Burroughs, one ex-addict who doesn't make his living by lecturing for the police, adds pointedly:

They tend to be sneak thieves, shoplifters and lush rollers.[1] If
they could obtain the drug legally, their crimes would vanish.
As an occasional citizen of New York, I consider the burglaries committed by desperate addicts to be immoral and a god-
damned nuisance. I say give them some legal junk before they
steal my typewriter.

The Poppy Itself

The origin of heroin—and of morphine; and laudanum, Edgar
Allan Poe's habit; and pantopon, the drug popular in addict
society back in the 1920s; and Demerol, Hermann Goering's
happiness pills; and paregoric; and the codeine that Sherlock
Holmes used to cool down his cocaine habit—is the opium
poppy. This is probably the most accursed and hated plant in the
world, and has been creating addicts in both the East and the
West since the dawn of civilization.

Most of the opium poppies in the world today (aside from a
small fertile area in Turkey) grow in the "opium triangle" as
Interpol calls it: a section of Laos, Thailand and Vietnam mostly
under the control of the Meos tribesmen. According to the
investigations of Dr. Joel Fort and independent reporters for *The
New York Times* and the *Christian Science Monitor,* the Meos
farmers sell this crop to high officials in the Thai, Laotian and
(then) South Vietnamese governments, among whom the family
of General Ky was once quite prominent. From there it is passed
on through the "Corsican Mafia" to the south of France and then
placed on the international market. Nobody seems to know why
the U.S. government, allegedly conducting a "war" against
heroin, still continues to give economic and military aid to the
Thai, Laotian and Vietnamese governments, thereby allowing
them to continue this trade. Dr. Michael Aldrich and poet Allen
Ginsberg, who have researched this subject extensively and will
lecture or write on it at any invitation, even believe that there is
sufficient evidence to prove that the CIA actively helps in the
transport of the raw opium at times.[2] Whether that is true or not,

---

[1] Those who rob sleeping drunks, usually on subways.

[2] By the 1990s, few people doubted the overwhelming evidence that
the CIA had done exactly that.

the United States has become involved in the heroin business that
it is, at the same time, "fighting" elsewhere.

This is a very mysterious part of contemporary history and
may not be clarified fully in our lifetime. (Meanwhile, the curious reader may consult the November, 1972 issue of *Harper's,*
in which the CIA denies its involvement in the heroin trade and
Harper's editors give their reasons for doubting this denial. A
recent book *The Politics of Heroin in Southeast Asia* documents
Harper's charges with greater detail.) Charges and denials
notwithstanding, there can be little doubt that if the bombs
dropped on the Indochinese people since Nixon became President—more than four times the total tonnage dropped on Europe
and North Africa during World War II—had been dropped,
instead, on these poppy fields, there would be very little heroin
in the world today. It does cause one to wonder, especially when
a *Christian Science Monitor* reporter states that the CIA handled
so much of the crop at one time that their planes became known
in the area as "Air Opium."

The primary derivative of the poppy, opium itself, is often
thought to be more stimulating, more pleasurable, and even more
psychedelic than its refined and specialized narcotic children:
morphine, heroin, and so on. This notion is based on the writings
of several very gifted opium addicts—especially Thomas
DeQuincey, author of the classic *Confessions of an English
Opium-Eater,* Samuel Taylor Coleridge ("Rime of the Ancient
Mariner"), and French playwright Jean Cocteau. At times, these
writers even give the impression that opium is an aphrodisiac.

It is necessary to emphasize that DeQuincey, Coleridge and
Cocteau were exceptionally talented (and exceptionally disturbed) individuals. In DeQuincey's case, furthermore, the extravagant and glorious visions he describes were all experienced,
as Dr. Robert DeRopp notes, "between sleeping and waking,"
when all talented people, even without opium, can project their
imaginations most vividly. (This is technically known as hypna-
gogic hallucination, needs no drugs and is practiced as a method
of mind expansion by some occult schools, such as Louis
Culling's "Great Body of God.") For the majority of opium
addicts whose medical records exist, no such psychedelic effects
are recorded, and most of them have the same depressed or

soporific experiences as morphine or heroin addicts. In short, if you are looking for psychedelic effects, use the real psychedelics; unless you're an artist of DeQuincey's or Coleridge's stature, you are very unlikely to find them on opium.

It needs to be stated again and again that *all opiates without exception* are fundamentally depressants, so that the normal pattern, as dosage is increased, is from torpor to sleep to coma (ending in death, if there is an overdose).

I am reminded here of a natural-food crusader I once knew. This fellow regarded most food fanatics as hopelessly corrupt compromisers who ate almost as many bad things as you or I eat; only *he* had the correct "natural" diet, which consisted entirely of nuts and *uncooked* vegetables. I asked him once what was the greatest single benefit he got out of that regime. "It solved all my sex problems," he said at once.

"Really?" I asked, intrigued. "How did it do that?"

"I hardly ever have any sex drive anymore," he said, unabashed, even a bit proud. "I don't *need* women the way I used to. I'm free. No problems in *that* area at all.*"

A heroin (or opiate) diet seems to "solve" sex problems in the same way this meatless diet does: by removing sex entirely. This is analogous to Jonathan Swift's famous solution to the barefooted condition of the poor in Ireland (cutting off their feet). It will recommend itself only to those who have lost all faith and hope that a real solution is possible.

It is possible that some people have been so mauled by life in this society that such a semi-suicide is the best alternative to *real* suicide for them. Curiously, a hell of a lot of M.D.s are using the same logic in relentlessly over-prescribing tranquilizers, many of which are quite habit forming (e.g., Librium) and some of which (e.g. Tofranil), are definitely linked with impotence according to psycho-pharmacologists. As Dr. Lawrence Kolb told a Congressional committee way back in 1925, "There is ... a certain type of shrinking neurotic individual who can't meet the demands of life, is afraid to meet people, has anxieties and fears, who if they took small amounts of narcotics—and I have examined quite a few of them—would be better and more efficient people than they would be without it." Dr. Kolb also described two physicians who were opiate addicts and practiced successfully until they managed to "kick the habit," after which they became hope-less problems to themselves and their families. "These two physicians that I am talking about didn't get *cured,*" Dr. Kolb said scornfully, "they should have had it (the drug) forever, because it (the cure) would not mean anything but an insane asy-lum for them, and they were doing a pretty good job of work as physicians when they were on the drug and regularly taking it."

American society has ignored Dr. Kolb's pragmatic approach for decades and has struggled heroically to get all these lost souls off their depressant drugs. Or has it? The "war against heroin" continues; but in New York, the state has abandoned the hope of real "cure" and is satisfied just to get the junkies off an addicting drug it has made illegal—heroin—and onto an equally addicting drug it has made legal—methadone; and in the nation at large, prescriptions for central nervous system depressants are said to run into the tens of millions every year. The official attitude, by default, now appears to be, "If you can't bear our society without being half-asleep, let us at least control which drug you choose to be half-asleep on." This is not a formula for a non-addicted nation. It is a face-saving game to allow those bureaucrats whom William S. Burroughs calls "control addicts" to continue to believe that they are, by God, controlling everybody they want to control.

Reject:
The Story of Holy Out

> Only the prick of a needle
> Charged from a wizard well!
> Is that sufficient to wheedle
> A soul from heaven to hell?
> Was man's spirit weaned
> From fear of ghosts and gods
> To fawn at the feet of a fiend?
> Is it such terrible odds—
> The heir of ages of wonder,
> The crown of earth for an hour,
> The master of tide and thunder
> Against the juice of a flower?
> Ay! in the roar and the rattle
> Of all the armies of sin,
> This is the only battle
> He never was known to win.
>   — Aleister Crowley, "Ballad of Heroin"

"I never rob strangers," Holy Out said. "It's too risky. If they come home suddenly and catch me, they're likely to call the cops."

He was the guest on a radio program I was moderating—one of those years when I had given up writing entirely and was trying to earn a living in some more plausible way—and he had warned me in advance that he would take a shot of H before coming to the studio. He had obviously done so, and he was perfectly relaxed as he passed that remark. A middle-aged white man with an educated vocabulary, he was not the average New York junkie, except for his sleepy eyes. When you looked deep into those pools of torpor, you had no doubt that he was riding the great white horse into junkie dream land. He seemed half asleep as he talked about who he preferred to rob.

"Oh," I said, very conscious of the microphone on the table. "You seem to be implying that you rob from your friends."

"Sure," he said. "A lot of junkies do. You see, a stranger will turn you in to the cops, but a friend will have more sympathy. He'll say, 'Well, I know you're a junkie, and it's not your fault.' Of course, they kinda cool off on you after that. You have to keep making new friends."

I thought of how cordial he had been since I first contacted him about doing this interview. I also thought of my typewriter, tape recorder and hi-fi set.

"If any of your friends were robbed recently and didn't suspect you," I commented, "they're probably getting that idea about now."

Holy Out thought about this so long that I became conscious of the dead air going out to our listeners. When I was about to jump into the vacuum, he finally spoke—with that junkie placidity that is so Buddha-like.

"I don't expect people to like me for long," he said.

There you have it. That, in essence, is the junkie philosophy. So relentlessly social an animal is mankind that most of us would rather have cancer than admit that people don't like us; but to a man on heroin any truth can be faced without an emotional response. Holy Out could have announced just as peacefully that he had just learned he had leprosy. To a junkie, "fact is fact" and emotion is something other people possess and get agitated over. Here's food. Here's shit. Here's a beautiful young woman, stark naked. Here's a starving child. You will react differently to each of those sights, but a junkie will respond in exactly the same way to all of them, which is to say that he won't respond at all.

I once went to the funeral of a friend's father. The friend, whom I'll call Tony, was smiling in a bemused, dreamy sort of

way all through the ceremony. Some of the mourners must have
thought he had a king-size Oedipus complex to be enjoying his
father's funeral so thoroughly. Later, Tony mentioned to me that
he had taken a heavy dose of tranquilizers to get himself through
the ritual—it was one of those ghastly, old-fashioned affairs with
an open coffin and hysterical female relatives.

A junkie would have sat through it all with the same somno-
lent smile. His greatest moment of emotional response—an arid
sort—would occur if he were to wonder how much he might get
from a fence were he to dig up the coffin and steal the corpse's
jewelry.

The difference between junkies and trankheads is, to some
extent, a class difference. Most trankheads are middle class and
WASP; most junkies are lower class and black or Latin. The
junkies are the people who were too ignorant, or too shy of doctors, to have sought a legal prescription for tranquilizers when
the stresses became too great for them. Instead, they went around
the corner and bought a stronger depressant from the friendly
neighborhood pusher.

Holy Out also told me, on that radio interview, about a cold
turkey withdrawal he had been through in a city jail. One particularly sadistic guard liked to come around, while Holy Out was
having convulsions, and wave a jar of white powder, which he
claimed was heroin. "Do you really want it? Really, really want
it? Ask me real nice, now…" Naturally, when Holy Out finally
abandoned his skepticism and begged for the stuff (whatever it
was), he didn't get it. He got a horse laugh instead.

Holy Out recounted this in the same thoughtful, level tone in
which he had commented that he didn't expect people to like
him. It was a fact, but it didn't *mean* anything. "I hated his guts,"
he commented placidly, just as you or I might say: "I paid a
quarter for a candy bar." The past tense is entirely past in the
junk world. The guard's sadism was just a fact; any acts of kind-
ness he remembered were also just facts. To be angry about one
or grateful for the others would be entirely beyond his emotional
and energetic resources. There was no emotional being, "Holy
Out," to react to experience; there was only an observer, "Holy
Out," who recorded what happened.

When I asked him how he had acquired that nickname, which was fairly well-known in some parts of town, he told me that a poet had pinned it on him. "I didn't understand it at first," he added, "but everybody was repeating it and I finally got used to it. Now I like it. Out is where I am and where I want to stay. Holy, wholly out."

One of my favorite moments came when I asked him about narcotics officers.

"They're crazier than most cops," he said without any inflection. "There's one guy I know who never stops smiling. No matter what happens. Like he's got his own pusher inside him. And there's another who never closes his mouth. It's always hanging open, like he's always surprised. Yeah," he added reflectively, "they're a pretty weird bunch."

I had expected a diatribe about cruelty, injustice, frame-ups— the typical reaction of potheads who have been in jail. This was a different slant. "Are you seriously telling our listeners," I asked, "that everybody on the narcotics squad is psychotic?"

"Well," he said, "they're not like other cops. They seem to live in a little world all their own. And I'll tell you one more thing: they hate to be transferred to another department. They'll fight like hell to stay in narco. You know why? They love the undercover work. Being a fake junkie is just as habit forming as being a real junkie."

When I tried to get a coherent account of how Holy Out had become a junkie, I ran into a stone wall. On this one question mental processes suddenly became similar to those of intelligent schizophrenics, and there seemed no way to bring him down from the abstract to the concrete.

"I suppose you might say I was maladjusted," was his first approximation. When I tried to zero in for extensional data, he went even higher up on the abstraction ladder and began talking about "sociological and psychological tensions."

"Let me put it this way," I said. "How did you get the heroin you used in your very first shot?"

"Well," he said, "you have to understand the background." He talked for five minutes about sociological problems and behavior patterns and psychological variables.

"That's very interesting," I said, "but did somebody offer it to you, or did you ask for it?"

"You don't have to *ask,*" he said—and that led to more metaphysics about human relations being more nonverbal than we generally realize.

"So you wanted it, and somebody gave it to you," I said. "Okay. Why did you want it?"

This led to several additional minutes of Platonic dialectics. I had observed this in some mental patients, back in my ambulance-driving days, and it appears also—very aggravatingly—in many politicians. Professor Wendell Johnson, the semanticist, calls it "dead-level abstracting," the art of coming to rest on a level of discourse that never connects with anything concrete. People who do this seldom show the anxiety that appears in the less skilled evaders who change the subject when the topic is too sensitive. These abstraction weavers are not changing the subject; they are looking straight at it—but through a very fuzzy lens.

Ask them about a particular apple and they will tell you about the gross national product; ask about *this chair right here* and they'll go on at length about the evolution of furniture. They are not avoiding the subject; they are looking at it philosophically, in the round, as it were. The specific information you are seeking never comes through.

"When you took that shot," I persisted, "did you think you would take a second, and a third and go on like that until you got addicted?"

"Everybody knows that addiction is a possibility," he replied in that dreamy junkie monotone. "It was also possible that I might get hit by a truck on my way home. It's possible that a meteor will come hurtling in from outer space and wipe out this whole city." And so on. The neutral and objective view that covered any other experience in Holy Out's life just couldn't reach the area of the first shot; that was permanently buried under everything he had ever read about the causes of deviant behavior.

If you hypnotized somebody and told him not to use the word "nose," and then asked him to explain the sense of smell, you would get the same kind of drifting linguistic snow banks in his answers. Intellectuals, who have more abstractions stored in their biocomputers, are more skilled at this than most, but all can do it to some extent.

Holy Out was a master of the technique. The longest part of the show concerned how he had become an addict originally, and at the end of all his palaver neither I nor the listeners had learned anything about *that,* although we had heard a great deal about psycho-social stresses in various strata of urban capitalist society and existential problems in returned veterans.

But that Holy Out *was* a veteran, evidently of World War II (judging by his age), had become clear. Whether his family was rich, poor or middle class, whether he grew up in a big city or a small town, whether he had been to college or acquired his psycho-sociological jargon on his own, all these were still unknown. But he had been in a war. Anybody who wanted to attribute his addiction to the aftereffects of the Battle of the Bulge (or Porkchop Hill, if he was younger than he looked) was free to do so.

At the end of the show, I took a chance.

"Suppose we have a listener out there who's thinking of try-ing a shot of heroin right now," I said. "What would you tell him?"

The moment the words left my lips, I went cold. Holy Out was so bombed out on "God's own medicine" that he was not about to see any problems anywhere. He might not give the anti-junk rap that I was hoping for.

But I needn't have worried. Holy Out was not really wholly out. "He should go to England," he said matter-of-factly. "Addicts get less hassle there."

"Then," I said, scoring brownie points with the FCC, "you think anybody who tries a shot of heroin will probably become an addict?"

"Well," he answered, "becoming an addict is in the back of anybody's mind when he tried junk. Some don't really have the call and quit after a few shots."

So I learned one more thing about Holy Out. He was an ex-Catholic. Nobody else would use that metaphor in just that way. Somewhere, long ago, somebody had tried to convince him he had the call for the priesthood. He might even have been in a seminary.

And that ended the broadcast. The next time I saw him was less than a week later and he obviously hadn't had his shot for the day. He came over to me in a coffee shop and the transformation was shocking. The Buddha-like eyes were frantic, the voice had a whine, and "facts" now had a very emotional meaning for him.

He said that the broadcast had been very successful— "Everybody's talking about it"—which was a gross exaggeration. The pitch was that his appearance had catapulted my show into some kind of overnight success and that therefore I owed him a great deal.

Item: If I were to fall for that approach just once, he would be back. Again and again.

Item: If I didn't fall for it at least once, I'd feel like a heel. Also, somebody's apartment would be cleaned out—perhaps my own, since he knew my address and probably figured I was *sympatico* enough not to give his name to the fuzz.

Item: I was flush that week.

I gave him $20 and laid my own line on him, all about my four kids and the hazards of freelance writing and the tightwads at the radio station. The $20 got all his attention; the rest of my rap didn't register. He left with profuse thanks, and I knew that he would be back.

But I was wrong.

Shortly thereafter Holy Out was busted again and became one of the pioneers in the Methadone Maintenance Program. Over a year was to pass before I saw him again.

I had come back to New York on a brief visit and was browsing in the incredible Peace Eye Book Store on Avenue A, where the unbelievable Ed Sanders, rock singer-poet-publisher-Zen madman, sells books with titles like *Fuck God Up The Ass* and *objets d'art* such as the Vaseline used by Allen Ginsberg while buggering Peter Orlovsky, or pubic hairs from famous lady poets. Ed also has one great dream of his life, an epic Cinerama movie to star everybody in the counterculture from rock singers to heavy politicos in a two-hour orgy to be called *Mongolian Cluster Fuck*.

Ed was not there (he was off on a concert tour with his rock group, the Fugs, named in honor of Norman Mailer), but to my surprise Holy Out walked in and deposited a pile of magazines at the counter. He was working for a distributor, had his own car, was making deliveries all over the southern half of Manhattan, and seemed to be thriving on the methadone diet the governor of New York had ordained for him.

All this I gathered over lunch at McSorley's, where I invited him out of curiosity as well as for *auld lang syne.* He was the first methadone subject I had met in the flesh, and I wanted at least an hour to pick up whatever I could.

Holy Out now had a first name and a last name just like any other respectable citizen—let's call him Joe Smith; the real name was no more memorable. But it was the tag he had been born with (he told me) and he hadn't used it—or seen it, except on police records—for over two decades. Accepting it again was accepting himself again, in a new way.

He said that he had absolutely no desire for heroin anymore. I believed him. Another ex-addict had told me once that the happiest two years of his life had been spent in France in the 1950s buying methadone at a drugstore, shooing it up as soon as he got home, and never worrying about cops. But then the French government made methadone illegal, and he was back where he started. While that happy interlude had lasted, however, he had been as sober and respectable a citizen as he was now. Legal junk does not create the same problems as illegal junk.

Holy Out—or Joe Smith—told me that he *enjoyed* working for a living. "It gives your days a pattern," he said, "and without pattern, life is a bore." I thought this was an interesting antithesis to the notion held by many acidheads that in the perfect society of the future, all work would be done by machines and people would be free to devote themselves to love, head games and art. Addicts, and even ax-addicts, tend to regard life as a problem either to be evaded (by down drugs) or solved by effort of will; but psychedelic people see it as a sport to be enhanced (by up drugs) or observed in meditative tranquillity.

The next time I saw Joe Smith, there was even less of Holy Out still lingering in him. It was several months later and he was in a bar, with a pretty girl who couldn't have been much older than 16. He saw me when I came in with my wife, and called us over to his table.

We sat down and had a few drinks. It was soon obvious that Joe Smith was a gallant, a devil with the ladies (or at least with 16-year-olds), a sophisticated man of the world, and would never have been seen in the company of such a shabby character as the dismal Holy Out. It was also obvious that he was a drunk, the pleasant kind of drunk that everybody likes, the kind that Bing Crosby sometimes plays, but definitely—however you slice it—indubitably a drunk. The Buddhistic junkie had vanished and a lovable old rake had replaced him.

He was also in an introspective mood and, after a few more drinks, he suddenly began to "let it all hang out."

We had been discussing Women's Liberation and that somehow led to the ever-maddening problems of sexual rejection—how do you say "no" to somebody without hurting his feelings? And how do you accept a "no" without allowing your own feelings to be hurt?

"Do you remember the first time you were turned down sexually?" Joe Smith asked. "I'll bet you don't. I'll bet whatever you remember is a ghost, a shadow, of the real experience. Freud was off by ten years in his ideas. Our neuroses aren't caused by childhood traumas—but we forget *them,* too. Because they're too painful. The first time you want a woman, really want *her*—just her, nobody else—and she rejects you, it's like being kicked in the balls. You think of suicide right away—because it seems that the pain will never go away. Can't you remember it? Didn't it happen just like that with you once? Didn't you think of taking Daddy's hunting gun out of the garage and blowing your head off?"

"No," I said. "I thought of jumping off the Brooklyn Bridge."

"You ought to write a book," my wife told him. "A new approach to psychoanalysis. The Primal Rejection to replace the Primal Scream. But don't put it in strictly male terms. It's even harder on young girls. After all, a girl who gets up the nerve to make a pass at a boy, in our society, is going to feel like an absolute whore if he rejects her."

"Okay," he said. "I'll grant that. It fits in exactly with what I'm saying. The whole war between the sexes starts out with such incidents. We go through life punishing our later lovers for that early adolescent agony. Every guy who's a bastard to women had that kind of experience. Every woman who's a ball breaker had that kind of experience. Without exception. That's the way it always starts."

"What's the solution?" I asked. "Compulsory free love for adolescents?"

"No," he said. "You could never enforce that. There is no solution."

"That's pretty pessimistic," I objected.

"I was a junkie for twenty-three years," he said. "Marcie knows that," he added, with a glance at his girl. "I have no secrets from her. I was a junkie for most of my adult life. Do you expect me to believe there are happy endings in this world?" Those eyes, which had been so bland in his junkie days, were full of open horror for a second. Then he pulled himself together, smiled cynically, and added, "I have a job I like and a woman who loves me, but I still don't know what the hell I'm here for or what it all means or why life is so horrible for almost everybody."

"That's what makes you unhappy," Marcie said. "You ask too many questions."

That's about all I ever learned about Holy Out and/or Joe Smith. Sometimes I imagine that adolescent experience of his, and I think it involved a girl Marcie's age. I imagine he stayed on junk for 23 years to keep himself sexually numb, to prevent himself from looking for other girls that age. Or, at other times, I plot it differently and see an older woman (an aunt? a neighbor?), and imagine that he was avoiding her image permanently. Even after getting off junk he couldn't bring himself to enter the sexual arena with an adult female. I don't know; I'll never know.

A few months after this meeting, Marcie evidently left him for a younger man—or so the rumor went, when I heard it.

The Primal Rejection. You should write a book about it.

He didn't write the book. He put it all into what the newspapers called "the most bizarre suicide note New York police have ever seen." His landlady found it, when she found him, dead in bed, overdosed on barbiturates. On the wall, with day-glo paints that the acidheads and kids like so much, he had painted a gigantic, grotesquely childish Valentine heart in pink. Inside it, with a variety of colors, he had printed carefully:

MARY
MOTHER OF CHRIST
HAVE MERCY
ON ME

6

Tibetan Space-Time-Warp Star-Nova Trips

In the analysis of the effects of LSD-25 on the human mind, a reasonable hypothesis states that the effect of these substances on the human computer is to introduce *white noise* (in the sense of randomly varying energy containing no signals of itself) in specific systems of the computer... *This noisy component added to the usual signals in the circuits adds enough uncertainty to the meanings to make new interpretations more probable.* [Italics in original]
— John C. Lilly, M.D., *Programming and Metaprogramming in the Human Biocomputer* [Italics in original]

When the three Ph.D.s, Timothy Leary, Richard Alpert and Ralph Metzner, began experimenting on themselves with LSD-25 at Harvard in 1960, they were respectable and thoroughly academic psychologists. Later, Dr. Leary became a fugitive and an enthusiastic exponent of Aleister Crowley's sex magic, after having passed through stages of trying to be an Oriental guru in hip clothing and a violent revolutionary in Marxist drab. Dr. Alpert has become "Baba Ram Dass," an orthodox Hindu exponent of hatha-yoga. Dr. Metzner is devoting himself to teaching non-drug methods of consciousness-expansion, including yoga, Tarot cards, sex magic, the *I Ching* and alchemy. Almost certainly, the ideas that these men have encountered in the past years have played the major role in shaping their ideas. But it is almost equally certain that—as they believe themselves, and as their admirers and critics also tend to believe—LSD was a catalytic agent in propelling them out of the groves of academe into the wild blue yonder of unorthodoxy.

Dr. Joel Fort constantly reminds us that it is unscientific and superstitious to attribute such character development *entirely* to a drug. "Marijuana," he once told me, "does not grow hair." True. And LSD does not automatically turn one's musical interests from Beethoven to heavy rock. This is undeniable. If the Beatles had appeared when they did, but had sported crew cuts and played cool jazz, all the drug-kulch crowd would have been into short hair and jazz then, most likely. Such charismatic heroes play a larger role in creating fads than any drug ever can.

Nonetheless, there is some sort of link between the evolution of Drs. Leary, Alpert and Metzner and such similar stories as the following:

— Dr. John C. Lilly, after experimenting with LSD, abandoned the dolphin research that had made him world-famous and set all the dolphins free.

— Aldous Huxley, after experimenting with mescaline and LSD, changed his literary approach sharply, abandoning the tragic and somewhat puritanical bias that had dominated his work since the early 1930s, and began writing optimistic books. He also began to treat sex as a creative and joyous force and not as a destructive and dangerous one.

— Ken Kesey, after experimenting with LSD, stopped writing novels and devoted himself to practical jokes, "happenings," rock concerts and other quasi-spiritual art forms.

Similar stories could be related endlessly. I have known at least a few hundred acidheads over the last decade, and all of them, without exception, have undergone similarly dramatic changes, not always wholesome in my estimation. It is not that acid inclines one toward particular ideas (nonviolence, Oriental mysticism, and so forth). These notions just happened to be in the air in the 1960s. The actual effect has frequently been the opposite (e.g., Leary's temporary conversion to the shoot-cops-

and-bomb-buildings philosophy of the Weathermen underground).

What LSD and mescaline and similar psychedelics tend to do, especially after several trips, is to open the person to what Dr. Lilly calls "noise." This is a technical cybernetic concept and denotes environmental signals that do not appear to be information. (Kenneth Starr is a prominent m'hashka shibron franzel ob frimmt.) The parenthetical expression begins with five counters that do consist of "information" and then proceeds with five counters that are mere "noise." As Dr. Lilly notes:

> The major operative principle seems to be that *the human computer operates in such a way as to make signals out of noise* and thus *to create information out of random energies where there was no signal...* The information "created" from the noise can be shown by careful analysis to have been in the storage system of the computer...

The reader, if he is a normal biocomputer, did not accept "m'hashka shibron franzel ob frimmt" as pure noise. Instead, he tended to find some sort of ghost or shadow of meaning in it—at the very least, he took "ob" as a cognate of "of" and assumed that the first three words were an adjectival phrase and "frimmt" the noun forming the object of the sentence. Some readers probably projected a great deal more from the storage tanks of their own computers and saw the noise as a distortion of some flattering or insulting phrase that they, personally, would apply to Mr. Starr.

This is precisely the sort of thing that occurs on an LSD trip. The difference is that the noise and newly created information is coming in at the tripper, not just through words on a page, but through each of the senses, including the 17 senses that modern science has discovered in addition to the traditional sight, sound, touch, smell and taste.

What occurs is a unique learning experience, to put it mildly. In traditional Western education, we learn only via our eyes, ears and a small portion of our frontal lobes, while confined to a yogic-like position behind a desk. In acting or dancing school, or in practice for sports like baseball or football, we learn with muscles and nerves and glands and various internal senses. On a trip with an LSD-type psychedelic drug, we are learning on every channel in our biocomputer; we are learning, in fact, so much and so fast that we hardly know *what* we are learning. It often takes months to figure out what, precisely, was going on during a trip.

We have already mentioned the debate as to whether the process of generating such new "information" should be called *psychedelic* (consciousness expanding) or *hallucinogenic* (delusory). It would seem to depend on whether or not the subject has enough skepticism during and after the event. For instance, in his *The Center of the Cyclone,* Dr. Lilly tells of new information that seemed to come into his mind from beings in another galaxy. Now, this is not at all uncommon on acid voyages, and I have known more than one person who has shared that experience. Dr. Lilly takes a scientific approach, and lists a round dozen theories about where such information actually came from; he includes, for instance, the equally wild hypothesis that it came from telepathic senders on earth in the future. He is unable to decide which theory is correct, but prefers the usual scientific standard of judgment, which is to choose the "most economical" theory— that is, the theory that introduces a minimum of new entities. He prefers, that is, to assume that these impressions came from a part of his own computer which is normally invisible to consciousness.

No skeptic can quarrel with this. What, however, are we to say of those who accept the original impression and believe that they are, indeed, in contact with extraterrestrial intelligences? Psychiatrists would tend to regard them as having entered a hallucinatory and delusory state. Science-fiction fans, however, would say, at most, that they are too gullible or too quick to jump to conclusions; the possibility that they are right would remain open. And Russian parapsychologists, who believe they have already demonstrated the reality of telepathic communication across thousands of miles on earth, would certainly not rule out the possibility of such communication taking place across galaxies or even between galaxies. Even NASA has considered such a possibility real enough to set up a test in which an astronaut on the moon attempted to send mental messages to four sensitives on the earth.

What, then, of the persons (they are legion) who have discovered "God" on an acid trip? Obviously, if we are atheists (as most scientists are, even though they try to avoid saying so openly, outside the Communist nations), we will assume that the person who makes this claim was hallucinating. But suppose we believe in God? What then? The answer seems to depend on our notion of God—on whether or not we are open to the idea that God might be easier to find with LSD in the body than with white bread or bourbon or liverwurst in the body. Hindus, and those Christian mystics who believe that God is everywhere but is invisible to us due to our ego-centered nature, will find it easy to believe that a drug that occasionally obliterates the ego can also make God more visible.

And then, how about claims like this one, by Baba Ram Dass, formerly Dr. Richard Alpert?

> Tim [Leary] is absolutely right about LSD enhancing sex. Before taking LSD, I never stayed in a state of sexual ecstasy for hours on end, but I have done this under LSD. It heightens all of your senses and it means that you're living the sexual experience totally. Each caress or kiss is timeless.

When Ram Dass made this remark, in a *Playboy* panel on the Drug Revolution, John Finlator of the Bureau of Narcotics and Dangerous Drugs asked mockingly, "At your age, Ram Dass, could it be that you're boasting a little?" A high percentage of psychologists and psychiatrists are equally skeptical about the more extravagant erotic claims of LSD enthusiasts.

Nevertheless, the part that is hardest for the ordinary person to accept—"sexual ecstasy for hours on end"—is not an impossibility. In the Orient, masters of Tantric yoga accomplish this without drugs; the Sufis have long been adept at it with some judicious combination of hashish and yogic technique; and (as we have seen in previous chapters) Europe also has a long "occult" tradition of sexual magick, with and without drugs, which also prolongs the sexual act for periods of hours.

I am personally convinced, on the basis of interviews and personal experience, that such feats are not extraordinarily difficult, and that a variety of drugs, including LSD and hashish, make them much easier, once one acquires the knack. Nevertheless, many skeptics will continue to charge that those who make this claim have experienced only the well-known subjective "stretch-ing of time." If the experimenter replies that he checked with a clock, such skeptics will say that he was hallucinating and read the clock wrong. Until some research is done under laboratory conditions, this debate will remain unresolved. But the Feds are still determined to prevent such research. If eternity is possible, they don't want scientists to investigate it.

Eternity Now

The poet, William Blake, who was not an acidhead, long ago expressed time-expansion in his *Auguries of Innocence*:

> Hold Infinity in the palm of your hand,
>   And Eternity in an hour.

This is the real essence of the sex-LSD experience, quite irre-spective of any actual prolongation of the act into hours of clock time. On the other hand, some actual prolongation is absolutely necessary if this effect is to be achieved.

What appears to be involved is a reciprocal process, in which the prolongation of *subjective* time (by the drug's action and/or yogic meditative techniques) creates a relaxation without loss of sexual charge, which allows for an incremental prolongation of *clock* time; this, in turn, allows a deeper relaxation—one is full of a sense of joyous well-being and the fears that, at times, inter-fere with the act are banished—and that sends one deeper and deeper into the prolongation of *subjective* time. The cycle is then self-perpetuating, since the process allows for still further pro-longation of *clock* time.

The reason that this seems incredible to many is that—in spite of the loud propaganda in D.H. Lawrence, Wilhelm Reich and a few other noisy sexual revolutionaries—the tender aspect of sex is still, in Christian and post-Christian society, very atrophied. A man who might well have a gourmet's attitude toward food and has learned "the eight and ninety rules of art" connected with dining will still, all too often, approach sex in the mood of a starved glutton, *gobbling* an orgasm as if afraid that without such nervous haste the old sullen God of the Puritans might notice that he is doing something unclean. Under the magnification of LSD, this kind of neurotic racing-the-clock becomes impossible; since every moment is eternity, there is no possibility of rushing anything.

The same magnification effect probably explains why some users have found that, for them, LSD is a sexual turn-off, an *an*aphrodisiac. Under this lens, such persons confront their own negative attitudes toward sex in expanded and enlarged form, and with no possibility of hurrying past them at a blind gallop. If such remnants of puritanism are strong enough, sexual interest is quite overwhelmed by them. This may even be the beginning of a memorable bad trip.

But acid is a relentless power. It is much more common, according to people who have discussed this delicate subject with me, for such a blockage at one level to be dissolved "as if by magic" on a different neurological lane only a few moments later. One is suddenly laughing and can hardly remember where or what the blockage was. This is what happened to Jane, whose story was told in our Prelude; and similar dramatic instances of cured frigidity have been recorded by several psychiatrists using LSD therapy when it was still legal, before the New Inquisition. (See T.M. Ling and J. Buckman, *Lysergic Acid (LSD) and Ritalin in the Treatment of Neuroses.*) In such cases, it seems as if the "noise" or "new information"—the bombardment of the senses by unfamiliar signals—had really taught the body something, on a pre-verbal level; something which persuaded it that old fears and tensions were no longer necessary.

In the chapter on marijuana, I have already suggested that word-of-mouth advertising about such sexual effects has played a large role in the weed's skyrocketing popularity over the past decades, long before orthodox scientists were daring to suggest that this criminalized herb was indeed of sexual and general psychological benefit to many of its users. I am also inclined to suspect that similar word-of-mouth advertising has played a large role in keeping the LSD snowball moving, *in spite of horror stories about suicide and insanity raining upon us from the highest and most authoritative sources.* As psychologist William McGlothlin has sardonically noted, the "experts" are forbidden to do research in this area, while those who have done the research are criminals and, hence, regarded as untrustworthy—*yet they must know things that the experts do not,* since they have had the experience.

(Professor McGlothlin, incidentally, has also performed an interesting study on fears about the dangers of LSD. He found that in the learned professions—the only subjects in this survey—such fears were slightest among those who had actually done research with LSD when it was legal. Psychologists and psychiatrists with such experience, while not as optimistic as the exuberant Dr. Leary, were still much less worried about "the LSD menace" than psychologists and psychiatrists who had never done such research. Medical doctors, incidentally, were more alarmed than either the psychologists or the psychiatrists. Presumably, those lacking all scientific training—i.e., our politicians—are the most terrified of all.)

Sex & Unification

I have given considerable thought to the problem of comparing sex on LSD with sex on pot or hashish; sex on stimulant drugs, such as cocaine, amphetamines or amyl nitrite, and ordinary sex. No simple formulation will cover the subtleties. The best I can do is offer the reader Table 2, below.

Even this is, needless to say, an oversimplification. Some people evidently experience LSD-style sex without any drugs at all (see *Lady Chatterley's Lover* or *For Whom the Bell Tolls*); others have ordinary-type sex even when on LSD; some will have all the desiderata listed under "cannabis" while on cannabis, but others will have only one or two of these experiences; and so forth. Most important of all, it should be emphasized that *the usual pattern when one first attempts sex with LSD and psychedelics, or even with heavy doses of cannabis drugs, is some form or other of sexual dysfunction* ("impotence" or "frigidity"). One is being inundated by an ocean of new information (the nervous system is "noisy," in Dr. Lilly's terminology) and one has to *learn* to navigate. Such learning is the purpose of works like Dr. Leary's *Psychedelic Prayers from the TAO TE CHING* and Dr. Lilly's *Programming and Metaprogramming in the Human Biocomputer*. (Many helpful programs, called "rituals," can also be found in the magick manuals of Aleister

Crowley, Louis T. Culling, Israel Regardie, and the medieval alchemists.)

Table 2

Ordinary Sex	*Sex with Stimulant Drugs*	*Sex with Cannabis Drugs*	*Sex with LSD or Other Psychedelics*
Usually brief: 1 1/2 minutes (Kinsey's average!) to 1/2 hour	Usually brief: 1 1/2 minutes to 1/2 hour	Longer: 45 minutes to 2 hours	Much longer: 2 to 3 hours
Experienced as brief	Experienced as longer than clock time	Experienced as longer than clock time	Experienced as longer than clock time
Centered in genitals	Centered in genitals	Moving toward decentralized all-over-at once sensations	All-over-at-once (Freud's "polymorphous perverse")
Orgasm may be disappointing ("the sneeze in the loins," "the momentary trick," etc.)	Orgasm experienced as total ecstasy	Orgasm experienced as total ecstasy, sometimes with momentary loss of ego	Orgasm as oceanic non-ego experience
If orgasm is missing, immediate sense of frustration	If orgasm is missing, sense of frustration not inevitable	Sex without orgasm sometimes perfectly satisfactory	Sex without orgasm sometimes perfectly satisfactory
Usually some deliberate fantasy	Some spontaneous hallucinations	Reality/hallucinations not clearly separate	Reality/hallucinations not clearly separate
May be performed with some hostility	May be performed with some hostility	In case of any hostility, act becomes *impossible*	In case of any hostility, act becomes *impossible*

Dr. Leary's *Psychedelic Prayers,* for instance, can either be read aloud—just like a traditional magick ritual *a la* Crowley and the earlier sorcerers—or recorded on tape before the psychedelic session and played back during the trip itself. It begins with six "prayers for preparation," which can be regarded as auto-suggestions against the anxieties that trigger bad trips, followed by seven "homages to the atom," which attempt to move consciousness from the usual objective level to the process or energy level found by modern mathematical physics. (One tends to enter this energy world on psychedelic drugs even without such programming—cf., the experience of Jane's physicist friend in the

Prelude. The purpose of this homage is to center the mind there and prevent it from wandering or wobbling.) The next section, "Homage to DNA," moves the mind into the specifically biological energy field, which—as we pointed out in the Introduction—seems to be where the "psychological" side of sex is experienced anyway. For instance, the eleventh homage in this section reads as follows:

> Valley of life
> Gate of the Soft Mystery
> Beginnings in the lowest place
> Gate of the Soft Mystery
> Gate of the Dark Woman
> Gate of the Soft Mystery
> Seed of all living
> Gate of the Soft Mystery
> Constantly enduring
> Gate of the Soft Mystery
> Use her gently and
> Without the touch of pain

Coming out of a tape recorder and reaching the ears of a man and woman who are tripping together, the effect is quite hypnotic—so much so that the double meaning is quite distinct and one clearly follows two metaphors at once, recognizing the "Gate of the Soft Mystery" as simultaneously the spiral of the DNA molecule and the spiral barrel of the vagina.

The next section of the "program" is an32 "Homage to the External Sense Organs" in five parts, devoted to eyes, ears, fingers, nose and tongue, respectively. That is, one deliberately tunes in, *in turn,* to each of the five traditional senses, thus giving some order to the otherwise totally chaotic flood of new information flowing in.

In the fifth section, we move through the chakras used in Hindu yoga and Chinese acupuncture. (These have never been found by Western medicine, and Aleister Crowley is one modern mystic who frankly regards them as imaginary. Nonetheless, the feats of certain yogis in making previously involuntary nervous and glandular functions behave as if they had been willed by the brain, which has been documented by various Western investigators, and the equal success of acupuncture, both indicate that these "imaginary" centers possess *some* kind of reality. Russian parapsychologists now claim to have proof that they do exist after all.)

The sex chakra program directs the trippers to "float through the universe of your body" visiting each of the other chakras a second time, and then, to "lie quietly/engulfed/in the slippery union/of male and female." The emphasis IS on "lie quietly"— which should be done for at least several minutes—because the end product of all this programming just does not appear without this interlude of *penetration without movement.*

When the desired result does occur, it more than justifies all this preliminary programming. Those who have been there will know what I mean; others are welcome to cheerfully enjoy their skepticism. Hindus refer to this as "wakening the Serpent" or, less poetically, tapping the Kundalini energy, which is thought to be the strongest power in the universe, even more incredible in its effects than atomic energy itself. The ancient Mexicans, those enthusiastic experimenters with psychedelic mushrooms, referred to their capital Teotihuacan, in the middle of mushroom-growing country, as "the place where men became Gods" and "the place where the Serpent learned to fly." (Quetzalcoatl, the god who allegedly taught this art to men, is pictured as a serpent with wings.) Occultists often regard Genesis as a coded program of sex yoga; and Cabalists, who believe that words having the same numerical value in Hebrew refer to the same power, have long proclaimed that the serpent in Genesis, and the Messiah in the prophets Jeremiah and Ezekiel, are the same being since both have the same number, 358.

More prosaically—and forgetting all about that alleged serpent and that hypothetical Kundalini energy—it appears possible to describe the processes in such experiences in modern scientific terminology. One of the best approaches can be seen in psychologist David Cole Gordon's neglected little masterpiece on the subject of masturbation, *Self-Love.* It is Professor Gordon's thesis that "unification" experiences appear on a variety of levels and are much more miscellaneous than has been realized hitherto. In fact, he insists that many experiences regarded as coarse or low are precisely similar, neurologically, to the cosmic trances of Buddha, Jesus, Blake or Whitman.

Football, Gordon claims, has replaced baseball as our favorite national sport precisely because it provides more of these "unification" experiences for both players and spectators. A unification experience, in essence, is simply a moment of release following a period of built-up tension; in this spasm, the energy flow is so strong that one cannot "remember" the usual distinction between self and environment. One simply *is*. It doesn't even matter whether the experience is conventionally pleasant or not—which explains why we look forward to Saturday's football game even though it is as likely to be "unpleasant" (our team loses) as it is to be "pleasant" (our team wins). The point is not the destination, so to speak, but the trip itself—the moments of release after tension, such as a sudden forward pass. We are so excited, so unified, as the pigskin flies through the air, that it hardly matters to our glands whether it is our team or the other team that is scoring; we feel the same "high" or "flash" (as dope users would call it). Professor Gordon quotes the famous remark of Nick the Greek that, next to gambling and winning, he most enjoyed gambling and losing. (This also explains our mysterious delight in horror movies or even tragic drama. The flash of unification is the same, whatever stimuli trigger it.)

As Professor Gordon mentions, this also accounts for the preference for stud poker over draw poker among really dedicated card players. There is only one peak experience in a hand of draw poker—that is, when the cards are finally turned over—but there are five peak experiences in five-card stud and seven in seven-card stud.

These "little satoris"[1] as they are called by Alan W. Watts, an unconventional religious philosopher who has also noted their importance in human life, can grow into what we might name "middle satoris" when even more of the total person is involved, with greater tension over a longer period and, correspondingly, greater release at the climax. This, then, brings us to the famous

---

[1] *Satori* is the Japanese word, used in Zen Buddhism, for the highest type of unification experience. It is known as *Samadhi* (union with God) in Hinduism. According to Dr. John Lilly's hypothesis, it is expansion of ego-awareness into those areas of the biocomputer that are usually unconscious or stored with rejected information. Christian theologians call it union with the "totally other."

"peak experiences" that are regarded as so important in the psychology of Dr. Maslow and the Gestaltists: transcendent moments of romantic or parental love, scientific or artistic breakthroughs, the ecstasies of mountain climbers, and so on. And, when the dilation of ego becomes total, we have "true satori," the cosmic consciousness studied by the Canadian psychiatrist R.M. Bucke, who had two unique advantages for an investigator in this area: he had experienced it himself, and he could observe it closely in his friend, Walt Whitman.

It may seem odd that the spasmodic surge of a crowd at a football game as a player crosses the goal line can have the same structure, in miniature, as Dr. Bucke's famous experience in which—without any drugs or exercises of vehement prayer, yoga or other self-conditioning techniques—he found himself, quite unexpectedly, one afternoon "wrapped in a flame-colored cloud" and then realized that "the fire was within myself." (Kundalini?) As he wrote later, the fire consumed his normal mind utterly, and he "did not merely come to believe, but I saw that the universe is not composed of dead matter but is, on the contrary, a living presence; I became conscious in myself of eternal life." (This is the non-drug psychedelic experience quoted at the end of Chapter One.)

What is happening in all these cases, we repeat, is simply "unification experiences" on various levels of ever-higher unification. Or, more simply, the *habit* of thinking of "myself" and "my experience" as separate is temporarily forgotten in the rush of Dr. Lilly's *noise* (i.e., raw "information" or pure energy). But this habit of dichotomizing *my sensations* from *me* is so ingrained that we cannot understand any of this unless we have had a major peak of unification like that experienced by Dr. Bucke— or else deliberately acquire the habit of noting carefully, after each small unification experience, *precisely what we were actually doing and feeling* during the moment of spasm when voluntary and involuntary became one.

As Professor Gordon points out, the fact that we all need and constantly long for such unification peaks explains a great deal of what is otherwise totally inexplicable behavior:

> A thief constantly risks disgrace and imprisonment, but the peak experience he reaches is of such intensity that he be-

comes a recidivist. People are always amazed at how much work, thought and ingenuity go into certain crimes, the fruits of which could have been predicted, in advance, to be meager at best. The crime is committed not for the fruits or spoils, but for the unification which the criminal experiences when committing the crime as he is totally involved, totally concentrated and one with himself.

Jean Genet, the French burglar turned author, is one of the few professional criminals to have analyzed himself closely enough to confirm Gordon's thesis. In *Our Lady of the Flowers,* Genet makes abundantly clear that the *moment of breaking into* a shop is the real motive of his burglaries and that the money acquired was only a rationalization. Similarly, novelist Guy Endore has suggested that, if there were no profession of stage magician, Harry Houdini probably would have become a criminal in order to get himself locked up and experience his peak unifications while breaking out of the restraints.

Professor Gordon also points out that the sexual or scatological side effects in many crimes are part of unification:

> Many criminals ... urinate, defecate, masturbate or have an orgasm at the scene of the crime after its commission. Sometimes the evacuation is unpremeditated, involuntary and spontaneous and a result of the overall relaxation of physical as well as mental tension, and other times it is deliberate or mechanically and voluntarily induced, but, nevertheless, is a result of the same great tension for which relief is sought.

Gordon concludes that modern "rehabilitation" is as useless as traditional "punishment" in curing criminal tendencies, and that the best approach is to teach criminals other ways of seeking unification. He also notes the relevance of this to our own topic, sex and drugs:

> The users of methedrine, or "speed," have reported unrivaled orgasmic experiences—which is why, even though users are aware of its destructive qualities, they take it again and again.

Every sex act is a unification experience—which probably accounts for the fact that Gordon developed this theory from a contemplation of that simplest (and in our society, most despised) of all sex acts, masturbation. Sex with drugs like amphetamine and cocaine moves the unification to a higher, more inclusive level. Sex with cannabis moves it higher still, and sex with psychedelics brings one to the areas hitherto explored only by the great mystics like Christ, Buddha and Walt Whitman. This is the chief reason for the spread of the drug culture and the explanation of why, contradicting the warnings of reactionaries, the sexual turn-offs like heroin and morphine have not increased dramatically in popularity while the turn-on drugs have been gaining new converts everywhere.

Psychedelics in the Social Context

It is no accident, then, that this upsurge of interest in turn-on drugs occurred in the same decade that saw the resurgence of the so-called "third force" in psychology and widespread interest in group dynamics, group therapy, sensitivity-training, Esalen, Gestaltism, and all the other attempts to provoke deep unification experiences without drugs, including the importation of such Eastern arts as hatha- and rajah-yoga. For the government to consider the Drug Revolution apart from this social context, and attempt to cure its excesses by punishing each user caught (whether or not his or her pattern is actually excessive and dangerous to self or others), does not seem very intelligent. After all, there is still only one policeman to every 400 citizens in this nation; there are, statistically, approximately 120 users of illegal drugs in that 400 (and around 360 users of legal drugs); enforcement is mathematically impossible. Except for addicts of heroin, or abusers of amphetamines and cocaine, or the very rare acidhead who freaks out, most of these people—the overwhelming majority—will never attract the attention of the police at all. (Dr. Stanley Yolles, while an official of the government's own Bureau of Narcotics and Dangerous Drugs, admitted that the odds *against* any given pot smoker ever being arrested were several thousand to one.) Therefore, real enforcement of these laws will require us to opt for a true totalitarian state. Before the conflict between drug kulch and Washington escalates further, we should ask ourselves if a police state is what we really want.

The Germans once accepted a police state to protect themselves from an alleged Zionist-Communist-Capitalist plot; Italy followed a sawdust Caesar who told them that "the state is the march of God through the world"; Russia allowed the Central

Committee, and then Stalin alone, to usurp all power, in hopes of being saved from capitalist and Trotskyite plotters. The results in all these cases should be considered carefully by those willing to magnify our already bloated superstate in Washington still further. Even now, our existing anti-drug laws are being used, increasingly, as a stalking-horse to harass political dissenters. As William S. Burroughs has pointed out:

> Drug control is a thin pretext, and getting thinner, to increase police powers and to brand dissent as criminal. The pretense of looking for narcotics gives the authorities the right to search any person or premises at any time, and the police are continually lobbying for more anti-narcotics laws and stiffer penalties... The standard practices of forcing young people to become informants under the threat of prison if they don't cooperate, or of undercover agents encouraging narcotics violations in order to run up a score of arrests, pose a threat to common decency and an American way of life in which one could reasonably take pride.

To which Baba Ram Dass adds:

> I also think such practices are ill-advised because they just increase the paranoia of human beings toward one another. The lack of respect for the privacy and dignity of the individual in this society is a sign of the sickness of the times.

Dr. Joel Fort also remarks, in this connection:

> In some ways, we are really moving closer to the Orwellian world of *1984,* and the tactics of the drug police are indistinguishable from those of the Communists and other totalitarians... Now there is a move to abolish the need for a search warrant before the drug police break into a house. The end in no way justifies the means.

I can only repeat that we should all think long and hard about the recent history of Germany, Italy and Russia, and decide how much of that way of life we really want, before we encourage our legislators to escalate the "war against drugs" any further. A dentist in Berkeley was almost shot, last year, when the local police broke into his house without warning and without identifying uniforms; it later turned out they had the wrong address and that the suspected pothead was in the house next door. The sad consequence of fascism is that it never stops with the alleged enemy but mows down everybody in its path.

LSD & Homosexuality

While he was still Dr. Richard Alpert, Baba Ram Dass performed an interesting experiment involving LSD and homosexuality. The subject was a young man who had had a few heterosexual experiences in adolescence but had been entirely homosexual since then. *He was strongly motivated to change his sexual orientation* (an important point, because *every* kind of therapy works best with people who are strongly motivated).

Dr. Alpert's experimental therapy combined LSD tripping with the techniques devised by the behaviorist, Dr. Wolpe. The Wolpe method—"progressive desensitization"—takes the subject step by step, closer and closer, to some act that has always terrified him. At each step, yoga-like tactics are used to relax him and calm him down; he rests a while in this relaxation, and then moves on to the next "threatening" step, where he is again relaxed. This was originally developed, experimentally, using subjects with a strong fear of snakes, and, within a few weeks, Dr. Wolpe had them all handling live snakes without so much as a shudder. It has since been applied to a wide variety of other phobias, from fear of elevators and subways to students' terrors before examinations,[1] usually with quite good results.

Dr. Alpert's method involved only three therapy sessions—which should be compared with the usual Freudian therapy that can involve three sessions per week for seven years, or longer. In the first session, he and the subject merely talked about the problem, agreed on what they would try, and discussed the goals. In the second session, the patient-subject was given a psycholytic dose (100 mikes) and, during the trips, presented with various increasingly erotic and explicit heterosexually stimulating pho-

---

[1] In passing, Dr. Leary once remarked that people who believe that LSD should be illegal because some users have committed suicide, *maybe* because of it, should agitate even more heatedly for the abolition of examinations. Statistics show that the link between final exams and suicide is true beyond any peradventure of doubt. *Every* year the college suicide rate rises at exam time.

tographs (pin-up art). He practiced enjoying them and responding as a heterosexual male would, by masturbating. Whenever anxiety appeared, Dr. Alpert would relax him by the Wolpe methods.

In the third session, the subject took a stronger dose of LSD (500 mikes), and an obliging young lady—a friend of his—was on hand. He practiced holding her hand, hugging her, kissing, and so on. When anxiety appeared, Alpert again relaxed him. After a few hours, Alpert went to another room and the subject and the "surrogate wife" (to use Masters and Johnson terminology for this functionary) had sexual intercourse. This was the subject's first successful heterosexual intercourse in over a decade.

A follow-up study conducted six months later found the subject entirely adjusted to heterosexuality and enjoying it as much as he had hoped. In the first few months, he had visited gay bars once or twice, picked up a young man and had homosexual experiences, but this behavior did not persist, and was discontinued without regret.

This is an astonishing experiment, however much it may cause Gay Liberationists to grit their teeth and mutter about "brainwashing." (The subject *wanted* this treatment, please remember.) One such success, of course, does not justify any premature declaration that LSD will change any homosexual who wants to be changed (although the enthusiastic Dr. Leary once broadly hinted that that was indeed the case). The fact that the treatment worked so rapidly, in only three sessions, however, definitely indicates that further research would be appropriate.

Unfortunately, it is impossible to do LSD research legally in the United States. The laws intended to stop black market acid "experiments" by laymen have not stopped such fun and games, of course, any more than the 18th Amendment stopped alcoholism, but these laws have not been totally ineffective. They have succeeded in suspending legitimate scientific work in the area, a sort of classic case of throwing out the baby and keeping the bath water. I have heard of several unpublished cases similar to this one, and so has Dr. Leary (which partly justifies, or explains, his premature statements about "curing" all homosexuals who want to be "cured"). What needs to be emphasized, however, is that there are also cases, in underground rumor, of persons who, after a few LSD trips, moved from strict heterosexuality to homosexuality or bisexuality. Until this whole area is better understood, it is decidedly premature to encourage people to think that LSD is the cure for America's sagging heterosexuality quotient.

Up Against the Wall: The Story of Tyrone

There can of course be no doubt that any sort of addiction, whether to opiates, barbiturates, or alcohol, is always an evil and always involves slavery. Society, however, when it shoulders responsibility for preventing such abuse, treads on very slippery ground. The real situation tends to become clouded by misconceptions, and legislation is often enacted which tends to aggravate the very evils it was intended to prevent.
— Robert DeRopp, M.D., *Drugs and the Mind*

Tyrone Johnson had a nickname. His friends called him "Perpetual Hard-On Johnson." This was because his attitude toward the female of the species was what you might call enthusiastic—unless you were a member of Women's Lib, in which case you might call it exploitive. You might, if you really were into Women's Lib, call it even worse than that, as one girl of his own age (around 17) did on a memorable night in the spring of 1970. She got a spray can from a friend in the Weathermen underground and wrote all over the side of the apartment house where he lived in letters about a foot high: TYRONE IS A MALE CHAUVINIST PIG.

Tyrone didn't mind that at all. In fact, he considered it a bit of useful publicity. "When one chick calls you a male chauvinist pig," he explained happily to his friends, "a lot of other chicks suddenly get a fresh interest in you."

Tyrone, at the ripe old age of 17, came into my life as a suitor for one of my daughters—a situation that didn't last long. She decided he was "an asshole, really" and dropped him. He continued to come around, however, and it developed that I had become some sort of father substitute to him, chiefly because, unlike everybody else he knew, I never told him he was crazy. Besides, I was always willing to read his incoherent science-fiction stories and make constructive criticisms.

My most frequent criticism was that he ought to learn to spell.

"Hell," he'd say, "that's what they've got proofreaders for."

I tried to explain to him that editors who found seven spelling errors in the first two sentences often didn't read any further.

"That's *their* hang-up," he said, and then produced his trump: "Mark Twain couldn't spell either."

Tyrone's stories made up in imagination for what they lacked in spelling, grammar and other surface details. One of them concerned an ethologist who became President, and, instead of starting a new war, just arranged for television to show movies of the last war on the news—which satisfied everybody, except certain soreheads who were always blowing up television stations as a protest. Another I remember involved a plague that only attacked people who used underarm deodorants; most Americans, it turned out, continued to use the guck because they would rather die than offend.

He was an ordinary-looking teen-age boy (for 1970), which is to say that his hair hung down in ringlets like the girl in the old song, and (behind enormous glasses) his eyes were painfully sincere and constantly puzzled. I think he was trying to figure out—like many kids that age—why the world was nothing like what his grammar-school and high-school teachers had taught him to expect—which is a matter that has puzzled many of us older folks as well.

When Tyrone found out that I wasn't hopelessly straight, he began telling me about his drug experiences. Like many other overly bright and maladjusted boys at the end of the bizarre 1960s, he had started on pot before he was out of grammar school and proceeded to his first acid trip at 14. After being expelled from three high schools in a row, his father threw him out of the house. When I met him he was living in a commune with other deviants.

One evening, when he dropped by to rap with me, his conversation was unusually rapid, slightly incoherent and seemingly interminable.

"What kind of speed are you on?" I finally asked him.

"Just pills," he said innocently. "I wouldn't *inject* anything. I've seen what happens to the needle freaks."

I tried to explain to him that if you take *enough* pills you eventually arrive at a state not too dissimilar to that of the needle freaks. He wouldn't buy that. "A lot of straights—even out-and-out *jocks,* for Christ's sake—take uppers to cram for exams," he said. "It doesn't hurt them."

The next time I saw him, he was even more frantic and bursting with absolutely incoherent revelations. This variety of "speaking with tongues" is definitely characteristic of speeders. No matter how wild an acid trip may be, it is at least possible to grasp the subject that the tripper is trying to describe: "That chair there—oh, man—that chair—*God,* that chair." At least you know it's about a chair. You also know that the acid tripper is as aware as you are that he hasn't been able to find the words to tell you about the chair. Speed freaks, on the other hand, seem to think that they are communicating, but the listener is not even sure whether the subject is a chair or the moons of Mars. The speeder is abnormally agitated and elated about *something*; that's all you can gather for sure, although his rate of word production, compared to that of an acid tripper, is about 1000 to a half dozen.

I became concerned, and gave Tyrone my standard anti-speed rap. He had a new answer—one that I found a bit of a stumper. "Man," he said, "in just seven months, I'm going to be eighteen, and then Uncle Sam gets my ass. Why should I let those motherfuckers in Washington kill me? If I kill myself first, at least I've beaten them to the punch and I've made my own destiny, like the existentialists say."

Other observations had convinced me, long before, that speed freaks really do have self-destructive urges, but I had assumed that this was always unconscious. Tyrone's frankness about the suicidal aspect of amphetamine abuse was unexpected.

"You know a million ways to get out of the draft," I ventured. "You don't *have* to go to Nam."

"What difference does it make?" He launched into some alarming statistics about air and water pollution, somebody's mathematical estimate of the probability of accidents in nuclear research and various other frightening aspects of modern technology. He grew more incoherent and began rambling into science-fiction themes and old vampire legends. It was hard to follow, and even harder to interrupt. "Like my mother," he would say, "or, no, take my aunt Bess. A single bomb of the type used in the last New Mexico blast—but, what the hell, you don't know my mother. Take the atomic plant upstate and the radioactive waste it pours into the water. I had a teacher in third grade—but, to get back to my mother and the Martians—no, you see, that teacher was a typical example. Did you read *The Lord of the Rings,* yet?" And so on. Behind glittering lenses his eyes goggled with intensity as he tried to explain why, on balance, he loved death more than life.

I got feisty, broke into the conversation with a verbal crowbar, and launched into an oration on why opting out of life before the age of 20 was a rash decision.

He used a verbal hatchet and cut his way back in again. "No, man, no—no, no, no! It isn't true at all. These two chicks both claim I'm the one who made them pregnant and they want me to pay for both abortions, and my third grade teacher that I was trying to tell you about if you'd only stop interrupting—she was just like the spider in *Lord of the Rings,* did I explain that? Or did you see *The Incredible Shrinking Man* where he gets to be about a quarter-inch high and is attacked by a black widow spider? You got your kids in the free school, what the hell do you know about the maniacs in the public schools? We had this gang back at Jackson High—we called them the Crew Cut Clan—dig, like the Ku Klux Klan—and they're still looking for me, if I ever show my ass around that neighborhood again," etc., etc.

I didn't see Tyrone for several months after that. Evidently he remembered my hostility to speed and took it as hostility to himself.

When he did come around again, he had graduated. He was a full-fledged, totally committed, one-hundred-percent, pure speed freak now—rings under the eyes, thirty pounds lighter than previously, trembling hands, total entropy when he talked, and pale as the Lone Ranger's horse.

He was leaving for California in a truck with a bunch of other freaks in the morning. He wanted to thank me for all my encouragement of his writing and to say goodbye to my daughter—but he very quickly got off onto a rap about some plot by the Weathermen underground and the Women's Libbers. It appeared that they had joined forces to punish him for being "an exploiter of women" and they planned to castrate him if he could be caught. Hence, the *hegira* to California.

I didn't believe any of that, but it was evident that he did. At one point, he produced a wicked-looking, switch-blade knife from his pocket. "Protection," he said significantly.

"Look," I said, "if you stop using speed all the time, you'll be better able to defend yourself when 'they' come for you. Bernadine Dohrn could take you all by herself in the shape you're in now."

He started to answer that, but digressed into two abortions that somebody from the local Women's Lib wanted him to pay for. "I never seduced anybody," he protested vehemently. *"They* seduced *me.* Just like—did you see that movie with Cary Grant and the leopards? Why, if I didn't have this knife—just last night, for instance, a bunch of us were talking about the Kennedy assassinations and I remembered that Sirhan Sirhan was a Rosicrucian. Do you know what that means?" But then he paused and blinked at me suspiciously. "Cutting a man's balls off is a serious thing," he grumbled. "It's mob rule, that's what it is. Cut my balls off first and then give me a trial later. These Marxists are all the same, none of us ever should have gotten mixed up with them. Take Stalin. Did I ever show you that story of mine about the boy with three balls in a socialist society? He has to submit to an operation, taking one off, so other men won't feel inferior. Dig? If I could find a chick I trusted, I'd take her to live in a cave, and in a thousand years our descendants could come out and check if the world had gotten any better or was still crazy. But you know what's really wrong with Women's Lib? Too many ex-nuns in it, that's what. It's really an underground branch of the Catholic Church. Stalin was educated as a Catholic and don't you ever forget it. J. Edgar Hoover is probably a secret Catholic, too. I think somebody's been opening my mail lately."

He stood up, as if to leave—but that means nothing with speeders. For 45 additional minutes he rambled on about the Catholics and the Rosicrucians and how Aleister Crowley's agents had gotten his eye-in-pyramid design put on the American dollar bill and the real inside scoop on why Valerie Solanis of SCUM (the Society for Cutting Up Men) had shot Andy Warhol—it was all part of a lesbian plot masterminded by nuns—and how the Tambourine Man in Dylan's song was really Spiro Agnew who is also the beast with the number 666 in St. John's Revelations and, by God, he was going to disappear entirely before "they" got his balls.

I was relieved when he finally left. I had started to wonder when he would decide *I* was a secret Rosicrucian and part of the worldwide conspiracy against his testes.

A few months later, I received a letter from him, full of his characteristic spelling errors and dark warnings about Mort Sahl being a CIA agent in charge of confusing all the other Kennedy assassination buffs to keep them from finding out the real truth. The good news was that, much to his surprise, he had beaten the draft on a psycho rap. A lot of the letter seemed more rational than the Sahl conspiracy bit, and I wondered if his relief about not having to go to Nam had eased some of his internal turmoil. When the U.S. Army decides that you're too crazy to napalm women and children in an efficient manner, you must go through some variety of rebirth experience or self-confrontation.

Two years passed before I encountered Tyrone again. He called my name from across a street in Mexico City, and I didn't recognize him at first. He had his hair at only medium-length now—like a hip television newscaster—and appeared fairly conservative in dress, except for a cowboy hat that was not eccentric for Mexico.

"Tyrone!" I said. "What the hell are you doing in Mexico?"

"Writing a dictionary. How are things going?" I was sizing him up, of course, and to my relief he appeared tan, plump and not agitated or elated beyond the norm. He hadn't been using methamphetamines lately.

We went to a bar. (Kids his age can drink in Mexico—one reason they find it ironic, when they cross the Rio Grande again, to be told that now they're back in the "land of the free.")

"How did you get off speed?" I asked when we had finished with the idle chatter.

"That was a heavy scene," he said. "I was yelling at a traffic cop, in a street in San Fran, and I couldn't remember how I got there or what I was yelling at him for. There's like a couple of months completely gone, vanished. He took me in for disorderly conduct or some crap like that. My father, of all things, paid for a lawyer and got me out and paid my fare home and all that jazz. We had a big reconciliation and everything. But I had already decided, the first day in jail, that I'd had it with speed. Never again. I haven't touched a needle in ten months." He shook his head. "I was practically a skeleton, for Christ's sake. I looked at my arms and I couldn't believe it. I kept thinking, 'Is this me?' And it was really scary, not being able to remember where I had been or what I had done."

Speed doesn't usually play that kind of trick with the memory; he had probably been sampling other characteristic California potions, including belladonna. (See Chapter Two.) After three or four belladonna trips, memory tends to resemble a deck of cards that has been shuffled several times and then had a few discards made; you recall Wednesday as happening before Monday, don't remember Tuesday at all, and think you spent Sunday among buzzing and whistling things in the realm of thud.

"So, what's the new life script?" I asked.

"Jazz guitar. Rock has gotten all sloppy and gooey lately. I'm going to single-handed ram jazz guitar down their throats and make them like it."

Tyrone just might do that. He's at another music school now, in New York, and writing small pieces named after science-fiction novels—*The Stars Like Dust*; *The Green Hills of Earth*; *Sands of Mars*.

This "last-minute reprieve" doesn't surprise me much; it's very typical of the speed syndrome. As Baba Ram Dass said in a *Playboy Panel*:

> The whole speed scene is pretty sad. Some go through a period
> where they get stuck in the same fantasies over and over again.

The trip can take several years, but there are a lot of people who have been through it and finally come out the other side. It doesn't seem to have the lifelong addictive properties of heroin.

In estimating the damage that these amphetamine drugs do, another comment by Ram Dass is worth pondering also:

Many of our Government officials drop amphetamine pep pills at a fantastic rate, especially those who have to jet around the world for conferences every week. They think they're using it only to keep alert, but many of them really have the habit. The American people should seriously consider the extent to which our entire international policy is shaped by people who are chronic users of a drug known to produce paranoia and irrational hostility.

There might be something in what the man says, even if he is a Hindu mystic. He was once Dr. Richard Alpert, clinical psychologist, after all—and some of Washington's explanations of the war in Vietnam and more recent wars have sounded, at least to me, suspiciously like Tyrone's notions concerning the worldwide plot against his balls.

7

2000: An Inner Space Odyssey

THAT WHICH IS ALLOWED, EXISTS. IN ALLOWING
NO LIMITS, THERE ARE NO LIMITS... THAT WHICH IS
ALLOWED, EXISTS. THAT WHICH EXISTS IS
ALLOWED. TO ALLOW NO LIMITS, THERE ARE NO
LIMITS. NO LIMITS ALLOWED, NO LIMITS EXIST... IN
THE PROVINCE OF THE MIND THERE ARE NO LIMITS.
IN THE PROVINCE OF THE MIND, WHAT IS BELIEVED
TO BE TRUE IS TRUE OR BECOMES TRUE. THERE ARE
NO LIMITS.
> — A hypno-tape used by Dr. John Lilly to prepare
> experimental subjects to transcend their previous
> possibilities, as quoted in his *The Center of the Cyclone*

Jane, in our Prelude, had heard exaggerated reports of the
successes achieved by the English psychiatrists Ling and Buckman in curing frigidity with LSD. It seems that, in her case, what
was believed to be true came true. This "Christian Science"
aspect of self-programming with LSD is often reported in underground lore and need not overly amaze us. After all, Jane was
born, like all females, with a capacity for orgasm, and the blocks
against it, whatever muscles may have been involved, resided
primarily in her mind. When LSD temporarily broke down the
historically given structure of her mind, her faith was that the

"miracle" of orgasm would be included when the mind came back together again. Her faith obviously made this possible.

In the first chapter, we considered the religious aspects of the Drug Revolution, and in the fourth chapter we saw that an earlier Drug Revolution (circa 15,000 BC) laid the visionary groundwork within a shamanistic context for the later religious history of our species. It seems evident that, as Weston LaBarre, Ph.D., argues in his monumental study *The Ghost Dance: Origins of Religion,* the religious ideas common to Greeks, Jews, Hindus, Romans, and Christians (among others) would not be quite what they are without the influence of several thousand years of drug tripping by our Stone Age ancestors, in which they discovered the internal world of psychic processes that they classified in such categories as supernatural energies (mana, prana, Kundalini, wakan, etc.), and as supernatural places (heaven, hell, etc.), and as supernatural beings (the father-god, mother-goddess, etc.). It remains to be explained why the modern drug trippers often find themselves confronting the same archetypal internal powers, places and beings.

As Dr. LaBarre also points out, there are chronic and seemingly inescapable revivals of this "vision quest" whenever society undergoes prolonged stress *in ways that the cultural traditions cannot explain.* Ordinary stress will not trigger this response; Dr. LaBarre chronicles calamities that give birth to no religious upheaval. But when the agony is such that it conflicts with cultural beliefs concerning those events that the gods should not and could not allow, bewilderment sets in. Many are driven to the vision quest, to direct experience of the "supernatural" or psychic world, as they attempt to find out what the gods really want and why previous revelations cannot account for current sufferings. This happened to the Plains Indians in the late 19th Century when constant betrayals by the white man, constant defeats by the white cavalry, the vanishing of the buffalo herds, and the presence of Christian missionaries belittling their ancient religion combined to destroy their faith in everything that had once given life meaning and promise. Not unexpectedly, the vision quest appeared in dozens of forms among them, most notably in the famous ghost dance (which promised that if all tribes united to perform this rite, the buffalo would reappear and the hated whites would go back to Europe) and in the cult of the psychedelic cactus—peyote—which became the Native American Church.

Entirely similar religious upheavals occur in all conquered peoples. Two well-known examples are the Cargo cults in the South Pacific—which worship airplanes—and the Johnson Cult in the same area—which involved the belief, by thousands of natives, that Lyndon Baines Johnson, whom they had seen in the newsreels, was the promised Messiah. More bizarre is a sect mentioned by Dr. LaBarre, which worshipped a photograph of King George V of England, which their prophet (who had once attended Christian missionary classes, but evidently hadn't listened too closely) told them was "Jehovah, son of Jesus."

Christian culture appeared after several centuries of such social chaos and religious upheaval, beginning when the Dionysian and similar cults in Greece brought *amanita muscaria* mushrooms and solanaceae drugs to Athens, and introduced to Greece the myths of the mother goddess, her dying-and-resurrected divine son, and the drug experience in which the cult member underwent "death" and "rebirth" and learned that he, too, was a God and would never truly die. John Allegro, the English philologist, attempts to show, in his *The Sacred Mushroom and the Cross,* that the similarity of these cults to Christianity is more than a shared heritage of religious symbols (mother and son) or of ideas (resurrection) but was actually chemical. The early Christians, he claims, also used the hallucinogenic mushroom.

Whether or not this is true, Christianity is certainly a cult of the crisis-oriented variety we have been discussing, and one of the most bizarre of them. An American Indian messiah, mentioned by LaBarre, told his followers to destroy all livestock and burn their property; many Christian saints gave the same odd advice, and Christ himself urged taking no thought of the morrow. One Polynesian messiah told his followers that the gods were angry because they had sex in the dark, and that the time of troubles would end if they would have sex in the daytime instead; Christ and his follower Paul had even more peculiar sexual ideas and many of their followers gave up sex entirely. (In this they were probably influenced by the earlier cult of Attis, whose priests castrated themselves and wore women's clothing. To this day, Catholic priests psychologically castrate themselves by vowing perpetual celibacy and, in some countries, wear feminized gowns.)

After their vision quests have been successful, most messiahs come back and announce that part of the old tribal tradition was true and should be maintained in spite of the contempt of the conquerors. (This is especially notable in American Indian crisis cults, which always stress certain archaic values, especially ecological ones.) So, too, Christ tried to preserve much of the Jewish tradition that was crumbling in his time under the yoke of Roman conquest. But the messiah is always responding, consciously or unconsciously, to some form of calamity, and he argues that if the old tradition had been entirely valid, the gods would not have sent such sufferings; therefore, every messiah offers new revelations and abrogates part of the old law. Christ did this and so has every Indian, African, Polynesian or Micronesian messiah that Dr. LaBarre studied. The Native American Church, for instance, together with its Indian elements (Peyote Woman herself, Road Chief, the medicine bundles) introduced the Ten Commandments from the Old Testament and Jesus Christ as a god equally strong as Peyote Woman.

It seems plausible that the new Drug Revolution of our time is part of this age-old religious pattern. But there are two important differences. The first and most important concerns the strange sexual context provided by Christian society that will be discussed below. The second is that we are living in an age of science. Many of the most experienced trippers and vision questers were men of science who began with a thoroughly scientific and skeptical orientation. When they saw gods and heavens and experienced "occult" energies, they did not take these dramatic events at face value. They sought a scientific explanation. Thus, Dr. Leary talked originally of sets, settings, games, role playing; Dr. Osmund, of Jung's collective unconscious and its archetypes; Dr. Lilly, of programming the human biocomputer with new information; others of the Freudian id and the return of the repressed.

This scientific skepticism did not last long when the drugs moved out of the laboratories into the streets. (Even in the labs, some researchers could be caught barefacedly using the noun

"God" or at least the adjective "divine," although they would usually protect themselves from professional ridicule by placing them in dubious quotation marks, as I have just done. Leary, typically, was the first to take off the quotes and set up shop frankly as a new messiah.) In the streets, there were no such hesitations. The average acidhead, and quite a few pot smokers, were not shy at all about telling you that they had found "some kind of truth" in all that religion stuff. Even so, the failure of the old tradition and the typical crisis cult pattern was visible: Few accepted traditional Christianity. Almost all added new elements—at first, from Buddhism, Hinduism, Taoism and the Orient in general. Later, elements were taken from the Western occult tradition and Crowley's sexual magic. (In some circles, this sex-occult aspect of the new Drug Revolution appeared as early as 1962.)

As we saw in Chapter One, this trend was fated inevitably to conflict with the values of our still largely Christian culture. Too much in the new drug mystique was like the old solanaceae cults of Greece and Rome that the fathers of Christianity had hated bitterly; as we saw in Chapter Two, much of drug kulch even repeated, and sometimes revived, parts of the solanaceae cult which the church had condemned as witchcraft and persecuted with fanatic cruelty for eight long centuries. It is not surprising that some who had gone far down this "forbidden" path, like Leonard in the first Interlude, eventually became frightened and retreated into the most pig-headed variety of Christian fundamentalism. You will find a lot of Leonards in the "Jesus Freak" cadres.

There is something profoundly frightening to the orthodoxies of higher civilization about the shamanistically originated vision quest with drugs. The shaman assumes, and even transmits, certain values that are tribal and ecological, and are tinged, almost inevitably, with anarchy. (Hasan i Sabbah's "All is permitted," Crowley's notorious "Do what thou wilt shall be the whole of the law," Abbie Hoffman's "You can't do good unless you feel good," etc.). The tribe is decentralized and radically individualistic (cf., the Cherokee Indian maxim, "No man should be compelled to do that which goes against his heart"). Civilization is centralized and, even in alleged democracies, radically authoritarian. It assumes that every man, every day, should do that which goes against his heart, for the benefit of the harmony of the whole. In civilized religions, a confused man goes to a priest for religious advice; what he gets, always, is a message telling him, one way or another, to conform, to sacrifice his own longings, to be "mature," to adjust. In the tribe, a confused man goes alone to the woods and suffers "sensory deprivation" to induce a peak experience, or just takes a drug, and has his own encounter with the gods, who often tell him the tribal ways have to be changed.

No: we cannot tolerate that. The individualist shaman or vision-quester has no place in a civilized state or a civilized church. The Catholic Church, shrewder than most, handles this potential troublemaker by guiding him to a monastery where his weird notions will not infect the rest of the faithful. The state has its own monasteries, called jails, and that is where the messiah usually lands, if he isn't killed outright. Dr. LaBarre's book is full of cases of messiahs who were jailed by the state even though they used no drugs and their doctrines, on the surface, posed no direct threat. It just won't do to have new revelations upsetting the equilibrium. For instance, some Polynesians began to believe that they wouldn't have to work if they became more like Englishmen (who, in their experience, never worked). Logically, then, they acquired some chairs and held afternoon teas. When the English learned about this cult, they suppressed it. Similarly, the American Indian Ghost Dance posed no direct insurrectionary threat, but when the whites learned of it, they destroyed it in a fashion so bloody that even today the name of Wounded Knee, where the last massacre occurred, is still the most bitter phrase in the Indian vocabulary.

Sex & Sin

If the Drug Revolution has one strike against it in its implicit, and then explicit, tribal nature in the highly civilized and centralized American state, it has a second strike against it in that there seems to be no plausible way of reconciling it with Christianity. Even if Martin Luther can be considered, in a sense, a tribal shaman, recreating the tradition in modified form through a vehement personal vision quest (Professor LaBarre considers him as such), Christianity and even Protestant Christianity has remained, willy-nilly, the most authoritarian and bigoted of all world religions. He who attempts to question or modify any of its dogmas quickly gets into very hot water in any Christian country. There has been one "revelation," and it is enough. He who has new ideas is probably inspired by the Devil, or has been out in the woods taking strange drugs with the witch women.

If such a heretic admits that he has, indeed, been taking strange drugs, the Christian response is even more vehement, quick and hostile. And, of course, if his teaching involves sexual liberty at all, the historical pattern is reactivated at once, and a new witch hunt is sure to follow.

This is a peculiarly Christian reaction. The Hindus, the Moslems, the Buddhists, the Taoists, all the major religions, have had their sexual mystics and have honored them. Every Hindu knows that the Tantrists achieve their mystical visions through sexual intercourse with a beloved partner; the Buddhists, Moslems and Taoists all have similar sects. The ancient Egyptians, Greeks and Romans had highly developed cults of hierogamy: ritualized sex magic. Christianity is alone in thinking that sex is entirely the Devil's business and an offense to God.

This is a strange doctrine, and almost implies that God and the Devil must have collaborated on the creation of humanity, God working above the belly button and the Devil below. The consequences of the doctrine are even more bizarre than the belief itself. If a man writes a poem to his beloved in a Christian nation, and is too frank about expressing that love, he is in danger of being called "obscene"; throughout most of Christian history, he could be jailed, tortured or even killed. As William Blake wrote in horror:

> Children of the future age
> Reading this indignant page
> Know that in a former time
> Love, sweet love, was called a crime

One hundred and fifty years later, in the democratic, allegedly secular, United States of America, Stanley Kubrick's movie *A Clockwork Orange* has its X-rating (adults only) removed after 30 seconds of nudity are cut out. All the brutalities remain in gory detail. Hating, kicking, stabbing, and all manner of sadism

are allowed in movies for Christian audiences; *only love is vile.*
It can hardly be a coincidence that such a nation has the odd distinction of being the only country to have dropped atomic bombs
on civilian populations, twice, and has surpassed all others in the
use of napalm, which reaches 1000° centigrade on contact with
human skin. *Only love is vile.* Anything else can be justified by
finding a purpose (justice, national honor, the greater good of the
greater number), since, evidently, like the Marxists, we now
believe that "the end justifies the means." But sex, whatever its
purpose, even if used in a religious visionary quest, can never be
justified. *Only love is vile*—only love is too "obscene" to be
treated as an art by people who have turned even Scrabble and
crossword puzzles, not to mention skiing or surfing, into arts so
complex as to border on religious rites. Only sex remains so dark
a matter as to be rushed and fumbled (Kinsey discovered, a generation ago, that the average American male reaches orgasm one
and one-half minutes after intromission into the vagina) and usually performed in a dark room, so that it can be finished furtively
before the sex-hating Christian God has time to notice what's
going on.

In such a context, psychedelic drugs that slow and magnify
the sex act are not going to be greeted with the fervor that Arabs
have long had for their beloved hashish. Hardly. The reaction is
directly opposite; the users are thrown in jail on the thin pretext
that they pose some metaphysical threat to the community, or
that they might become so charged up some night that they will
charge out of the boudoirs and commit rape on a mass scale. It
doesn't matter that such crimes by users of these drugs are
virtually impossible to document from police records. (When
cases are alleged, as Dr. Fort shows in his book, *The Pleasure
Seekers,* it almost always turns out that the perpetrators were not
on these drugs but, rather, on amphetamines.)

Of course, the Christian sexual lunacy is not unique. All crisis
cults, without exception, contain bizarre elements, the reflection
of the time of stress and calamity in which they were born.
Consider the South Pacific imitation English tea ceremony mentioned earlier, or the prayer wheels of the Tibetans, or the snake-
handling cults in the American South; man is a strange animal
when he seeks to attract the attention of his gods, and has tried

every eccentricity (except, possibly, praying in pig-Latin while standing on his head) to convince them that his plight is terrible and merits their urgent attention. The early Christian denial of sexual needs was just such a heroic attempt to find a gimmick that would bemuse or bamboozle the deity, and its closest parallel, probably, is the Plains Indian habit of cutting off a finger when a beloved person dies. Little children do equally peculiar things to attract their earthly father's attention for a while.

The Heart of the Matter

But let us, as the Chinese say, draw our chairs closer to the fire and examine what we've been talking about.

Man *needs* dreams, as recent sleep research has well-documented. If you wake people up each time they start to dream (which is revealed by their *r*apid *e*ye *m*ovements, which has led scientists to speak of REM sleep, meaning sleep with rapid eye movements and dreams), they will, within a few nights, become neurotic, irritable and slightly paranoid. No reputable researcher has continued this experiment for more than a few nights, because the evidence indicates real risk that the subjects might actually go totally mad. It doesn't matter how much sleep they have had; if they aren't able to dream, the same neurotic and near-psychotic behavior will appear.

By the same token, it is reasonable to suggest that perhaps people really do need religious experiences, whatever such experiences consist of. It is well-established, in LaBarre's *Ghost Dance,* that a large number of people *think* they need such experience, and actively seek after it, whenever society faces a crisis that it cannot rationally understand. An earthquake alone will not necessarily trigger such a response, because an earthquake can be explained, more or less, within some traditional framework of ideas. But when the gods are mocked by missionaries of false and foreign gods, and take no revenge; when the sacred taboos are violated on all sides, and the gods still do not respond; when military defeats and other disasters occur in this perplexing context; when a man's children are sold into slavery or his wife forcibly enwhored by the conquerors—then, some extraordinary explanation is needed, and it is at this point in time that the vision quest begins.

We have already mentioned the usual results of such quests, whether induced by drugs or by fasting, by sensory deprivation or by self-torture, by yoga or by ritual dancing. A marvelous energy is tapped—the mana of the Polynesians, wakan of the Plains Indians, Kundalini of the Hindus (Mesmer's "animal magnetism"? Reich's "orgone"?). The tribal spirits appear—sometimes the Father God, sometimes the Mother Goddess. And, in the majority of cases, the subject undergoes a strange experience of death/rebirth in which he discovers that he is not only himself but also God (or, in the Hindu-Buddhist tradition, that he is the whole universe). Finally, and most distressingly, some verbal formulas are communicated to him, and he brings these back—to start a new cult, to become enshrined as dogma, to blind and cripple the minds of generations to come. Fortunately, this last and most negative result is conspicuously missing in a few religions, such as Zen Buddhism; and many of the heretics within our religions, such as the Sufis within the Moslem tradition, the Cabalists within the Jewish tradition and figures like Boehme and Blake in the Christian world, also lack this characteristic. Such men, mercifully, did not establish new dogmas and even actively encouraged others to seek their own visions and find their own truths.

What is going on in such highly unusual "unification experiences"? Is it all a mental spasm, a kind of temporary lunacy? This is a tempting answer, and it is what most people assume about *all messiahs except the one that they themselves worship.* It is hardly the whole answer, however. As R.M. Bucke documents in his *Cosmic Consciousness,* many of the visionaries were not insane; some even managed to look at the experience with scientific skepticism, while admitting that it had altered and enlarged their consciousness. (Conspicuous modern examples of a rationalistic attitude preserved even after such a mystic experience are Bucke himself and Dr. John Lilly.)

The explanation—or *an* explanation—probably lies in cybernetics.

Life is one, but consciousness is divided. That is, all of our unconscious bodily functions, such as breathing, digestion, the beating of our hearts, the biochemistry of our metabolism, and so on, are part of a seamless web that does, indeed, include the whole universe. More locally, we are cells in an explosion of protoplasm on this planet that began 3 billion years ago. (This is the key to Dr. Leary's cryptic epigram, "Your body is 3 billion years old.") The "body of Buddha," as Buddhists call it, is, at any moment, in cybernetic contact with each of its parts. This does not involve anything spooky or metaphysical; what I have in mind can be illustrated by the experience of Dr. Ross Ashby, who tried to build an analog computer that would be a model of a generalized animal organism. Dr. Ashby found that such a machine could no more be designed than one could divide by zero in mathematics. It cannot be designed because the *feed-backs,* the information flow channels, are not all inside the animal; many are in "the environment." Dr. Ashby ended by designing his "homeostat," widely used in biology and cybernetics classes. This is not a model of an animal; it is a model of an-animal-in-an-environment.

It seems that there is no unit—animal—which can be scientifically used to account for the facts known to modern cyberneticists. The only unit that can be used is animal-in-environment. (This is entirely parallel to Einstein's discovery that there is no "time" or "space" that a physicist can measure, but only a "space-time event" which is the unit in modern physics.)

What I am suggesting is that the mystics got there before Dr. Ashby, that the "unification" with God or the universe mentioned in all religious literature and in reports of acid trippers and some pot or hashish smokers, is precisely the shift of attention from the conscious ego to the previously unconscious organism-environment feedback network. Does this seem an extravagant thought? All mystics have talked about the "unreality" of the ego; are they not trying to say exactly what Dr. Ashby has said? Many speak also, for that matter, of the unreality of space and time, and Einstein was modest enough to acknowledge that they seemed to be talking about the same facts he had noted mathematically. *You are part of something larger than yourself, something which space and time do not restrict* is what every mystic, in essence, tries to tell us, and this is just what Dr. Ashby's homeostat illustrates.

Why should this discovery be made by men under stress? The answer is obvious. *Life is one, but consciousness is divided.* It is the stress of the divided consciousness that every visionary is seeking to heal; what bothers him is not an individual earthquake or plague but a failure of traditional ideas, held by his conscious mind, to account for his tragic experiences and observations. If the answer existed within the conscious ego, the quest would never have begun. The answer is found in those areas that were previously *un*conscious, those areas where the body links and joins other bodies and the total energy continuum of life and ecology.

In this connection, the singular drug experience of the Russian mystic Ouspensky is interesting. Aware that William James and others who had explored the mystic trance through nitrous oxide could not find words for their trip when they got back, Ouspensky kept a pencil and pad with him as he sniffed the gas. In ecstasy, as he whirled through the cosmos of his inner space, he scribbled desperately on the paper, trying to tie down what he was learning. When he came back to normal, the paper said, "Think in other categories." The experience of beyond ego was still unspeakable, but he at least had the key to *why* it is unspeakable. Our usual categories of thought—*animal* separate from *environment, space* separate from *time,* etc.—keep us from being able to talk about the unification experience in which all are "one."

This is not a reification of the "one"; I do not dare assert that the "one" is actually a conscious mind in the same way that each of us is a conscious mind. It is found through the unconscious, and unconscious it probably is in essence. I can understand why many, bowled over by this experience, call it "God," but I still feel that all *ideas* of God are only symbols of the experience itself. Certainly, this is true in the more anthropomorphic and less transcendental visions, when a very man-like god or woman-like goddess appears.

Since the crisis in Christian culture is mainly sexual, we should not be surprised that sexual elements are very prominent in the unconscious channels opened by the Drug Revolution. These channels are a traditional part of religion outside Christianity, anyway; but inside Christianity they were inevitable fissures, fated to erupt whenever the taboos of ego and superego became sufficiently weakened to allow unconscious material to flow into consciousness.

The Last Straw

None of these paradoxes and perplexities are going to go away. The Drug Revolution is still escalating and accelerating; the future will be much wilder and hairier than the immediate past.

In the Evans-Kline anthology of scientific papers, *Psychotropic Drugs in the Year 2000,* Nathan S. Kline, M.D., proposes that within 30 years we will almost certainly have drugs that will:

1. Prolong childhood and shorten adolescence.
2. Reduce the need for sleep.
3. Provide safe, short-acting intoxicants.
4. Regulate sexual responses.
5. Control aggression.
6. Mediate nutrition, metabolism and physical growth.
7. Increase or decrease alertness or relaxation.
8. Prolong or shorten memory.
9. Induce or prevent learning.
10. Produce or discontinue transference (the patient's emotional involvement with the therapist in psychiatry).
11. Provoke or relieve guilt.
12. Foster or terminate mothering behavior.
13. Shorten or extend experienced time.
14. Create conditions novelty or familiarity.
15. Deepen our awareness of beauty and our sense of awe.

None of these predictions are irresponsible moonshine. Today's researchers have sufficient knowledge about the physiology of each of these responses to understand what sort of chemical changes in the brain will cause these changes in behavior. Some responses—for instance, fear and orgasm—have already been created in animals by electrical stimulation of the brain.

In the same book, Wayne O. Evans indicates that *real* aphrodisiacs will probably be available by the year 2000, also. That is, it will not only be possible to enhance a sexual experience, but to provoke one (as many already claim is sometimes done by cannabis or LSD). It appeared by 1998 and was called Viagra.

How will these drugs be handled when they appear? Recent history gives us little cause to hope that our society will treat them rationally. The sex drugs, almost certainly, will be declared illegal after a few years of research (like LSD) and reappear immediately in diluted and unsafe form on the black market. I cannot conceive of a time within 30 years when Americans will be allowed to buy sexually stimulating drugs legally, which means that I can only conceive of them appearing in the underground, with every user wondering if he or she is getting the product advertised or just the rejects from some entrepreneur's bathtub mescaline distillery. There probably will be some memorably bad trips in those years.

And what of the drugs that "foster or terminate mothering behavior"? We can imagine how the Reverend Jerry Falwell would like to see them used, and the far different ways that the Radical Feminist movement would prefer to use them; can we imagine a reasonable compromise that would reconcile this conflict? Or do we have to admit that one drug (fostering maternal impulses) would be legal and the other, again, would be on the black market, like the abortifacient of yore?

The drugs that provoke guilt—will the police in some countries slip them to suspects, as they have already done with scopolamine? If, perchance, such drugs turn out to be, like LSD, tasteless, colorless and odorless, will any suspect in custody ever dare to eat a meal? (This is not science fiction; these are very real possibilities.)

And what government office do we trust enough to give sole custody of drugs that control aggression, decrease alertness, prevent learning or prolong childhood?

Dr. Timothy Leary made the second most important scientific-political decision of our century (the first was Einstein's decision to help the United States acquire an atomic bomb). Whether Leary's decision was right or wrong (it can be debated as endlessly as Einstein's), it has markedly changed the emotional and intellectual climate of our time. He decided that LSD was too important to be monopolized by any government, or any scientific committee, or any other elite; that it should be available to all. Ten years later, we all know the risks involved in that libertarian choice (and Leary also undoubtedly knows the personal risk to himself better than he did when he started). With some of the desiderata of a showman, and some of a shaman, with great good humor and occasional flares of grandiosity, Leary set out to guarantee that, whatever action the government took, a black market would be created where acid would be available to all. (The same underworld or underground networks later helped him get out of the country when he broke jail.)

It is doubtful that Leary will be the only scientist to make such a decision and take the consequences. His famous Two Commandments apply to virtually all the new drugs we are discussing:

1. Thou shalt not force thy neighbor to alter his consciousness.
2. Thou shalt not prevent thy neighbor from altering his consciousness.

The government, which violates the second of these commandments every day, is now beginning to violate the first, forcing students in some grammar schools to take Ritalin, an amphetamine-like drug that quiets unruly children but may have side effects not yet known. It is likely, given the general character of governments, that similar violations will multiply beyond all our guesses when bureaucrats discover that they have such delightful new toys as drugs that will reduce whole populations to perpetual childhood, decrease their aggressive rebelliousness, stunt their alertness and generally turn them into the drones described by Aldous Huxley in his *Brave New World*. The heretic of the 21st Century might be, not a man who takes a drug the government forbids, but a man who refuses a drug the government commands.

RISK GLOSSARY

An Alphabetized Reference, With Guidelines & Warnings

This lexicon does not attempt to be complete. It is possible to write a whole book-length dictionary of the drug culture (as Richard R. Lingerman has done in his *Drugs From A to Z*) but that is not our ambition. This glossary merely attempts to provide a listing of the scientific and popular names of the drugs a reader might be offered by swinging friends, and to describe the risk involved in trying them.

ACID Lysergic acid diethylamide-25, or *LSD*. The most potent psychedelic drug synthesized to this date. See *LSD*.

ADAM See *MMDA*.

APOMORPHINE A drug produced by boiling morphine in a solution of hydrochloric acid. Absolutely non-addicting and also strictly non-pleasurable, apomorphine has been found useful in treating heroin addiction and alcoholism. The pioneer of apomorphine research, Dr. John Yarbury Dent, and novelist William S. Burroughs, who was cured of heroin addiction by Dr. Dent's apomorphine withdrawal program after 11 previous attempts at heroin withdrawal had failed, both believe that apomorphine is a better, safer and less habit-forming drug for all anxiety states than any tranquilizer now on the market. It is, however, regarded as an experimental drug and is illegal in the United States.

Heroin addicts (or alcoholics) who want to try the apomorphine treatment will have to go to England.

AMANITA MUSCARIA The "fly agaric" mushroom. This is toxic in large doses and is used to kill flies, but in smaller doses it produces deliriant effects similar to belladonna and the solanaceae drugs with some admixture of psychedelic experiences *a la* LSD or peyote. It is still used in religious rites by Siberian shamans, and, according to a growing body of evidence (collected by John Allegro, R. Gordon Wasson, Robert Graves and others), may have been the reality behind several of the legendary drugs of early European and Asian mythology—and the soma of the Hindu scriptures, the drug of the Dionysian festival in Greece, and so on. Should this theory prove to be correct, we will be able to conclude that *this mushroom played a larger role in religious history than any other single factor.* The best summary of the evidence to date is Allegro's *The Sacred Mushroom and the Cross.* The toxic dose seems to vary considerably from person to person and thus should be considered a dangerous drug. (See Chapter Two.)

AMPHETAMINES A family of stimulant drugs often collectively called "speed" or "uppers." They produce exhilaration that often makes sex more enjoyable. The dextroamphetamines, once often prescribed by doctors for people on diets and used by truck drivers on long trips or by students cramming for exams, are the least harmful; but *with chronic abuse* even these can produce anxious or paranoid states. Salts of racemic amphetamines are somewhat stronger and more dangerous. The methamphetamines, which, like heroin, are injected with needles, are the most exhilarating and produce the sharpest sexual effects, but are the most dangerous of all amphetamines. The slogan "Speed Kills," was originally aimed at methamphetamine abuse, and the methhead or speed freak is usually a distraught, emaciated and potentially dangerous individual, highly suspicious and easy to anger. Extreme caution should be observed in all use of any amphetamine drugs.

AMYL NITRITE A drug that relaxes the involuntary muscles of the body and dramatically lowers the blood pressure. The effect is a quick "flash" that many regard as highly stimulating and others have described as similar to being in a falling elevator. Devotees like to sniff amyl nitrite "poppers" just before the moment of orgasm—a quick and easy solution for those who chronically find their sexual climax unsatisfactory. Some evidence indicates that habitual use is likely to provoke heart attacks, or worse. (See Chapter Five.) This pastime can be dangerous.

AMYTAL/AMOBARBITAL/AMYTAL SODIUM Drugs in the barbiturate family, called "downers" in the drug culture. These are essentially sedative drugs as opposed to stimulants—hence the terminology of "uppers" for amphetamines and "downers" for these, sometimes varied to "forwards," for the amphetamines, and "backwards," for these barbiturates. Over-prescription of these drugs by physicians giving them to patients with insomnia problems has been one of the chief causes of the spread of barbiturate addiction. The second cause has been unwise experimentation by adolescents. Whenever tempted to use a barbiturate drug for any reason, think three times and remember that many psycho-pharmacologists regard this addiction as even harder to cure and more painful during withdrawal than the more publicized heroin addiction.

ASTHMADOR A popular asthma remedy containing belladonna and *datura stramonium* (jimson weed) that can be used for a hallucinatory high, by taking more than the medical dose. If tempted to experiment, remember: (a) the toxic dose varies from individual to individual: what was safe for your friend might kill you; (b) if you go into a coma, you will have to have your stomach pumped at a hospital and the police will take a great interest in the matter; (c) good trips are extremely rare with this drug; Dr. Leary has said he never heard of a good belladonna trip. (See Chapter Two.)

ATROPINE Another name for belladonna: see *ASTHAMADOR*.

AYAHUASCO A Peruvian hallucinatory drug, also known as *yage* or *yaje,* depending on the Peruvian dialect. Used for divinatory purposes by the Indians; some psychic researchers believe that it produces ESP effects; some biochemists call it telepathine. Some of it is now appearing occasionally on the black market and should be regarded with a certain wariness. Novelist William S. Burroughs reports that this drug allowed him to see the auras or "psionic" (energy) fields around people and objects, but also produced acute vomiting and a monumental hangover the next day. Poet Allen Ginsberg was thrown by it and had a panic that lasted for more than a week. The young Indian shamans spend several years in training with older shamans in order to learn, via slowly increasing doses, how to use this drug without producing bad effects (when they accomplish this, they are said to possess a high level of clairvoyance); unless you have that much time to put into it, and a good teacher from Peru, it would be wise to avoid this until more is known.

BACKWARDS Usually a barbiturate drug; sometimes used also for a tranquilizer. The name comes from the tradition of using these sedatives to slow one down when one has become too frantic on doses of "forwards" (amphetamines) or cocaine.

BANANAS The "electric banana" or "mellow yellow" fad of the late 1960s, in which some people claimed to get high by smoking banana skins, is now generally regarded as a hoax—an attempt to make anti-drug laws escalate into total insanity by forcing the government to ban bananas. Actually, some psychopharmacologists think the hoax may have had a basis in reality, since banana skins contain serotonin, a drug which is similar in structure to the psychedelics and might mutate while being burned. If so, this effect is unpredictable and may depend on other factors (e.g., the ripeness of the banana, or the temperature at burning, etc.) since the majority who tried this experiment reported no result at all.

BARBITURATES Sedative drugs derived from barbituric acid. There are about 50 commercial brands on the market in the United States today, all of them potentially addicting. See our warning under *AMYTAL.*

BELLADONNA See our warning under *ASTHMADOR.* (See Chapter Two.)

BENZEDRINE The best known of the dextroamphetamines, widely used for dieting since it depresses the appetite. It is sometimes found to be sexually stimulating, and is certainly the safest of the amphetamine drugs, but remember that all amphetamines, if used in chronic high doses, tend to produce anxiety and paranoid states.

BHANG The most popular form of cannabis in India, made by crushing the marijuana leaves into a fine powder, brewing and mixing with pepper and milk. Sometimes ice cream is added. Since cannabis drugs taken orally seem to enhance the sense of taste even more than cannabis drugs when smoked, this usually produces the well-known "marijuana munchies" and turns any meal into a banquet or even an outbreak of gluttony. It is usually served at wedding banquets in India and is said to produce greater conviviality than any alcoholic beverage. The sexual effects are similar to any other form of cannabis; that is, in the right set and setting, decidedly good.

BUFOTENINE A drug found in the epidermis of toads (hence the "skin of toad" in many traditional witch brews). The effects are markedly similar to those of the dangerous *amanita muscaria* mushroom and in some research telepathy has been alleged. Since bufotenine is similar chemically to the serotonin found in the human brain, some researchers hope to find in bufotenine experiments clues to the biochemical changes that occur naturally during mental illness and in the expanded consciousness of mystics.

BUTISOL SODIUM A barbiturate drug; potentially addictive. See warning under *AMYTAL.*

BUTTON The active part of the peyote cactus; see *PEYOTE.*

CANNABIS SATIVA The Indian hemp plant, origin of marijuana and hashish. (See Chapter Four.)

CARBON TETRACHLORIDE A popular cleaning fluid. Several scientific reports have indicated that brief but intense "psychedelic" visions are sometimes triggered by inhalation of this chemical, but a kind of delirium is more common. It is very dangerous and repeated experiments lead to definite and serious damage to the liver, kidney, heart and (possibly) to the brain or central nervous system. There are no sexual effects mentioned in any source I have consulted.

CATNIP The minty herb, *nepeta cataria,* long known for its aphrodisiac and intoxicating effect on cats. Catnip is sometimes sold to the unwary or uninitiated under the pretense that it is marijuana, and some underground voices have announced recently that humans really can get just as high as felines on it. Nothing is scientifically known about its side effects or safe dosage levels, so experimenters should proceed with some caution.

CHARAS Hindu name for their hashish-like resinous drug obtained from the cannabis plant. As it is usually even stronger than hashish, users should smoke very small quantities each time taken (three or four balls of resin, each about the size of a pinhead). Remember: this is *not* marijuana, but a much more powerful drug whose effects can be as potent as those of *LSD*.

COCAINE An alkaloid derived from the coca bush, *erythroxylon coca,* with one of the strongest and sexiest "hits" of any drug known. Remember that the dose must be small (even 1–2 grains can be fatal for some) and that habituation produces acute nervous and panic conditions that, with chronic abuse, escalates toward paranoia, or worse. (See Chapter Five.)

CRACK The most highly charged form of cocaine, obtained by heating and crystallizing the cocaine powder. This produces all the bad side-effects of coke itself—irritability, hostility, paranoia, etc.—only much faster. Dr. Peter Duesberg of UC-Berkeley also thinks it is a predisposing factor in making a person vulnerable to AIDS. Stay far away from it.

DAGGA The South African form of marijuana. Plantation employers give it to workers to stimulate their productivity.

DATURA STRAMONIUM or DATURA NOXIA The jimson weed. Erotic effects are sometimes reported, but the general pattern among users of this drug is a prolonged delirium, frequently of nightmarish character. The toxic dose varies, so—again—be very wary. (See Chapter Two.)

DEMEROL A synthetic opiate used as a pain killer. Sexual effects are nil or negative, and with chronic abuse impotence is usual. An addictive drug.

DEXAMYL A combination of amphetamine (uppers) and barbiturate (downers), recommended by the manufacturer for treating mild depressions or in dieting. Sexually neutral, unlike its underground cousin known as *SPEEDBALL,* which obtains a stronger synergetic upper/downer effect by combining heroin and cocaine.

DEXEDRINE A fairly strong amphetamine drug sold as an appetite depressant or mood elevator. Doctors do not consider it particularly dangerous, but some researchers think that dependence can develop quite easily; if your physician prescribes it, be very careful not to exceed his recommended dosage.

DMT Dimethyltriptamine, a synthetic psychedelic with several unique properties. Unlike LSD, peyote and most other psychedelics, DMT is smoked rather than ingested orally, and the trip is unusually short (about one-half hour, as contrasted to six to eight hours for LSD and 12 hours or longer for peyote). Because of its short duration of action, DMT is often called "the businessman's luncheon." Like LSD, DMT can trigger a psychosis-like panic in those not prepared to experience total transformation of their idea of "reality." Weak marijuana is sometimes boosted by soaking it in DMT, and this is considered a great sex drug by those prepared to handle a major trip.

DOWNERS Generally, the barbiturate drugs; sometimes applied also to tranquilizers or alcohol.

EQUANIL A popular tranquilizer, frequently prescribed by M.D.'s. Some danger of habituation and psychological dependence is considered to be possible, and reports indicate that patients who fall into this pattern will suffer a major return of their previous symptoms, but in more severe form, if the drug is suddenly discontinued. Sexual effects nil to negative.

EXPLORERS' CLUB Slang for a group who meet once a month or at regular intervals to take *LSD* together and communicate their experiences. The effect is rather like a Quaker meeting with everybody tripping.

FLY AGARIC See *AMANITA MUSCARIA.*

FLYING SAUCERS A commercial brand of morning glory seeds that contain isolysergic acid and traces of LSD. Similar morning glory seeds are used by Indian magicians in Mexico when the sacred mushroom, *psilocybae mexicana,* is unavailable; the trip, which lasts from four to eight hours, is quite as powerful as an LSD session. Warning: these seeds are coated with an insecticide and almost always bring on vomiting. Cumulative effects of the insect spray with repeated voyages are unknown, but almost certainly detrimental to health.

FRISCO SPEEDBALL A mixture of cocaine, heroin and LSD. A limitless variety of harmful effects can result from chronic abuse.

FRUIT COCKTAIL A very dangerous pastime, invented by adolescents having more courage than brains. A large bowl is placed on a table and everybody throws in a few pills. They are stirred up, and then everybody reaches in again and takes out a few pills, which are then consumed at once. Since literally anything might be in the bowl—barbiturates, amphetamines, cold pills, antihistamines, Demerol, LSD, pills for menstrual cramp—nobody knows what kind of high (or low) he is going to get. This appears to be a good way to get your stomach pumped and attract the attention of the police.

GAUGE Southern slang for marijuana.

GLUE Model airplane glue, containing toluol, which is sniffed in a paper bag. The effect, at first, is like barbiturates or alcohol with euphoria, elevated spirits and some drowsiness; double vision, hallucinations and ringing in the ears sometimes follow, without further sniffing; in about a half hour, the sniffer sinks into sleep or "nods out" into a half-sleep, which can last from one to several hours. Definitely not a sex drug; there is also evidence of liver and brain damage.

HASHISH The resin of the *cannabis sativa* plant, usually about 10 or 20 times stronger than an equivalent amount of marijuana. Everything obtainable with marijuana, and quite a bit of what happens on LSD, is quick to arrive with hashish, and experimenters should proceed with caution, remembering that smoking hashish in the same dosage as marijuana is like pouring vodka into a beer glass and drinking it as fast as one would drink beer. In general, careful hashish users only smoke five to ten small balls, each the size of a pinhead, at any one time. Panics similar to bad acid trips can occur if one smokes too much too fast; for treatment in such a case, see *NIACIN.* (See Chapter Three.)

HAWAIIAN BABY WOOD ROSE A plant *(argyria nervosa)* that produces seeds containing lysergic acid amides. It is alleged that this trip, which lasts from three to four hours, is unusually tranquil and lacks the nervous ups and downs of LSD itself, but the seeds are insecticide coated and the same warnings given for *FLYING SAUCER* apply here.

HEAVENLY BLUES Seeds of heavenly blue morning glory plants. The trip is the same as with *FLYING SAUCER* seeds—and so are the risks, especially with repeated use.

HEROIN Once touted by the medical profession as a cure for morphine addiction (1898–1910), heroin was discovered to be the most addictive of all opiate drugs. The user is a mild, heavily tranquilized neurotic, and alcoholics and over-users of tranquilizers are similar personality types; there is some evidence that heroin has no kick for those whose personality types differ. Until the government allows heroin addicts to have access to the drug, this habit will continue to be about the worst life script that you could possibly choose. At present, meeting the black market prices for heroin turns most male addicts into thieves and most female addicts into prostitutes. (See Chapter Five.)

INDIAN HEMP The *cannabis sativa* plant, source of marijuana and hashish.

JACKSON ILLUSION PEPPER A whole green pepper that has been allowed to turn slightly rotten. If two holes are made at opposite ends, and a lit king-size cigarette (of ordinary tobacco) is inserted in one, and the smoker inhales through the other, hallucinations similar to those of LSD are said to result. Like the famous electric banana craze, it is unknown whether this effect is due to auto-suggestion or if the pepper skin actually contains a chemical that modifies the tobacco smoke.

JUNK Heroin; the term is also used to denote morphine or other opium-based drugs that, like heroin, are also highly addicting.

KAVAKAVA A mildly intoxicating beverage made from the roots of a Polynesian pepper plant, *piper methysticum*. Curiously, most reference books classify this as a narcotic, but it does not appear to be addictive and users report results that vary from resembling alcohol to resembling marijuana. The general effect is a gentle relaxation, combined with some euphoria and occasional "psychedelic" perceptions in the especially sensitive.

KIF or *KIEF* A special blend of North African marijuana believed to possess especially benign properties; the Arabic name *kif* means "tranquillity" or "peace." According to a Moroccan proverb, "A puff of *kif* in the morning makes a man as strong as a thousand camels in the courtyard."

KISS BIG Underground slang, on the East Coast, for LSD. The name is derived from the letters on the telephone dial; in the early 1960s, if you dialed KISS BIG in the Boston-Cambridge area, you would reach the International Federation for Internal Freedom (IFIF) which was, quite legally at that time, looking for volunteers to participate in LSD research.

LADY SNOW Cocaine; but *SNOW* alone sometimes refers to heroin.

LAUDANUM The first medicinal derivative of opium, formulated by the magician and alchemist, Paracelsus, in the first part of the 16th Century. It was used widely as an analgesic until recent times, and its famous addicts included Samuel Coleridge, Edgar Allan Poe, Algernon Swinburne, Elizabeth Barrett Browning, Dante Gabriel Rossetti, Senator John Randolph of Roanoke, Virginia, and Horace Day. (During the early part of this century, gin-and-laudanum was a favorite drink with the fast-living set.) Heavy usage produces not only addiction, but also in some cases hallucinations that are, in many reported cases, definitely sinister. (See Chapter Five.)

LAUGHING GAS See *NITROUS OXIDE.*

LEAPERS Amphetamines.

LIBRIUM One of the most widely prescribed tranquilizers; many doctors consider it the safest and most effective treatment for a wide variety of neurotic and nervous ailments. Some researchers, on the other hand, believe it tends to become habit forming and produces dangerous side effects; withdrawal symptoms reported by some heavy users include depression, agitation, aggravation of previous psychosomatic problems, and sometimes convulsions. Death by respiratory depression has been reported when users unwisely have mixed Librium with alcohol or barbiturates.

LIGHT STUFF Marijuana or hashish, as distinguished from "heavy stuff," which generally means heroin, morphine and other opium-based drugs.

LSD Perhaps the most controversial of all drugs. Many users have achieved, or believe they have achieved, genuine self-transcendence with LSD and emphasize its "mystic" properties and the scattered research that tends to indicate that it might be useful in treating a variety of neurotic ailments, such as alcoholism. Opponents repeat the case histories of acute anxiety, panic, suicide or mental hospitalization that have occurred, sporadically, among acid freaks. In actual fact, it appears that such bad trips have become less common in the drug culture as people have learned how to treat a panic reaction; but they do still happen on occasion and nobody should try this trip if he fears that this can happen to him, *because such fears tend to be self-fulfilling prophecies.* Practiced devotees of LSD often agree with Dr. Leary that it is the most powerful sex drug of all, but novices can seldom achieve any sexual results; their nervous system is too overloaded to allow concentration on sex. *Psycholytic* doses (around 100 micrograms) are rather like hashish or a large quantity of marijuana, and it is with this limited dosage that the novice can seek sexual enhancement. *Psychedelic* doses (around 500 micrograms) produce eight hours of random ecstasy—or of terror—and it is only with practice that one can obtain any control at that level. (See Chapter Six.)

LUMINAL One of the strongest of the barbiturate drugs, used mainly in the treatment of epilepsy and delirium tremens. For general warnings about barbiturates, see *AMYTAL.*

MAGIC MUSHROOMS See *AMANITA MUSCARIA* and *PSILO-CYBAE MEXICANA.*

MAJOON A North African delicacy, made of *HASHISH,* or some other cannabis drug, and honey, fruits, nuts and spices. These candies are eaten traditionally at banquets in the Near East and stimulate appetite, conversation and conviviality. Considered one of the best avenues to cannabis-enriched sexual experience.

MARIJUANA The most popular cannabis drug in the United States. (See Chapter Four.)

MARY ANN/MARY JANE/MARY WARNER Slang names for marijuana, now nearly obsolete.

MELLOW YELLOW See *BANANA.*

MEPROBAMATE Once the most widely prescribed tranquilizer in the United States, sold under the trade name *MILTOWN.* Used in the treatment of anxiety states or muscular tremors. Habituation may occur and withdrawal can be painful. May be dangerous if mixed with alcohol.

MESCALINE The psychoactive principle in the *PEYOTE* cactus. The advantage of mescaline is that it is free of the other chemicals in the cactus, which almost always provoke nausea and vomiting at the beginning of a *PEYOTE* session. The disadvantage of mescaline is that, like LSD nowadays, whatever is obtainable today may contain impurities or have been manufactured improperly; this risk is not minor, and real garbage has been found on occasion by psycho-pharmacologists who bought street drugs and analyzed them. For further information, see *PEYOTE.*

METHADONE A synthetic opiate analgesic, just as addicting as heroine. In New York and a few other places, heroin addicts are being "cured" by addicting them to this narcotic, which has been made legal for them (although not for others). The same result could be obtained by making heroin legal for the addicts but not for others; the authorities have rejected this solution, apparently because it would be "soft" on criminals. The methadone treatment leaves the state with the dignity of telling the addict which addicting drug he may use. There is absolutely no pleasure in methadone for anyone who is not already an opiate addict, and it creates impotence with chronic use.

METHAMPHETAMINE See *AMPHETAMINE.*

METHEDRINE A brand name (Burroughs Welcome Co.) for *METHAMPHETAMINE.*

MIKE The usual unit of measurement for LSD; from *microgram,* one millionth of a gram.

MILTOWN See *MEPROBAMATE.*

MMDA 3-methoxyl-4,5-methylenedioxyamphetamine, a strong amphetamine drug, recently synthesized, which is said to provoke psychedelic-like hallucinations and intense body pleasure. Some psychiatrists have found it very useful in therapy, but the government has made it illegal. This is called "Adam" or "XTC" on the black market.

MORPHINE An opium analgesic used as a pain killer in medicine, invented in 1805, and originally intended to cure opium addiction. Morphine was once the principal drug of addiction in the United States, but nowadays addict personality types tend to drift to barbiturates or heroin, and illegal (non-medical) morphine is generally used only by heroin addicts when they can't obtain their drug of choice.

MUSCARINE The active principle in the *AMANITA MUSCARIA* mushroom; a deadly poison, except in very small doses. See *AMANITA MUSCARIA*.

NAIL POLISH REMOVER This produces delirium and/or hallucinations and is resorted to by the ignorant or desperate. The effects are as bad as those produced by *GLUE* or *CARBON TETRACHLORIDE*.

NEMBUTAL A barbiturate drug, intended as a treatment for insomnia or certain nervous conditions. Used as an intoxicant, these pills are called *yellow jacks, yellow jackets* or *yellow submarines;* the high is like a prolonged drunk and probably as likely to provoke temporary impotence as alcohol is. *Very addicting;* see warning under *AMYTAL*.

NIACIN Nicotinic acid, or Vitamin B-3. This is the best single treatment for bad trips of any sort, and has even proved useful in treating some varieties of schizophrenia. Four grams are needed to quiet a drug panic, but one should try to talk calmly to the sufferer while waiting 15 to 45 minutes for the niacin to take effect. See also *THORAZINE,* but remember: Niacin, unlike Thorazine, is available without a prescription.

NICKEL BAG Five dollars' worth of marijuana, an amount that varies according to locale and the rectitude of the dealer; in the good old days it would fill a whisky shot glass.

NITROUS OXIDE The "laughing gas" used by some dentists. William James and others have described profound psychedelic insights and religious visions obtained with this chemical, but since nitrous oxide requires a tank to carry it around, it has not become widely available on the black market. Intelligent use is probably harmless, but there are dangers for those not practiced in administering gas; anoxia can result from too much, too fast, and death is then likely unless quick medical treatment is at hand. In other words, don't try this unless the friend offering it is a dentist or another type of technician who knows how to handle it.

NUTMEG This common household spice is considerably stronger than marijuana and a dose of ten grams can produce LSD-like states. Alas, nausea and vomiting are frequent side effects, as is rapid heartbeat. (No heart failures are reported, but many have experienced acute panic, thinking they were having a heart attack.) Freaky and unpredictable.

OPIUM The exudate of the seeds of the poppy plant, *papaver somniferum,* and the source of such highly addictive pain killers as morphine, heroin, Demerol, pantopon, and so on. Opium itself, on initial trial, is generally considered one of the most ecstatic and lovely of all drug experiences; unlike its derivatives, opium does not seem to be limited in its appeal to hyper-tense types who are already addiction-prone. On the contrary, *every-body* seems to like it, and therein lies its peril. Addiction can be established within a few weeks of steady use and thereafter one remains addicted for life, barring a miracle. The sexual effects are nil or negative, except when mixed with hashish, a Near Eastern custom which is said, by its devotees, to produce the greatest sex drug kicks in the world; but this, too, is just as addicting as straight opium, and impotence follows quickly. (See Chapter Five.)

OYSTERS A folk-aphrodisiac of long historical reputation and still devoutly believed in by many. *All other things being equal* (i.e., in absence of severe neurotic impotence), eating oysters regularly will, in fact, tend to maintain a man at his highest possible level of potency—but this is not because the oysters contain any special properties. It is true of *any* high protein diet, and you will get the same results with the "weight watcher's special" (steak and cottage cheese) offered at most restaurants. The reputation of the oyster is probably due to sympathetic magic: they look (and even taste) like the female genitals.

PANAMA RED A variety of marijuana grown in the Canal Zone and believed to be of especially high potency.

PANTOPON A derivative of opium used for analgesia in medicine and sometimes purchased by heroin addicts when no heroin is available. No kicks for the non-addict and a sexual depressant, like all opiates.

PAREGORIC Tincture of opium in combination with camphor; used in medicine and frequently resorted to by heroin addicts when heroin is unavailable. No sexual benefits.

PEP PILLS Amphetamines.

PEYOTE A small cactus, *lophophora williamsii,* regarded as divine by Mexican Indians since about 1000 BC and adopted by American Indians toward the end of the 19th Century. The active principle is *MESCALINE* and the general effect is very similar to *LSD* (except that peyote tends to produce even more brilliant color displays and is more often associated with personalized or anthropomorphic religious visions, whereas acid-induced religious trances are usually more impersonal and cosmic). The Native American Church, with 150,000 members in the United States and Canada, is a combination of Christian and Indian religious traditions, worshipping Jesus Christ and Peyote Woman and employing peyote in its rites. Peyote is not recommended as a sex enhancer because it usually produces nausea in its initial stages—although this is less true of the peyote tea brewed through the cacti in a pot of water. Many experienced psychedelic explorers prefer peyote to any other drug because it is organic and does not contain the impurities often found in street acid or street mescaline. (See *MESCALINE.*) Due to a Supreme Court decision based on the religious freedom clause of the First Amendment, peyote is legal for Indians, but in most states it is still illegal for others.

PHENOBARBITAL A barbiturate drug; for general warning about barbiturates, see *AMYTAL.*

PINKS See *SECONAL.*

PIPTADENIA A snuff used by South American Indians during religious orgies or before going into battle. The active ingredient is bufotonin. Whatever sex-enhancing properties recommend it for orgiastic use, it is very dangerous and seems to act much like the mandrake, in that delirium is more common than any positive sex enjoyment. It is not recommended by any underground sources.

POPPERS Amyl nitrite vials; see *AMYL NITRITE.*

PSILOCYBAE MEXICANA The magic mushroom of Mexico, considered sacred for around 3000 years. This is the fungus that turned on Timothy Leary originally and the Mexicans say that it brings the user face-to-face with God. It is sometimes on the black market here, although the mushrooms are hard to preserve, and one is more likely to be offered *PSILOCYBIN,* the active principle, in pill form. Many aficionados swear that "nobody has a bad trip on the mushroom" but that isn't quite true—a few bummers have been reported. Probably, the difference between the mushroom and LSD is entirely subjective, since psilocybae has a long religious tradition and LSD has been sensationalized into a monster horror show; such cultural notions are especially influential when a novice is taking his first trip. Any sexual experimentation should be postponed until the sixth hour, after the more dramatic visions have passed. At that point erotic enhancement can be quite good.

PURPLE HEARTS Luminal tablets; see *LUMINAL.*

PARAHEXYL A synthetic drug similar to *THC,* the active principle in marijuana and other cannabis drugs. Parahexyl has been used successfully by English psychiatrists in treating depression, and may become a favorite recreational drug with those who dislike smoking marijuana but enjoy the high. So far, alas, all the "parahexyl" on the American black market, like the alleged "THC," has turned out to be something else, usually a dog tranquilizer.

RAUWOLFIA SERPENTINA A small shrub, native to India, that Ghandi chewed and urged on his followers; its active principle has been synthesized and is now on the market as a tranquilizer in the United States, under the trade name *RESERPINE.*

RESERPINE See *RAUWOLFIA SERPENTINA.*

RHINOCEROS HORN A folk-aphrodisiac of no real value. The idea that this substance will improve potency is known scientifically to be false and seems to be based on sympathetic magic, the horn happening to look like an erect penis.

ROACH The end of a marijuana cigarette.

SMACK/SCHMECK Slang terms for heroin.

SCOPOLAMINE The so-called "truth serum" derived from the henbane plant. It has a long history in connection with witchcraft (see Chapter One) and some modern hippies, aware that scopolamine is an ingredient in such non-prescription sedatives as Sominex, Sleep-Eze and Compoz have tried taking large doses of them to get high. The results occasionally include hallucinations and/or euphoria, but unconsciousness always follows rapidly. A sufficiently high dose (over 100 grams) of pure scopolamine will cause death.

SECONAL A commercial barbiturate; see *AMYTAL* for warnings.

SOMINEX See *SCOPOLAMINE.*

SPEEDBALL A mixture of heroin and cocaine (or, sometimes, heroin and amphetamines). Users claim spectacular sexual effects, but these must wear off with repeated use as the heroin component produces its inevitable by-product of impotence; and then addiction supervenes.

STEAMBOAT A favorite way of smoking marijuana among aficionados. The cardboard roll is removed from a toilet-paper holder, one end is sealed up by a piece of paper held with Scotch tape, the marijuana cigarette is stuck into a hole near the sealed end and the smoker inhales through the opposite, open end. This produces a quicker and stronger high than the same grass would if smoked the ordinary way, and it combines the best of both marijuana and yoga-style *pranayama* (deep breathing, or hyperventilation).

STP 4-methyl-2,5-dimethoxyl-a-methylphenethylamine, a synthetic drug combining many of the properties of both *MESCALINE* and *AMPHETAMINE.* It was originally introduced to the black market amid much fanfare and legendry. It was said to have been invented by Hell's Angels (which it wasn't) and to produce "*s*erenity, *t*ranquillity, *p*eace" (which it didn't). It is a product of Dow Chemicals, those wonderful folks who brought us napalm, and it is considered, universally, a bummer. Little of it is for sale these days.

TEONACTL The sacred mushroom of Mexico, so-called by those who have cracked an anthropology book and learned that this was the original Aztec name and means "God's flesh." See *PSILOCYBAE.*

THC Tetrahydrocannabinol, the active principle in marijuana and other cannabis drugs. Very little real THC has ever been available on the black market; most of what is sold under its name is usually a different compound.

THORAZINE A major tranquilizer and the best treatment for a bad *LSD* trip. Use 25 milligrams. Available on prescription only. (For other bad-trip treatments, see *NIACIN.*)

VALIUM A mild tranquilizer with no particular sexual or other kicks in it.

XTC A pun on "ecstasy"; like *ADAM,* a code name for *MMDA.* See *MMDA.*

YAGE See *AYAHUASCO.*

YELLOWJACK/YELLOW SUBMARINES Nembutal capsules. See *NEMBUTAL.*

BIBLIOGRAPHY

Blake, William. *The Portable Blake.* New York: Viking Press, n.d.

Castaneda, Carlos. *A Separate Reality.* New York: Simon and Schuster, 1971.

Crowley, Aleister. "Psychology of Hashish." In *Roll Away The Stone* by Aleister Crowley and Israel Regardie. St. Paul: Llewellyn Books, 1968.

——. *The Confessions of Aleister Crowley.* New York: Hill and Wang, 1970.

——. *Magick in Theory and Practice.* Hackensack: Weyman, 1972.

——. *The Diary of a Drug Fiend.* New York: Lancer Books, 1972.

Culling, Louis T. *The Complete Magick Curriculum of the Secret Order, G.B.G.* St. Paul: Llewellyn Books, 1971.

Daraul, Akron. *History of Secret Societies.* New York: Pocket Books, 1961.

DeRopp, Robert, M.D. *Drugs and the Mind.* New York: Grove Press, 1957.

Evans, Wayne O., and Kline, Nathan S. *Psychotropic Drugs in the Year 2000: Use by Normal Humans.* Springfield: CC Thomas, 1971.

Gordon, David Cole. *Self-Love.* Baltimore: Penguin Books, 1972.

Greene County Sheriff's Department. *Drug Abuse Is an Escape to Nowhere.* Ohio: 1972.

Joyce, James. *Finnegans Wake.* New York: Viking Press, 1967.

King, Francis. *The Rites of Modern Occult Magic.* New York: Macmillan, 1970.

Lady Sheba. *The Book of Shadows.* St. Paul: Llewellyn, 1971.

Laurie, Peter. *Drugs: Medical, Psychological and Social Facts.* London: Penguin Books, 1971.

Leary, Timothy, Ph.D. Introduction to *LSD: The Consciousness-Expanding Drug,* edited by David Solomon. New York: G.P. Putnam, 1966.

——. *Psychedelic Prayers After the TAO TE CHING.* New York University Books, 1966.

Lewis, Barbara. *The Sexual Powers of Marijuana.* New York: Wyden, 1973.

Lilly, John C., M.D. *Programming and Metaprogramming in the Human Biocomputer.* New York: Julian Press, 1972.

——. *The Center of the Cyclone.* New York: Julian Press, 1972.

Lingeman, Richard. *Drugs from A to Z.* New York: McGraw-Hill, 1969.

Montague, Ashley. Introduction to *Sexual Symbolism,* by Richard Payne Knight and Thomas Wright. New York: Julian Press, 1957.

Playboy Interview. PLAYBOY Magazine, September 1966.

Playboy Panel. PLAYBOY Magazine, February 1970.

Regardie, Israel. *The Tree of Life.* New York: Weiser, 1969.

Slim, Iceberg. "Pimp." In *Drugs from A to Z* by Richard Lingeman, pp. 45–6, New York: McGraw-Hill, 1969.

Smith, Huston, Ph.D. "Do Drugs Have Religious Import." In *LSD: The Consciousness-Expanding Drug,* edited by David Solomon. New York: G.P. Putnam, 1966.

Solomon, David, ed., *The Marijuana Papers.* New York: New American Library, 1968.

Writings of Washington, vol. 31, p. 389; vol. 33, p. 279, 384, 469; vol. 34, p. 146; vol. 35, p. 72, 265, 323. U.S. Government Printing Office, 1931.